From Peddlers to Merchant Princes

Also by Penrose Scull

Great Ships Around the World

From Peddlers
to Merchant Princes

A History of Selling in America

by PENROSE SCULL

with PRESCOTT C. FULLER

FOLLETT PUBLISHING COMPANY

Chicago, New York   1967

3/28/85

Library of Congress Catalog Card Number: 67-20837

First Printing

Manufactured in the United States of America

Design by Gordon Martin

Follett Publishing Company
1000 West Washington Boulevard
Chicago, Illinois   60607

T3265

Foreword

From Peddlers to Merchant Princes is the first comprehensive book of its kind ever written. Many years ago Cicero declared, "Not to know what has been transacted in former years is to continue as a child. If no use is made of the labors of past ages, the world must remain always in the infancy of knowledge." This book is a narrative account of events that played an important part in the growth and development of our free enterprise system.

Salesmanship has come into its own in the twentieth century. It has inherited tradition. The remarkable exploits of our forefathers as related in Penrose Scull's book point up the romance and adventure in the history of selling in America. This is the story of enterprise, foresight, and hard work on the part of progressive merchants and businessmen since our nation's infancy. The salesman and merchant today are heir to a profession carved out of pluck, imagination, and just plain hard work centuries ago. Still the fundamentals of selling remain the same as in the earliest days of American history. And the importance of selling is as great as ever before. Methods have changed in many ways, but the output of American industry must still be sold.

Many books have been written on salesmanship. Most of them have been inspirational; others have been based upon the experiences of their authors. Each of them has served a worthy purpose in interpreting the basic elements of selling. Textbooks have also been produced by authorities on the subject; among these *Successful Salesmanship*, written by Paul W. Ivey, Ph.D., while he was a professor of merchandising at the University of California, stands high in the field of academic training on the subject. Dr. Ivey might well be considered the Rockne of teachers of the fundamentals of salesmanship to students interested in selling as a career.

From Peddlers to Merchant Princes is an engrossing narrative that will help the reader attain a better understanding of a "working democracy" and the dignity of the individual in an economy that exists because of the efforts and enterprise of many individuals. Readers in this country, and those abroad, will understand from this book that the competitive system, or what we might call the "selling system," is the one true way to freedom from want and economic instability.

Salesmen and merchants are still making history. In our present age we are constantly refining and polishing the processes of marketing through study and training. No profession requires more individualism, initiative, self-control, and self-development than salesmanship, as *From Peddlers to Merchant Princes* so lucidly points out in the following pages. This is a book that will inspire its readers and stimulate in salesmen a new pride in the work they perform.

—Robert E. Palmer, President
Robert Palmer Corporation

Preface

Like most books, this one has a hero: the American salesman. To tell his story, Mr. Scull sometimes personally, sometimes vicariously, rummaged attics, basements, and vaults for original source material. Generously, files and archives were opened, rare books lent, queries painstakingly answered. As a result, a unique portrait has emerged, more detailed even than he dared hope when he began to compile and expand a series of vignettes written originally as sales-training articles for the Robert Palmer Corporation.

Over the years, as we researched these articles, delving deep into the fascinating lore and legend of business Americana, we inevitably found ourselves with far more interesting and significant information than these articles could contain. At the same time, as vignette after vignette began to appear, each one adding a brush stroke to the composite, comment seemed to come from every side: "They ought to be in a book." Now they are.

In particular, we wish to thank Frank Wetzel of the Lincoln Educational Foundation in New York City; Dr. M. G. Garagosian, who did much of the contemporary research; the personnel of historical societies and libraries; business firms large and small that have shared with us their corporate sales experience; the publishers of *American Heritage*, in which an abridged version of the chapter on early Yankee Peddlers appeared under the title "Pack Road to Yesterday." Finally, I should like to express my personal thanks to Prescott Fuller, who completed the final chapter from the notes of Mr. Scull.

—Mrs. Penrose Scull

Table of Contents

x

From Peddlers

to Merchant Princes

No Carriage Trade

*The first Americans were a poor people
with very little cash income and less
money to spend for luxuries.*

THE EARLY SETTLERS of America were, for the most part, farmers, tradesmen, and craftsmen. They were not wealthy men. The people of the nation that today is the world's richest did not start out rich. First as colonists, and later as adolescent freemen, Americans had very few coins to jangle in the pockets of their homespun jeans. A few amassed tidy fortunes from the early fur trade, from whaling, from the West Indian commerce in salt, fish, rum, and molasses. A handful of others were comfortably well off, having brought money with them from their homelands. But, generally speaking, there existed no hard core of what today would be called the "Big Rich." The vast majority of our people were stony broke.

What is more, practically no one believed that America would ever be wealthy. Nothing seemed to point to a destiny other than that of an agricultural nation strung along the Atlantic seaboard. Here a settler could expect to scratch a subsistence out of the rocky soil of New England or do somewhat better, with less backbreaking toil, raising tobacco, hogs, and cotton in the Southern colonies. It

Out of the wilderness the early settlers hewed the trees for homes, for stockades, and for boats to ply the rivers and bays which were their lifelines to a tenuous civilization. Each stroke of the ax or oar brought them closer to the powerful America they fought for, and never knew.

was a way of life offering a satisfying amount of adventure and freedom to those who chose it, but it portended little in the way of financial reward.

The West and the Midwest—all the immense and unknown region that lay beyond the hazy shoulders of the Appalachians—were, by eyewitness accounts and widely circulated rumor, poor and formidable lands of well-nigh impenetrable forests, vast plains of coarse buffalo grass, and barren stretches of utterly worthless desert. For all the seaboard settlers knew about them, the West and the Midwest were of little value so far as natural resources were concerned. Besides, the French, English, and Spaniards had mapped out great chunks of those areas as their domains, though they were in no great hurry to exploit their American real estate in face of the vigorous opposition from the Indians, the tempestuousness of the climate, and their own preoccupation with Continental wars.

It is quite understandable why the North American colonies were as poor as the proverbial church mice. They were settled during an era when fabulous riches were pouring into the royal coffers of the European monarchies. A dazzling stream of bullion, specie, precious stones, silk, ivory, and spices flowed to Europe from the treasure-rich Indies, Africa, and the Orient. And what did the threadbare Americans have to contribute to this exotic commerce? Not much. As the Spaniards had long ago discovered to their annoyance, after a tedious and thirsty search for the Seven Cities of Cibola, North America appeared to have very little that was worth carrying back to the old country. To be sure, the sea swarmed with fish to assuage the hunger of man; the bays and estuaries from Maine to the Virginia Capes were alive with remarkably large and succulent lobsters, crabs, oysters, and

The scenery in America, such as the Delaware Water Gap, was magnificent, but there was very little known natural wealth to enrich the first settlers.

other shellfish. The land itself was well covered with useful timber, although none of it was thought to be as desirable as the teak, mahogany, and sandalwood to be had in other parts of the world. Once cleared, the land gave promise of yielding a surplus of agricultural products. In addition, there was an abundance of meat animals and wild fowl, and here and there were deposits of granite, limestone, and low-grade iron. But more than a century and a half was to elapse before America would be known to be providentially bestowed with natural riches such as man had never before stumbled upon.

Taken all in all, the known riches were not the sort that appealed to the expensive and fastidious tastes of the merchant princes of, say, London and Amsterdam. Consequently, the early Yankees had no part in the silk-stocking trade with Europe but were obliged to take their humble wares around to the back door and barter them for the humdrum goods wanted at home in the colonies.

Thus the principal assets the first Americans had to work with were their natural talents and skills, and once a settler arrived on these shores those talents and skills had to be put to work quickly. The survival of the individual rested largely upon his ability to contribute to the meager wealth of the community. A farmer settling in Connecticut with little capital and a large and hungry family had no time to lose in clearing the land of rocks and trees and putting a hoe to the ground to raise a crop. An impecunious cabinetmaker landing at Boston or Philadelphia had no time to waste before he set about making, and *selling*, furniture so that he could procure food raised by the farmer. And the tradesman who had brought with him from Europe a few hampers and bundles of trade goods had to set up shop immediately and begin the slow turnover of his meager capital.

This was a basic, but rickety, foundation upon which to establish the economy of a new nation. In sharp contrast to the established order of trade in Europe, our farmers, tradesmen, and those who tinkered at making things had no "carriage trade" made up of a fabulously rich aristocracy upon which to lean for support. There was no wealth in the country, no economic aid from abroad, no openhanded grant of money or goods from nations seeking our allegiance. We were very much on our own, as individuals and as a nation.

In the long run everything worked out for the best. One result of these austere and often frightening conditions was that a man, in order to survive, had to exert extraordinary skill and perseverance in raising or making things and disposing of them so that things raised or made by other people could be purchased. When Samuel Sanford, who operated a gristmill on Pootatuck Brook at Newtown, Connecticut, accepted flour from farmers in payment for his services as a miller, it became incumbent upon him to sell the flour to someone else before the weevils got at it.

All of this placed an emphasis on selling such as existed nowhere else in the world at the time. Every American who had something to dispose of, whether it was a sack of potatoes, a barrel of salt fish, a beautifully made chair, a beaver hat, or a gallon of rum, had to do a job of selling. While it is true that most Americans wanted or badly needed the things that other men had for sale, it is not true that this created a seller's market. Purchases or barter deals were made only after very careful deliberation. Considerable persuasion was required to convince a farmer that he should part with eighteen shillings for a pair of new boots, or to convince a merchant that it would pay him to run a small advertisement each week in the Boston *Commercial*. Owing to dire economic necessity on the part of the seller, there was an urgency to closing a sale. If the sales presentation lacked polish or an insight into the psychology of motivation, it was successful more often than not chiefly because what a man had to say

The Americans built their settlements along the tidewaters and amid the forests and turned to creating our first industries, which included lumbering and shipbuilding. Timber and salt fish from the northern colonies and tobacco from Virginia were the first products sold to foreign markets. These exports earned the money needed to purchase from abroad clothing, household goods, sugar, coffee, and other essentials.

3

about his product was said with enthusiasm and without any beating about the bush. When Americans with goods for sale made long trips to Europe, to the West Indies, or to the hills of Vermont, they were not bashful about asking for an order. In those days when liberal expense accounts and equally liberal drawing accounts were unheard of, such amenities as the long lunch with a prospective customer and frequent call-backs were luxuries very few could afford.

The stringency of money had another far-reaching effect upon the beginnings of our economy. Since there were few rich people to sell to, there was obviously no sense in producing a limited volume of luxury goods to be sold at high prices. The alternative was to produce goods in volume to be sold at the lowest possible price to the greatest number of people. This was a brand-new idea, unknown —or at least unexploited—in Europe. It was the start of mass production for the mass market, and throughout the colonies hundreds of men fiddled with all sorts of new contraptions—their object, to

invent equipment that would make five candles in no more time than it took to hand-dip one or to turn out six wagon wheels a day instead of two.

On many occasions the inventive genius of the colonists resulted in an outpouring of goods that overburdened the primitive facilities for distribution. When Ezekiel Reed, after much experimentation, hit on a workable design for a machine that could turn out one hundred million tacks a year, he created quite a problem for himself. The mountains of tacks were in Bridgewater, Massachusetts, but his customers were scattered over several hundred thousand square miles of rugged territory. Without men to sell and distribute the tacks, Reed's machine and its prodigious output were worthless, even though there was a good market for these

At left: "American Farm Scene No. 1," published by N. Currier. Below: early markets were primitive. The Fulton Street market in New York City, shown here circa 1834, became one of the largest and busiest in the country.

Whaling was one of our first major industries and the source of our first modest fortunes. It was a hazardous trade that flourished for more than a century, during which time millions of barrels of whale oil were sold in the home market and for export to Europe.

machine-made tacks because they were priced at a fraction of the cost of tacks made by hand.

In many ways the problems of sales, merchandising, and distribution in colonial days were greater than the problem of production. These are still the major problems, and have been so throughout our history. Farmers and ranchers have raised a prodigious larder of foodstuffs. We have drilled, mined, and sawed mountains of raw materials. By 1857 we had invented so many things that there was serious talk of closing the government Patent Office because, so it was said, by then everything possible had been invented. But the Patent Office

remained open and we continued creating products and discovering new ways to make more and more of these products faster than ever before.

Our free-enterprise system has continuously lived with the threat of collapse under the sheer weight of its productive capacity. Ezekiel Reed was a minor genius because of his workable idea to produce millions of tacks, but he might have ended in debtors prison had not other men come along and marketed those tacks for him. The bulwark against chaos and the dull thud of collapse has been the American system of selling, merchandising, and distribution. The whole idea of mass production would have foundered had we not had the talents and energies to develop systems of mass marketing and selling. The ways in which we created, through salesmanship and imaginative merchandising, our mass market for products, services, and ideas is an inspiring and important chapter in our history.

8

Seagoing Salesman

To Marchantes as a Patterne he might stand,

Adventring Dangers new by Sea and Land.

—EPITAPH OF CAPTAIN RICHARD LORD

NEW LONDON, CONNECTICUT, 1662

UNQUESTIONABLY, the colonial seafarers who traded along the coast and at ports overseas were among the first American salesmen. The colonists from Europe had no sooner recovered from the fright and misery of the long trans-Atlantic voyage than a goodly number of them began to build a fleet of cockleshell ships and put out to sea again. Within ten years after Salem had been founded by John Endicott, shipbuilding was a thriving industry there, with the men of Salem making bold plans for sending their ships as far away as the West Indies. Every settlement had its fleet of pinks, bugeyes, snows, and other types of small ships for the nearby coastal trade. Two years after Boston had been settled, a shipload of salt fish and furs was dispatched from there to Virginia; several years later a Boston ship sailed across the Atlantic to Tenerife, where its cargo of New England corn was exchanged for wines, fruit, sugar, and ginger. By 1665 more than three hundred New England-owned vessels were sailing in the trade with the West Indies and Europe. By 1717 better than two hundred vessels annually sailed from New York with export cargo, and about as many more cleared from Philadelphia.

American clipper in a Caribbean port, painted by Gordon Grant.

It may be argued, as has been done, that the captains of those vessels were not salesmen in the real meaning of that word but traders who bartered rather than sold their outward cargoes for return loads. However, that would be splitting hairs. Any profitable transaction, whether it involved cash or barter, called for salesmanship of a high order, and since it is a notable fact that the American sea captains were on very rare occasions participants in unprofitable transactions, either at home or abroad, those men are entitled to charter memberships in the sales profession. Early American trade was, in fact, the result of salesmanship, not the cause of it. A man who had the gumption to gather together a shipload of Maine granite and set sail along the coast to dispose of it at a profit was a salesman, although by custom and tradition we might think of him primarily as a sea captain or trader.

The captain of a vessel loaded with a cargo of corn or barrel staves or salt fish faced a complex situation that taxed his talents as a merchandiser and salesman. First, he had to be reasonably certain he was setting his course for a market where he could dispose of his cargo. Then, since there existed no established world-wide price for his wares, his bargaining powers established the value of his cargo. The price of corn, for example, was set, not by cabled quotations from the Chicago Board of Trade, as is done today, but by what the captain held the corn to be worth and how much the buyer would agree to pay. And since in all probability very little actual cash would be paid by the buyer, the captain had to accept goods to be disposed of when he returned home. He was, in short, not only a seller but a buyer as well, and to fail in either of these capacities meant a financial loss for a voyage of anywhere from two months' to two years' duration.

9

Consider, for example, the anxieties that plagued the captain of a Salem sloop that sailed to Bermuda in 1636 with a cargo of corn and salt pork. For these two commodities his Bermudian customers offered oranges, limes, and potatoes in lieu of cash. Upon the captain's judgment and the islanders' bargaining abilities rested the ticklish determination of how many oranges and limes constituted a fair swap for a bushel of corn and how many bushels of potatoes were worth a barrel of salt pork. And there were other considerations. Only a few people in Salem were wealthy enough to afford the extravagance of buying oranges or limes. If the captain took too many of these fruits, he would swamp the market and be forced to sell them at less than cost. But how many oranges would be too many? And how many might spoil on the trip home? And if he took fewer oranges and loaded up with potatoes, would he glut the Salem potato market?

Imponderables like these haunted the Yankee seafarer who doubled in brass as shipmaster and master salesman. Nearly all he had to work with were the price his ship's owners had paid for the cargo and the wages and other costs of the voyage. It was up to him to bring back to his home port a cargo which, when sold, would bring in more money than had been invested in the voyage.

POOR SAM HILL

On a sultry day in July 1817, Samuel Hill, captain of the brig *Packet*, was ready to put to sea for a voyage from Boston to Chile and then on to Canton. Before casting off, Hill received the following instructions from the owner of the *Packet*:

"Should you find the Ports of Chile open for a free trade with Americans, you will trade at such ports as you deem safest & best for the Interests of the voyage . . . taking care in all cases to sell for cash in hand, and to give such samples, or make such exhibit of the Goods you sell, as not to lay yourself liable to disputes about the weight, measure, or quantities afterwards. . . . It will be very desirable that I should have as early Information as possible of the State of the Markets in South America, and of the State of the Country at the time you write, and probable State of the Country, one year or more afterwards, in fine, your own deliberate opinion as

to the State of the trade & permanent situation of the Country, and in order that I may have the best possible Information, I should recommend your causing to be prepared pattern cards of every article of European fabrick, with marginal marks, describing the length and breadth of each kind of Goods, with such explanations & remarks, as to the quality and quantity which may be sufficient for the market, as well as enable me to form a Correct Judgment of the trade, & of the Goods suited to the market, and in order that I may not be disappointed in receiving this information, it may be well to send home by some whaling or other vessel one of your trusty, Intelligent, confidential men charged with this information. . . .

"On your arrival at Canton you will dispose of the cargo which you may have on board on the best terms you can, & invest the proceeds thereof in a return cargo of such articles, & in such proportions as you deem best adapted to this market, and such as will meet the most ready sales here, taking care not to trust your property in the hands of anyone. . . .
Israel Thorndike—OWNER

Poor Sam Hill. Not only was he expected to sail the *Packet* safely on a voyage halfway around the world and back; he was also to serve as the owner's salesman, buyer, banker, market analyst, and observer of short-term and long-range political and economic trends in Chile. In addition, he was expected to prepare a sort of "Seller's Guide" of articles suitable for the Chilean market and to collect samples of European goods selling well in that country so that enterprising Yankees in New England could copy them.

Hill's voyage to Chile was routine enough. The *Packet* inched her way through the doldrums with as little delay as possible, and she rounded the Horn with no more than the usual buffeting encountered in that miserable stretch of water. It was after she arrived in Valparaiso that Sam Hill's troubles began in earnest, and in some ways the fate that befell

Selling a cargo to best advantage in a foreign port and buying salable goods required a knowledge of the market both abroad and in the colonies. American ship captains were notably successful.

10

him was of his own making. Two years previously, when on a voyage to Chile in the *Ophelia,* Hill had written to his owners with unrestrained enthusiasm: "The high Price which many articles of Merchandise could command at present in Chile offers a Powerful Inducement to adventurers, but none can be introduced except by Contraband, or Smuggling, and in this way I think a Cargo of 50 or 60 thousand Dollars or even much greater amount might be disposed of in Chile and with very little risk and not much delay."

With this letter Hill had submitted a list of articles suitable for smuggling into Chile, including cottons, silks, teas, furniture, Malacca canes, and "50 Dozen Ladies Silk Shoes, assorted: 7 or 9 inches in length generally."

Just why Hill did not follow his own suggestion and attempt to smuggle his goods into Chile when he arrived in the *Packet,* we do not know, but this much is clear: had he done so at the propitious time, he might have spared himself a heap of trouble and delay. In any event he decided to play it straight, and sailed into Valparaiso harbor as a legitimate merchant come to trade with the Chileans.

Hill could not have arrived at a more inauspicious time. The country was in the throes of one of its more or less chronic civil wars, this one between the Patriots (the rebels) and the Republicans (the ins). There was considerable fighting in the north and a fairly good chance that the Patriots would break through the Republican defense and swoop down on the port of Valparaiso and the capital city of Santiago. To make his arrival even more untimely, the country was badly jolted by a severe earthquake several days after the *Packet* anchored. Nonetheless, Captain Hill dutifully rented a horse and jogged the seventy-five miles to Santiago to see about disposing of his cargo.

In Santiago the outlook for trade was darker than the reports and rumors in Valparaiso had foretold. Families of wealth and those whose political faith was Republican were preparing to light out for the Argentine border if the Patriot forces overwhelmed the Republican army. Consequently, the merchants in Santiago were reluctant to commit themselves to purchases of large stocks of goods and were even more reluctant to pay cash for any merchandise

they might be persuaded to take. It was a melancholy prospect for a man with a shipload of goods to sell, but there was little Hill could do to extricate himself from this unhappy predicament. There was no other market for his cargo within five thousand miles; the goods aboard the *Packet* were intended for Chile and were unsuited for the Canton market, so he could not proceed to China. He could not go north up the coast of Chile, where he might have traded his cargo for copper, for the northern ports were in the hands of the Patriots, who had served notice that they intended to seize any neutral property they could lay their hands on.

In short, Hill was stuck with a bad situation and he did the only thing he could under the circumstances. He rented a store in Santiago where he could display his merchandise to the merchants, climbed aboard his horse, and painfully made the journey back to Valparaiso to unload the *Packet* and get his goods through the customs. On November 19 Hill's merchandise was in Santiago and he made a sale of sixty thousand dollars' worth of goods to D. A. Barros, Balero y Bezanilla. On the twenty-seventh, after much scurrying around for customers, Hill got an order for twenty thousand dollars' worth of goods from Ambrosio Aldunati. Each buyer was an old and respected merchant with a good credit rating, and each agreed to pay for his purchases in thirty days. Meanwhile, however, the revolution was reaching a crisis and the affairs of the Republicans were going badly. Trade slowed from a snail's pace to none at all, and the thirty days came and went with no payments by Hill's two customers.

In February, according to Hill's daybook, he "earnestly pressed those merchants who had been the principal purchasers of our Goods to make payment for the Same . . . but such was the State of the Market that they had not & could not sell any considerable portion of those Goods at anywhere near the price they had paid, or agreed to pay for them, nor even at a discount of twenty-five percent, and although they were absolutely unable to pay their acc'ts. at present I might rest assured that I should suffer no loss on their account. . . . I finally succeeded in collecting about $10,000 on Aldunati's acc't. & $5000 on Bezanilla & Balero's acc't. For the

Yankee captains often took their wives along when they went to sea. Seated in the main cabin, whose luxurious furnishings included a piano, a captain poses with his wife and dog.

residue I was obliged to be contented with promises for the present, as there was no Remedy."

In March, Sam Hill believed he had found a remedy after all, or at least a way to speed up the sale of the remainder of his merchandise. He hired a carpenter and converted part of his wholesale showroom into a retail outlet, a move that actually did not help sales very much but did get him into an uncomfortable situation with the Tribuno de Consulado for selling at retail goods entered into the country specifically for sale to wholesalers and merchants.

In August—almost nine months to the day after the *Packet* had arrived at Valparaiso—Captain Hill gathered together all the cash he had been able to collect and, leaving his showroom in charge of a Mr. Robinson, rode over the Santa Lucia mountain range, climbed aboard his ship, and sailed for Canton.

In time—and it was a protracted length of time even in those days of long voyages and negotiations —Hill completed his business in Canton and returned to Chile. During his absence the war had ended and most of his goods had been sold. The merchants were able to settle their accounts, and although his room in Valparaiso was broken into and nineteen hundred dollars was stolen from his money chest, the Chilean venture came to a reasonably profitable conclusion. But the dozen or so round trips in the saddle between Valparaiso and Santiago were not quickly forgotten, and Hill, upon his arrival in Boston, wrote in his journal: ". . . of my health I cannot speak much, it having been impaired during my severe journeys on horseback to which I was of necessity exposed in the course of my business."

ADVICE ON TRADING

Some years after Captain Hill's unhappy experience in Chile, in 1854, Arthur L. Payson, a Boston merchant-shipowner, anticipated the need to impart as much advice as he could to Oliver H. Underwood, serving as supercargo aboard the bark *Eagle*. Payson was sending a cargo of goods to Turkey and ports in the Black Sea during the height of the Crimean War and was well aware that anything might happen beyond the ordinary perils of the sea when the *Eagle* arrived in that troubled area. Thus he set down, in considerable detail, the various courses of action for Underwood to pursue in his efforts to profitably dispose of the goods aboard the *Eagle* and purchase a cargo for the voyage home:

"When you have reached Constantinople you had better call on Mssrs. Matthien Bros., my correspondents there, and ask them to advise you regarding the state of the market, for the articles composing your cargo, and what prospects there may be for its immediate sale; letting them understand that you have not determined to sell it in Constantinople, but may proceed on to some port in the Black Sea, which will stimulate them to give you as favorable a report of the market as possible. . . . It would be well for you on your first interview with them, to let them understand that you are perfectly untrammelled, but that my wishes are, that in case they do as well by you as any other house, that you should give them the consignment, of your cargo, in case you find it necessary to sell it through any firm in Constantinople.

"You had better call on Messrs. V. Azarian Sons & Co. to whom I enclose a letter of introduction, and from whom you may possibly obtain some in-

Shown in this harbor view of Valparaiso, Chile, are the high, wrinkled Andes over which Captain Samuel Hill of Boston made many uncomfortable trips on horseback during the long months it took him to sell his cargo in Santiago.

14

formation that may prove of use to you; I do not wish you upon any account to transact your business with them, nor had you better even let them know the quantities of each article you have on board, for they will doubtless do all in their power to injure you, and the object of your visit to them must be to disarm them if possible, by inducing them to hope (without committing yourself, however) that they may possibly obtain the management of your business. . . .

"The Cavenish Tobacco you will probably be obliged to sell in small lots, partly in Constantinople to the ship chandlers, store keepers, etc., to merchant vessels, captains, or the pursers of the men of war, either in Constantinople or the Black Sea, and perhaps even, some of it to the army sutlers in the Crimea.

"The crackers of different kinds will be probably satiable [sic] to the same people and I should think might be wanted at the Eng. and French army hospitals.

"The cigars ought to sell remarkably well; a part of them in Constantinople, but by all means retain a part for the Crimea, if you go up there.

"So much will depend upon circumstances, upon your arrival in the East, that everything must be left to your discretion. You must bear in mind that you have the vessel by the month, and can do whatever you please with her, while others will be obliged to discharge their cargoes in Constantinople, you can go to any port that you see fit for my interest, so that you have every means at your disposal, to make the most that can be made in that part of the world with your cargo. . . .

"Regarding your return Cargo, obtain all the information possible in Constantinople regarding Wool, either of the City of Angora or Crimea. Box Wood, Otto of Roses, Oil Geranium (worth $2. per oz. here), Canary Seed, Hemp Seed, Gum Tragacanthe, Vallonea, Opium, Nut Galls, Yellow Berries, Filberts from Trebisond, Hemp from Sinope, and see what arrangements could be made for collecting an assorted cargo of these goods, while you are absent in the Black Sea, so as to have them already on your return to Constantinople. . . .

"Should you succeed in reaching any of the ports in the Black Sea, which you must try to do, if such a course does not appear totally inconsistent with my interest, endeavor to pick up a cargo there, for it may be that the war has caused an accumulation of the products of the country and that wool, and perhaps Linseed, Hemp, Flax & Iron, may be obtained there at a very low cost. Neither is it unlikely that in ports where the allied fleets are wintering, a cargo of Old Iron, Brass or Copper or Rigging & Junk, might be purchased very low indeed, and even lots of goods seized by the allies in Sebastopol, might be obtained on fair terms. . . . Should you however find nothing in the Crimea to make up a return cargo, and you learn that Odessa has been taken by the allies, you had better by all means proceed to that port, where there is every probability that a cargo of some of the articles already mentioned, may be purchased. . . .

"Be careful not to commit yourself in any way, or afford any pretext to the English, French or Turkish forces, to seize or stop your vessel, or in any other ways cause you trouble. You will treat all officers with whom you come in contact with respect and politeness, assuring them that your voyage is a perfectly legal one, intended for the peaceful object of opening a commercial intercourse between this country and the Black Sea, that you have no wish or intention of breaking any blockade, or violating any laws whatsoever, and requesting any information which they may be able to give you, to enable you to keep strictly from allowing them any cause of complaint; in your negotiations with any of the English or French commissary generals, or any other officers of those nations; you had by all means better be open and straightforward in all your dealings; but, in your communications with merchants, Brokers, Ship Chandlers, and the people of the country who you may employ as interpreters, guides or laborers, you must be very careful not to be deceived, as they will take every advantage in their power of you, and will endeavor to influence you as their interest may dictate, and will not hesitate to give you false information of every kind, to undervalue your goods, and overvalue their own, to charge you double and treble prices for labor, and articles that they may furnish you, and in fact fleece you in every imaginable manner if you allow them so to do; for the inhabitants

16

At Constantinople (the harbor is shown here) the sale of the Eagle's *cargo and purchases of goods for the Boston market was left to the discretion of Supercargo William Underwood, who had no knowledge of how the Crimean War was going when he sailed from home.*

of the Levant have the reputation even among the shrewd nations of the Mediterranean, of being the sharpest & least scrupulous in all commercial transactions.

"In Constantinople it will probably be necessary for you to employ somebody as a guide throughout the city, and an interpreter in your dealings. Be careful not to disclose your projects to any such person, as he may be paid as a spy upon you. . . .

". . . You will write me as often as you think you can convey any information of interest, choosing the speediest route in order that the letters may reach me as soon as possible. Do not entrust any of your letters to any one for the mail, but always put them

into the Post Office yourself. My letters to you will all be addressed to the care of the U.S. legation at Constantinople and not to Messrs. Matthien Bros. & Co. In the Black Sea find out from the English officers the best way of forwarding your letters and at Trebisond, or any other small ports if you require assistance for this or any other purpose always call on the English Consul in preference to any other, as you will find them generally most intelligent and mostly merchants and by far more honest than the most of the acting Consuls of other nations. . . .

"I think of nothing to add but to warn you once more against the danger you incur from the want of honesty of the nations in the East, and wishing you all possible success, and a pleasant passage, I am, Yours truly, Arthur L. Payson."

Such letters as those to Captain Hill and Supercargo Underwood were not extraordinary. All shipowners issued similar instructions on sailing days, the tenor of such orders serving as a stern reminder that the success or failure of the voyage depended

17

on the man representing the owner and how well he exercised his judgment and talent for trading in foreign ports. A captain worth his salt was expected to be a good horse-trader when he went ashore.

HORSE-TRADING IN MARTINIQUE

In some cases ship captains literally did engage in horse-trading. In 1806 the brig *Betsy* sailed from Salem with a deck cargo of horses. Her destination was the French island of Martinique. Horses and mules were readily marketable in the West Indies, and a sea captain with a flair for horse-trading could sell his animals at an exceedingly good profit. Thus, when the *Betsy* arrived at Martinique, the captain left his mate in charge of the ship and her cargo and boldly went ashore in the role of a Yankee horse-trader. It must have been amusing to watch the old salt prying open a horse's mouth so that prospective

buyers could examine its teeth, and to hear his exposition about withers, fetlocks, and other vital points of the animal's anatomy and ancestry.

At any rate, the captain discovered that the French buyers had had some experience with sea-going horse-dealers from New England and were in no hurry to do business. They were slyly aware that it cost money to keep the *Betsy* idle at anchor and the longer they waited, the more it would cost the captain to feed and tend his cargo. If they held off buying long enough, the shipboard supply of hay and oats would be used up and the captain would be forced to a more favorable appraisal of

Weights, measurements, and quality were always checked when a captain did business ashore. Here a barrel of sugar is being weighed on the docks.

18

the value of his horses. So day after day passed, while the disconsolate mate watered and tended the horses and dutifully entered in the ship's log this laconic message: "Cap't gone ashore again to sell horses."

Eventually the horses were sold at a profit, the *Betsy*'s decks were scrubbed down, and once again the crew breathed clear, clean salt air untainted by the pungent odors of the paddock.

ITINERANT MERCHANTS

Some two hundred years ago, Captain Ephraim Bartlett, owner and skipper of the schooner *Squirrel*, worked his ship up the winding Connecticut River as far as the town of Hartford. Aboard was a cargo of salt cod, ironware, pottery, cloth, and powder and shot, all of which, upon arrival, he set out in an eye-catching display on the deck of his ship. During his stay in Hartford, people from the city and the surrounding countryside and peddlers stocking up for their next trek clambored aboard the *Squirrel* to see what Salesman-Captain Bartlett had to sell. They gawked at his merchandise, haggled over prices, and muddied up his deck, but they bought his goods. Some paid cash, but most offered corn, pelts, hides, and salt pork, all of which Bartlett cheerfully accepted until his ship was filled, whereupon he sailed to New York and re-opened shop there on the decks of the *Squirrel*.

Wherever he went, landlubbers quite properly addressed the master of the *Squirrel* as "Captain," and when he died his obituary dutifully referred to him as having been a master mariner. All of which was as it should have been. But Bartlett was more than that. He, like so many others, was an itinerant merchant whose ship was his shop.

So, too, was Enoch Reed, who brought his sloop *Tender* to Hartford with a cargo of rock salt, which he let be known he would trade for flaxseed. He took the flaxseed to Ireland, where he sold it at a profit, then proceeded to England to buy a general cargo of goods for the West Indies, where he purchased sugar, rum, and molasses to carry home to America. Such triangular voyages were exceedingly profitable to captains with a knack for buying at a low price and a flair for selling at a better figure.

SEAGOING ICEMEN

Captain Frederick Tudor was a man endowed with a sharp eye for a chance to turn an honest dollar. Tudor was a visitor to tropical ports in the early 1800s, long before the discovery of the process for manufacturing artificial ice. In all areas in the world where temperatures remained higher than thirty-two degrees Fahrenheit, men lived and died without the benefit of ice and the cheerful tinkling of it in their mugs of rum—a deplorable situation that set Tudor to thinking as he quaffed a tepid drink in Havana. He thought of the ice a foot or more thick on the ponds of New England and of the icehouses there where ice, cut in blocks from the ponds in winter, was bedded down in sawdust and stored for use during the summer months. If ice would keep for months in an icehouse, Tudor reasoned, it would keep in the hold of a ship if it were well packed and the hatches were carefully battened down.

Naturally, there were problems and risks. If the ice melted during the voyage, the tons of water sloshing around in the hold might cause the ship to capsize in a heavy sea. And once the hatches were opened upon arrival at a tropical port, the ice would melt quickly. But then, it would sell quickly too, and in all likelihood more quickly than it melted. It was a dazzling scheme, and the more Tudor calculated his costs (nominal) and what his profit would be (exorbitant), the more irresistible became the urge to make an experimental trip south with a cargo of frozen water.

One bit of encouragement for his scheme was recorded in Tudor's diary: "A French lady Mad. H. now in Boston & acquainted at our house from Trinidad assured me that ice creams were carried there when it was in possession of the English in pots packed in earth or sand & from Europe a voyage 'at least one third longer than from the United States.'

"But of all the greatest confidence arises from what a french gentl. I think Maj. R. mentioned at our house. I observed to him that I supposed he never saw ice in the West Indies—he replied that he had frequently seen it in very small quantities on the ends of the boards that were discharging from the holds of American vessels. The boards had

SHIP ICEKING OF NEW YORK CAPTAIN BARTLETT

The Tudor Ice Company built three beautiful ships, one of which, the Ice King, *is shown above under full sail. Before the age of ice-making machinery these big ships, plus others chartered by Tudor, carried ice cut from New England ponds to tropical countries.*

been shipped from hence in winter & that the little ice that could have adhered to them should not have melted in the holds of the Vessels seems surprising."

In New England Frederick Tudor's idea was viewed with skepticism. He was told he was carrying a Yankee notion too far and would be well advised to stick to cargoes of cod and salt pork.

Tudor's detractors proved right—at first. He loaded one hundred and thirty tons of ice aboard the brig *Favorite* and sailed on what turned out to

be an unusually slow passage to Martinique. Most of the ice melted during the voyage; the remainder melted quickly in port, where there were no facilities for rapid unloading and proper storage.

Undaunted by his out-of-pocket loss of forty-five hundred dollars and the taunts of I-told-you-so when he returned home, Tudor fitted out the *Trident* as an ice carrier. She was better insulated than the *Favorite* and Tudor bought ice that was not less than twenty inches thick instead of the nine or ten inches customary for the domestic market. Tudor sailed the *Trident* to Havana, where he delivered enough of his cargo intact to impress the Spanish authorities with the possibility, as well as the desirability, of such a trade. Over well-iced drinks Tudor finagled monopoly privileges that virtually made him Cuba's iceman, in anticipation of which

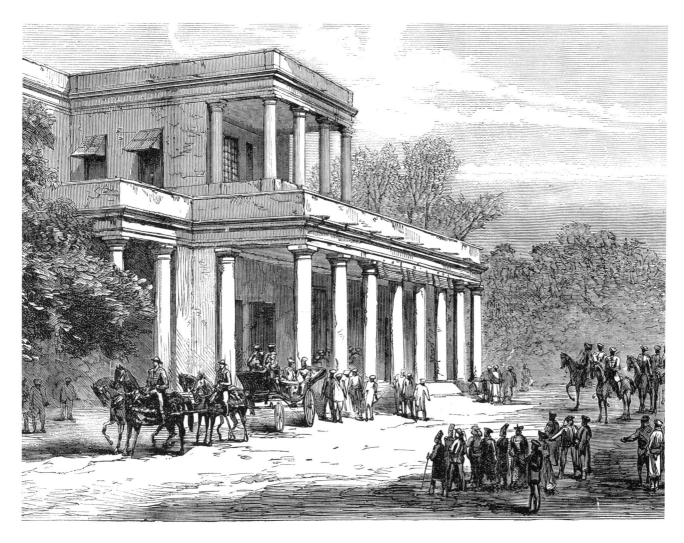

Captain Tudor was internationally known as the "world's iceman." The princes and other nabobs in India were among his best customers, and the ice he delivered to Bombay and Calcutta cooled the drinks served on festive occasions at residences such as the one shown in this sketch.

the authorities agreed to erect a suitable storage house for his future cargoes.

Tudor's ice business flourished for many years and he became known as the world's iceman. He built icehouses at Kingston, Martinique, and other West Indian ports. A few years later he played a long shot and sent the bark *Madagascar* on an experimental voyage to Rio de Janeiro. The profits were more than satisfactory, and other ships were dispatched to Brazilian ports. In 1833 Tudor made the first shipment of ice to India in the ship *Tuscany*.

The voyage out to Calcutta was made in four months and seven days, during which the *Tuscany* crossed the equator twice. About half the tonnage of ice was lost in transit and during discharge in Calcutta, but the remainder was sold at a price high enough to earn a profit on the voyage.

A Mr. J. J. Dixwell, who acted as Tudor's agent in Calcutta, was swamped with questions and a few complaints about this strange cargo from America. The query most often put to him concerned the best method of keeping ice after the customer had purchased a chunk from the icehouse, although it was not uncommon for Dixwell to be asked if ice grew on trees or shrubs and could such plants be brought to India. The complaints came from the uninitiated who left ice in the sun and felt defrauded when they found only a damp spot where the ice had been. Many demanded their money back.

The ice trade grew phenomenally, as did the number of Tudor's competitors once they realized he had a good thing going. In 1846, 175 ships sailed with 65,000 tons of ice for export. The numbers increased to 363 ships and 146,000 tons by 1856. A great many of these ice cargoes were delivered to such faraway ports as Cape Town, Bombay, Calcutta, Rangoon, Singapore, and Melbourne, and to cities on both coasts of South America. On very long voyages the average wastage was about 40 per cent, but since ice sold for as much as fifty-six dollars a ton in such places as Calcutta and a ship earned money for a return cargo of regular trade goods, the ice trade was a profitable one. The high-water mark was reached in 1880 when 890,364 tons of ice were forwarded to foreign destinations in 1,735 ships.

Then, suddenly, disaster struck. The winter of 1880–81 was unseasonably warm, causing a failure of the New England ice crop. Ice for export was scarce and soared in price. This was the moment the first inventors and manufacturers of artificial ice-making machinery had been waiting for. They moved into the market and sold their machines around the world. The natural-ice trade never recovered from this crop failure and within a few years it had entirely died out.

The foregoing are accounts of the adventures of only a few seagoing salesmen. There were thousands of men like them and most were eminently successful. In time, however, as overseas business became more firmly established, shipowners made fewer demands upon their captains to act as both mariners and salesmen. Agents were appointed in foreign ports to handle the customs details and to act as brokers in the sale of cargoes and as buyers for return cargoes.

Foreign agents more than earned their commissions. They had on-the-spot knowledge of local customs regulations and of the avariciousness of the customs officials. They knew exactly how many palms to grease, and how well, before a ship and its cargo arrived. They knew the local merchants and at what point, up to a split second, to stop dickering over price and conclude a sale. Furthermore, they knew where and how goods to be shipped back to

At San Francisco (below) and hundreds of other ports around the world the disposal of a cargo at a profit depended largely upon the captain's prowess as a salesman.

Exasperated sea captains learned to be patient when transacting business with local customs-house authorities. There was no way to hurry a customs official who took diabolical pleasure in lingering over the red tape of his office and the processing of innumerable documents and permits.

the owner's home port could be bought most advantageously. In a matter of days a good agent could transact business that might take a captain, feeling his way through a maze of local customs and red tape, a month or more to accomplish.

And so, at about the middle of the last century, ships' captains, once among America's most successful salesmen, were established in the role of masters and navigators. Salesmanship and mercantilism became the business of others.

24

The Peddlers

For more than two hundred years the peddler with a pack on his back or a wagonload of Yankee notions was an indispensable man in our system of distribution.

THE SEA AND THE BROAD BAYS and rivers sweeping far into the continent offered the early American colonists their easiest and cheapest highroad for commerce and communications. There were literally tens of thousands of miles of shore line that could be reached handily by boat; yet, owing to some streak of adventurousness and independence in man's nature, it was not long before a number of restless people packed their scanty possessions and struck out for the heavily wooded, hilly interior.

As these defectors from the tidewater areas moved inland, cleared their land, and established outposts of civilization in western Massachusetts or Virginia and along the Mohawk Valley in New York State, they presented a challenging opportunity to other men whose minds were occupied with trade and commerce. A farm family could build its own cabin, raise its food, knock together furniture, and weave cloth, but there were some things they could not raise or make with their hands. Each farm, each grist mill, each nucleus of some future village had its constant need for a supply of worldly goods, just as each had a surplus of produce to be sold in the

A peddler showing cloth to a girl in a farm kitchen.

seaboard markets. These outposts constituted a market that could not be ignored—and they were not ignored long. Soon stout-legged men were hoisting trunkloads of merchandise on their backs and trudging off into the pathless forests to trade with the people who had moved inland.

These were the peddlers. For the next two centuries they were to follow doggedly in the shadows of the far-wandering Americans as they rafted down the Ohio and Mississippi rivers, trekked along the Wilderness Road and the Santa Fe Trail, and ultimately moved in on the Spaniards on the far side of the Rockies in California.

Considering the number of easier and more sedate ways there were to earn a living, one wonders why men chose to become peddlers. In almost every respect it was a dog's life, knocking around the raw back country of America. When the peddlers went out on the road, they were quite literally on the road—afoot, sloshing through ankle-deep mud in winter, or scuffing up a cloud of dust in summer. They were snapped at by vicious dogs, shot at by Indians, nipped by frost, and pounced upon by hijackers. Many were bitten by rattlesnakes and all were feasted upon by fleas, gnats, mosquitoes, bedbugs, leeches, and other flying and crawling tormentors.

Despite these occupational hazards, there were many overriding reasons why so many men chose such a precarious profession. Adventure was one of them, and from all accounts the peddlers encountered enough of that. A chance to get about and travel was another; early Americans had a consuming curiosity about the make-up of their country, and for a man with a restless foot, peddling supplied plenty of exercise. As early as 1800 several thousand peddlers were roaming the New England country-

side and pushing into the Middle Atlantic and Southern states.

The main reason for "going peddling" was opportunity. A young, healthy man who wanted more from life than the dull chore of pushing a quill in a counting house or milking cows on a farm chose peddling as the road to opportunity. It was a business that required no previous experience and very little capital. A peddler could quickly learn his trade as he made his rounds, and for as little as ten or twenty dollars in cash he could buy enough stock to set himself up in business. If he was known to local merchants to be honest and conscientious, he could usually get stocks of merchandise on consignment.

There was no lack of opportunity for ambitious peddlers, as the market for their goods was rapidly expanding. Many peddlers accumulated enough money after several years on the road to retire from traveling and settle down at home as merchants or

At farms located a day's journey from the nearest store, the arrival of a peddler was a welcome event that drew the attention of the entire family. Most of the articles shown in the sketch at the right, including the book the housewife is reading and the chair (which came unassembled), were purchased from peddlers.

traders. Thousands of others spotted remote villages and crossroads that might someday become bustling centers of trade and transportation. They returned to such places and settled down. Some opened stores and became prosperous merchants. Others became jobbers and wholesalers, while still others acted as selling agents for firms whose goods they had once carried on their backs.

John McKnight of Hartford, mentioned in the *Colonial History of Hartford*, came from Glasgow in 1738, bringing with him English goods valued at £60 sterling, "which he traveled with and Disposed of in this Colony. After two years' experience

ington, who was one of the promoters of the Central Pacific Railroad, peddled his way across the continent to San Francisco. B. T. Babbitt, whose soap became a household word, began his business career as a peddler. Abijah Smith of Derby, Connecticut, returning from a peddling trip into Pennsylvania, brought with him several bags of anthracite coal. After the people of Derby had burned these curious black stones in their grates, they wanted more. Smith ordered anthracite shipped by boat from Pennsylvania and built up an enormous business in coal throughout Connecticut. In the 1850s a western Massachusetts manufacturer of tinware, sheet iron, and copperware had sixteen peddlers on the road and did an annual gross business of close to one hundred thousand dollars.

A noted historian, Lewis B. Atherton, in writing about the main "migratory merchants" of the 1830s, remarked:

"Some men started as peddlers and through economy were able to open stores. Jared Warner, who became a successful merchant and dealer in produce and lumber in Wisconsin, peddled goods in his early business career.

"His outfit consisted of merchandise bought in Pittsburgh at a cost of $324.71—horse at $45, wagon at $6 and harness at $14. Approximately half his goods were bought on time. He started westward with his merchandise and a cash reserve of $2.15, which had increased to $260 at Terre Haute, Indiana, four days before he started home. Warner travelled from six to twenty miles a day on the trip west, going through Ohio, Indiana and Illinois.

"His outward journey covered a distance of 620 miles and was made in a little over two months' time. The route home was shorter than the one he had followed on the outward journey, and Warner made fewer stops to trade along the way. His stock had been replenished by small purchases in Richmond and Indianapolis, but it is likely that his merchandise had been sold down to the point where it was useless to try to continue regular sales. The Day Book does not give complete figures on the trip, and it is impossible to tell how much he profited from his three months of trading. By 1836, however, he was operating a store at Canfield, Ohio, and his future journeys were confined to occasional trips up

as a trader, he was associated with Robert Sloan, a Hartford merchant. Then he went to New Haven, where he built two ships of about 250 tons each, and was clerk of the company that extended Union or Long Wharf. Later he returned to Hartford. At one time he had large means, and gave financial aid to the government; but he suffered from the depreciation of old tenor [old legal tender], and by being 'unhappily bound for another man.' In 1774 he petitioned the General Assembly for a peddler's license, intending to return to his early occupation. When he died in 1785 at East Windsor, the *Courant* termed him 'an eminent trader' to which his extant account books bear witness."

Adam Gimbel, whose descendants founded the famous Gimbel Brothers department store in New York City, peddled notions in Indiana before opening a dry-goods store at Vincennes. John Jacob Astor peddled bakery products on the streets of New York before going into the fur trade. Collis P. Hunt-

and down the Ohio River, for the purpose of buying and selling produce and merchandise."

NECESSITIES AND FRIVOLITIES

The first of the Yankee peddlers carried a general line of housewares and notions. Pots and pans, axes, nails, thread, buttons, scissors, thimbles, and combs were among the fastest-selling items. The biggest profits were earned on such frivolities as bits of lace, ribbon and fancy cloths, mirrors, spices, tea, coffee, toilet water, and nostrums. Fiddle strings and spectacles were other popular items.

There were limits, naturally, to the load of these things a man could carry or stow on his horse. Such weight and space limitations led some of the peddlers to become specialists in certain lines. Instead of loading up with a hodgepodge of general merchandise, the specialists handled spices only, or tinware, or herbs and medicines. In later years there were clock peddlers, furniture peddlers, sewing-machine peddlers. There were even peddlers of wagons and carriages—men who hitched together a string of three or four vehicles and drove them around until they found buyers for the new rigs.

There was no end to the peddlers' ingenuity in finding customers. They tracked down the remotest farmhouse and loneliest cabin and turned up at every fair or carnival. In the Deep South they paddled up and down the rivers and bayous in canoes and drew their customers from plantation mansions and shanties by blowing on a bugle or a conch shell. But mostly the peddlers walked, pacing off the long lonely miles with their heavy loads on their backs, the dream of riches easing their way.

The peddler's trunk was a long, rather narrow box usually made of tin. A strong peddler starting out on a selling expedition carried two such trunks, one on each shoulder. The stowing of merchandise in these trunks was a major undertaking requiring great skill. Dishes and pans of varying size were nested. Into pots went buttons, pins, nails, and rib-

As long as the peddlers stayed in the back country (above), they were free men, but when they sold door-to-door in towns and villages, local merchants raised a fuss. Many towns banned peddlers; others required the itinerants to obtain expensive licenses. Below: peddlers in the wholesale district of New York.

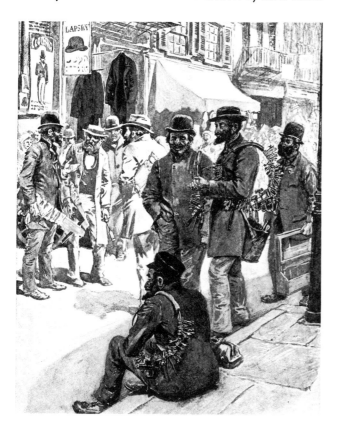

Peddlers gladly accepted rags in trade for their wares. Rags were readily salable to paper manufacturers at a handsome profit. The man in this sketch (right) appears to have got a good-sized bundle in exchange for the pan the farm woman is holding.

28

The peddler charged a high markup on everything he sold, but he earned it. A family might spend several hours ogling all the wondrous items in his wagon but buy only two or three dollars' worth of goods, paid for partly in cash, the balance in homemade items, pelts, or produce, which the peddler carried back to town and sold. One peddler who had accepted eggs in payment for his wares lost the profits for a two weeks' trip when his wagon upset and the eggs were smashed.

bons. Gingham and bright calico were wrapped around long-handled forks.

So packed, each trunk weighed up to fifty or sixty pounds. And, paradoxically, the more a peddler sold the heavier his trunks became, for, often as not, the buyers had only grain, honey, furs, and homemade woodenware to exchange for the peddler's goods. These products, which often weighed more than those the peddler had sold, had to be carried back

30

to his home base and sold to merchants and whole-salers. How successfully the peddler sold these country wares determined his ultimate profit.

There were compensations, however. Wherever the peddler called he was a welcome visitor. House-wives stopped their work, men came in from the fields, children gathered round when the trunks were opened. There was no great hurry. Everyone wanted to see all the fascinating goods and hear every scrap of the latest news. And the peddler was in no hurry either, for he welcomed a chance to rest his road-weary legs. If it was morning when the peddler arrived, he could usually drag out negotiations long enough to be asked to stay for the noon-day meal, and if he arrived in the afternoon, there was a good chance of an invitation to stay over for supper and the night. One peddler who pushed his luck too far staying on the road until late fall got snowbound in an early blizzard and spent three days at a farm in Illinois.

As roads improved, some peddlers rode on horse-back, carrying their wares strapped to their horses. Others used wagons capable of carrying fair-sized loads. These improvements in transportation increased the importance of the peddler in our early commerce. He was able to go farther, carry more stock, and take a greater volume of goods in trade or barter.

But the peddlers still had their troubles, as the following letter written by a peddler of bonnets to his supplier in western Massachusetts attests:

"Tioga June 22nd 1830 NYK
"Sir.

"From Bainbridge I arrived here today at 12 o'clock by driving 12 miles yesterday in the rain. In consequence of the heavy rains that have fallen in this country the past ten days the roads are *tremendous* bad they are so rutted that I have been obliged to fasten a roap to the top of my box and hold on. I have just met with a Dry Goods Pedler who trades through all parts of Pennsylvania. he says the roads are much worse than they are here however I am not discouraged yet, my horses stand it well except they are galled a little by driveing yesterday and today in the rain & for Bonets I have found no chance for any sales of consequence yet.

"The Small Pox is spreading over this country. "don't send out another Pedler with so high a box.
In haste yours
Rodney Hill
"I am in good health."

A SELLER'S MARKET

By early March, after a winter of isolation, farm families were eagerly looking for the man with the packs on his back. Long before his arrival they had carefully listed the wares they *must* have—a dozen buttons, a paper of pins (very expensive in those days), a new jackknife, two pewter mugs, six needles—and as an appendage to that list of essentials there was a much longer list of the things they would *like* to have.

The meeting between a farm family and a peddler was a lively swapping session, with the peddler in the much stronger position to get the better of every transaction. First of all, he was working in a seller's market. His wares included items the family could not do without. Then, too, he was selling to people who understandably were eager to add the slightest luxuries to their meager possessions. People possessing so little found it difficult to resist a jew's-harp for the children, a stick of candy, a bit of gay ribbon or lace, or a pretty piece of chinaware to set on the bare mantel over the kitchen fireplace. Sales resistance was low—even among the most frugal—and country people were uninformed about goods and prices.

A peddler could hold out for a 600 per cent markup for pepper, blandly explaining that the price was high owing to an obscure war at sea which had shut off imports from the Spice Islands. So, too, could he justify exorbitant prices for other articles by fixing the blame on the British king or the avarice of the merchants of Boston, New York, or Philadelphia. His customers were in no position to dispute his laments about skyrocketing prices in market places, and they frequently paid through the nose for the things they bought.

But when it came their turn to offer goods to the peddler in payment, farm families invariably found that the demand for such things as they had for barter was poor indeed. Honey might be a drug on the market according to the peddler; the mer-

The crab man

The howling man

The pepper-pot woman

chants in town were not much interested that year in coonskins and beaver pelts or handmade chairs. If the peddler was to be believed, he could resell such items only at very depressed prices, hardly more than it would cost him to transport them back to town.

Very often a peddler would deliberately mark up an item unrealistically so that he could magnanimously come down to, say, one half the figure and still make an exorbitant profit—a process of repricing which was an exhilarating experience for both the peddler and his customer.

THE PEDDLERS: PRO AND CON

A magazine article published at the time when peddlers were swarming over the land had this to say about peddlers and their profession:

"The Yankee Peddler must be a man intimately acquainted with 'human nature'; and his manners must be of that flexible kind which adjusts itself to all ages, both sexes and to all conditions. He must be grave and respectful with the clergyman, intelligent and polite with the squire, shrewd with the lawyer, jovial with the publican, frank and insinuating with the farmer, and full of flattery and devotion to the girls. . . .

"Some individuals devote themselves to a particular article; one man is a faithful follower of

City street vendors were a particular kind of peddler. The four shown here, including a woman, are hawking their products on the streets of Philadelphia during the Centennial Exposition of 1876.

Father Time, and deals only in clocks. Much dreaded is he by many that fear him, distrust him, yet patronize him. Another deals in confectionery; he is a favorite with the girls, with whom he drives sharp bargains while the 'old man' is absent in the 'field'; a present of an ounce of snuff wins the heart of the 'old lady.'

"The tin pedler, who barters his wares for rags in lieu of money, is a man in very bad repute among housewives; and yet somehow or other he contrives to do a thriving business. 'The horrid tin pedler,' as he is called, rarely calls at a house without effecting his object; and many a lovely housewife's sideboard would look grim and dismal were it not replenished and rendered glittering by the visits of the tin pedler.

"Shrewd and calculating, cunning and overreaching as he is apt to be, yet the pedler is not without his good qualities and benefits to the housewife. His life is not a life of ease—he is subject to many vicissitudes; and to bear up under all, he must be a resolute and enterprising man of character; for if he deals dishonestly, he will very soon run out his routes, and come to the end of his chain.

32

"We are inclined to think that pedlers, as a class, have been unjustly condemned by the community. The tricks of a few individuals have been charged on the entire class, whereas the truth probably is that there is no more unfair dealing among the pedlers than among any other class of tradesmen."

There is plenty of evidence that peddlers could be masters of the art of deception and overpricing, and unquestionably a minority of them were first-class bums and crooks. The drunken brawls, bloody fights, and shady deals they were involved in were well publicized and drew sharp blasts from newspaper editors. Many inns and taverns posted notices bluntly announcing that peddlers were unwelcome. Throughout the land peddlers were scorned by many pious people as ungodly ne'er-do-wells only a cut or two better than gypsies.

Another important consideration, portending the war that was to divide our nation in the 1860s, was political. In the South it was not unusual to refer to the peddlers as "those damn Yankees from Connecticut," and as far back as 1820 the following editorial, headed "Unpleasant State of Society," appeared in the *Niles Weekly Register* in Baltimore:

"Some of the southern states are jealous of the designs of the 'northern traveling pedlars'—they are said to have increased of late to an 'alarming degree,' and a writer in a Charleston paper says—'If, as may be the case, these men should be *political* missionaries, they cannot be stopped too soon in their nefarious career. . . . The doctrine of the Missouri question [whether Missouri should be admitted to the Union as a slave state] is not yet, I hope, erased from our remembrance.'

"As *pedlars*, we have not the least objection that these people should be kept out of all the states, except their own. The traffic is injurious to the interests and the morals of society, and many of them are dealers in counterfeit notes; but as 'political missionaries'—the idea is too absurd to be conceived, except in the mind of one who trembles at the falling of a leaf. It is like the story which was 'right soberly' told some years ago, that Napoleon had contrived the subjugation of the United States, by the introduction of his myrmidons as dancing masters and barbers!—except that it may be honest, while the other was deliberately wicked and false. Buy Jonathan's wares and truck or trade with him, and he will never abstract his mind from his business to the Missouri question, depend upon it!"

But for all the unsavory publicity generated by the few bad eggs among them, the peddlers served a useful purpose. Importers and small manufacturers depended upon them to distribute a large portion of their goods. Several million people relied on these wandering merchants to bring them the goods they needed and to carry away the things they had produced. This army of walkers represented a primitive and inefficient way of carrying on trade, but when the peddler's trunks were opened and he began his persuasive sales pitch, as one historian has remarked, "wants dawned on the minds of the household that they had never known before."

The peddler's salesmanship and physical endurance kept alive the first stirrings of our industrial economy. He has gone now, but for two hundred years he was an important man among men engaged in important affairs.

A tin peddler on the road.

34

Back-Yard Industries

*Men with a talent for tinkering began making
things in their homes or in small back-yard shops,
and going out to sell these items spelled
the difference between commercial failure
and production expansion.*

IN TIME, as the country people of our nation became more adept at making things at home for the ever growing American market, some of them began to realize it was not sufficient to rely on a peddler to distribute and sell their products. Production in many of these home manufactories was exceeding the quantities a peddler could handle and those manufacturers who lived fairly near a village that was quickly growing into a town, or lived in the more thickly settled farm areas, quite rightly concluded that they could increase their sales if they themselves journeyed about to sell their goods.

Levi Dickenson, a Yankee farmer in Hadley, Massachusetts, decided one year to raise a half-acre of broom corn, which, when harvested, he made into some two hundred brooms—more than any one peddler could physically handle. So Dickenson struck out on his own. He packed the brooms into a cart and went peddling in neighboring towns. Soon he had sold every broom at a "goodly" profit. Encouraged by the success of this venture, Dickenson planted a full acre of broom corn the next year

"The Village Blacksmith," lithograph by Currier and Ives.

and persuaded some of his farmer neighbors to do the same. Each year more brooms were made in Hadley and each year Dickenson and his neighbors set out to sell them. In short order Dickenson and his enterprising neighbors had saturated the local market; thus, before long, they were traveling as far as Pittsfield and New London and even to Albany and Boston. They sold their brooms house-to-house, to local merchants and to wholesalers—and they succeeded without benefit of the peddler as an intermediary.

Benjamin Wood, Jr., up in New Hampshire, worked as a cooper during the winter, making butter tubs, cider barrels, leach tubs, and cheese hoops. As a side line he made goose-quill pens, dippers, wooden bowls, shaving mugs and other woodenware. In the spring, Wood went off for three or four weeks to "voige," as he termed it, to sell his woodenware and quills to the farmers in the hills.

As early as 1794, Samuel Yale of Meriden, Connecticut, had established a small factory for the making of pewter buttons and afterward for the production of other small articles of metal. His business had begun with the making of cut nails, partly by hand and partly by machine, each separately headed.

Farther south in Connecticut, James Benedict manufactured boots and shoes in a small shop adjoining his home in New Canaan. What made Benedict an outstanding bootmaker was that his boots came in four styles. In his day only a handful of American bootmakers made ready-to-wear shoes, and of them Benedict was perhaps the only one who cared about style and size. It was the custom then to make boots to the approximate size of a customer's foot and to ignore completely all thought of style; so long as a person could manage to get his foot into a shoe, it was considered suitable. Moreover, Benedict concentrated on the high-price market and sold his output in New York City to merchants who catered to a clientele of some wealth.

Today New Canaan is a commuter suburb of New York, forty miles from Grand Central Station. Back in 1780 New Canaan was far out in the country; the trip to New York was more of an ordeal than flying to Europe now—and it took longer, too. Undoubtedly Benedict left home at the crack of dawn and covered the ten miles to Stamford on horseback or by cart. At Stamford he boarded one of the many packet boats that sailed Long Island Sound, linking New York with towns and villages along the Connecticut and Rhode Island shore lines. If all went well and the winds held steady, the packet boat tied up at an East River dock on Manhattan Island sometime early in the evening. More than likely, Benedict put up at one of the inns on

Pearl Street or on Broadway. And we can easily imagine that upon arrival he was wearied from his travels and went to bed early, though the hubbub of city traffic may have kept the countryman awake longer than was his custom.

All these things we can readily picture, for descriptions are available of the places Benedict passed through, the boats he traveled in, and the inns where he stayed. What we must imagine are Benedict's calls on the shoe merchants of New York. What did he say in his sales presentation? How did he convince the merchants that the public would buy "shop-made" shoes in those days when most shoes were made to order? How firmly did he resist the buyer's insistent charge that his prices

The old lithograph published by N. Currier shows a farmer loading his wagon with surplus crops, which he will sell at the local market.

36

were too high, times were hard, money was tight, and prices were falling? Very likely sales resistance today is the same as in Benedict's time. If one of his customers could step out of the wings of the musty past and confront a shoe salesman making his rounds, the salesman would undoubtedly hear what he heard only last week on Fifth Avenue, or on Chicago's State Street, or along the Miracle Mile in Los Angeles.

Benedict must have been as good a salesman as he was a shoemaker, for his business flourished and volume crept up year after year as he continued to coax orders from his New York buyers.

The first hatmaking shop in America was operated by another Benedict—Zadoc—who began his business in 1780 in Danbury, Connecticut. He employed one journeyman and two apprentices, whose combined efforts produced eighteen fur hats a week. Benedict bought furs from peddlers and local farm-ers and sold his hats locally and throughout southeastern Connecticut. In time he extended his marketing area to include New York, Philadelphia, and points south as far as Charleston and Savannah.

FROM BACKYARD TO BIG TIME

Two Irishmen, William and Edgar Pattison, who settled in Berlin, Connecticut, were the first men to capitalize in a big way on the growing market for tinware. They went to Boston and bought a stock of tin imported from England, brought it back to Berlin by cart, and in their shop knocked together an inventory of pots, pans, basins, cups,

Troy, on the upper Hudson River, was a strategically located funnel for the products of the upper New England home industries that were headed for the New York City market.

Deep-sea fishermen were Captain Crandall's first customers. Later he enlarged his market for fishing lines to include sportsmen who fished for the fun of it.

and teakettles. They then peddled these goods while their sister supervised the work of several apprentice tinsmiths who had been employed to help with production.

It did not take long for word to get around that the Pattisons had a salable line of goods, and peddlers from all over the state came to Berlin to do business with William and Edgar. Through their peddlers the Pattisons expanded their sales to cover most of what was then the American market. Every fall twenty-five or more men loaded with Pattison tinware headed south on a fifteen-hundred-mile house-to-house selling odyssey. By the time they got as far south as Georgia they had sold their stock and turned north to deadhead back to Berlin for a fresh supply. This long walk home empty-handed seemed like a waste of time and manpower to the Pattisons, and they decided to do something about it. When the peddlers left Berlin the next fall, the Pattisons sent a half-dozen of their tinsmiths and a supply of tin plate by boat to Savannah, where the tinsmiths set up shop and worked through the winter months making a supply of tinware for the peddlers to pick up and sell on their return trip north in the spring. Other tinsmiths were sent to Montreal, where they made pots and pans to re-

38

plenish supplies of the peddlers covering the northern territory for the Pattisons.

This jumping-bean type of operation by the energetic Pattison brothers was the forerunner of the branch plant. It enabled them to sell everywhere without having to charge "prices slightly higher south of the Potomac" or "north of Albany." The Pattisons never had any difficulty finding enough men to sell their products, for they had leveled out the peaks and valleys of seasonal sales and supplied their men with goods to sell on a year-round basis.

In Rhode Island, Captain Lester Crandall also was confronted with a seasonal lull in his business but one which he could not do much about. Crandall was a commercial fisherman and could not go out to sea during the winter months when storms swept along the Atlantic coast. Like most commercial fishermen in the 1820s, Captain Crandall made his own fishing lines during the off season, twisting them with the aid of a large hand-operated wooden wheel set up in the back yard of his home in Ashaway. Crandall's lines were considerably better than those made by other fishermen along the Rhode Island coast, and when many of the old salts asked him to make lines for them at reasonable prices, Crandall decided he would do better as a full-time line maker than as a fisherman. He gave up the precarious life of deep-sea fishing and, in 1824, with his son, A. J. Crandall, established the Ashaway Line & Twine Company, thereby becoming a manufacturer, which, in those days, was almost as precarious as being a fisherman.

Tucked away in the archives of our historical societies are literally hundreds of records of such small-time entrepreneurs who contributed their handicraft to the commerce of the nation. We know how these people worked and the tools and raw materials they worked with. We know, in many cases, how much business they did and how greatly or inconsequentially they prospered. But all we can learn about their selling and merchandising techniques are generalities. The records merely show that a man took his products and went "voiging" among his neighbors or that another man took his wares to the city to sell them. We do not know how Captain Crandall and his son developed sales for the Ashaway Line & Twine Company, but after the initial orders from local fishermen were filled, sales along the coast undoubtedly developed from word-of-mouth appreciation of Ashaway fishing lines. And apparently both Crandalls realized there was a good market for their lines among sports fishermen throughout the country. Just how they went about reaching this market is not known, but it is reasonably certain that one of the two men made a trip to New York to call on sporting-goods dealers, for several such dealers carried Ashaway lines as early as 1830.

THE FREE TRIAL AND INSTALLMENT BUYING

Occasionally, the records do give us an insight into the sales techniques used by a pioneer entre-

Farmers in rural New England had very little cash income. Most of their buying from men such as Eli Terry or Benjamin Wood was on a barter basis or with long-term installment payments. Purchases were made only after long and soul-searching deliberation.

preneur. One of these men whose techniques we know something about was a Connecticut clockmaker named Eli Terry, a man whose curiosity had been aroused by Eli Whitney's ideas for the standardization and interchangeability of parts used in manufacturing processes.

When Eli Whitney quit the South in disgust and abandoned all hope of collecting a penny of royalty from the hundreds of blacksmiths who had copied his cotton gin, he moved to New Haven and, in 1798, began manufacturing muskets for the U.S. Army. At that time, muskets—or any other product, for that matter—were the work of individual craftsmen. A gunsmith was a highly skilled artisan who made one complete gun at a time. Naturally, production was slow and costly, and no two guns were exactly the same. Barrel lengths varied slightly, as did the bores. Some triggers pulled hard, others soft, and the sights were not always perfectly aligned.

Whitney changed all this. He hired carpenters who did nothing but turn out wooden stocks; other men made the barrels or the firing apparatus or the triggers. Still other men assembled the finished muskets out of these standard-sized parts. This was not the world's first application of assembly-line production, but it was one of the earliest and certainly one of the first successful operations of its kind in America. Eli Terry watched with awe and admiration the performance in Whitney's plant and forthwith decided he could make clocks in the same way.

So, using the assembly-line technique, Terry produced four identical clocks. Then he packed them in a saddlebag and set off across the wintry hills of the Connecticut River valley on a sales trip among the farmers.

If Terry had not been a smart merchandiser, the chances are his trip would have been unsuccessful, for he ran headlong into sales resistance. Several prospective customers to whom Terry and his merchandise were unknown asked what guarantee there was that the clock would go on ticking after Terry had ridden off. These farmers had been stung before with shoddy merchandise sold by itinerant peddlers, and a timepiece with its intricate workings was something that might well break down very quickly.

Terry struck a bargain with these doubting Thomases. He would leave the clock and if it gave good service, he would collect payment on his next trip along that route; if the clock proved faulty, the customer would owe him nothing. It was a flabbergasting offer, and even the most skeptical were hard put to find a flaw in it. Thus Terry became the first man in America, so far as is known, to offer merchandise on a free-trial, no-money-down basis.

Other prospects on whom Terry called doubted they really needed a timepiece. In those unhurried days country people arose with the sun and went to bed when it got dark. Admittedly, a clock would be a nice thing to have, but a man hardly needed such an expensive luxury to tell him when it was time to get out of bed in the morning or when he was sleepy at night. To these people Terry made his same free-trial, no-money-down offer. It was a stratagem that seldom failed, for after a month with a clock in the kitchen, a farm family was loath to part with it. Its faithful recording of time might have been unimportant, but there was a warm and comforting friendliness about its quiet tick-tock.

The introduction of the assembly line and mass production, as in this shoe factory, added to the already difficult problem of selling and distribution.

41

Parking was no problem for this salesman, but getting enough orders from country stores to keep his plant operating was a real worry.

Few clocks were returned to Terry as he made his rounds to collect them or his money.

Leaving his clocks on a free-trial basis was not Terry's only sales approach. He sprang another innovation on those prospects who liked his clocks but lacked the wherewithal to pay the twenty-five dollars he had set as his price. That was more hard cash than many families saw in a month's time, and this paucity of money, Terry realized, would greatly restrict his market. On the other hand, he reasoned, he could double or triple his sales if he accepted a small down payment and arranged to collect regular installments on each of his trips through the country. So far as can be determined, Eli Terry was

the first man really to push installment buying.

By linking the advantages of the assembly line to his bold and appealing sales plan, Terry quickly became the world's largest maker of clocks. Within three years he had sold five thousand—a truly staggering quantity for those days—and had cut the price to an amazingly low five dollars.

TWO SMITHS WHO MADE GOOD

There were many other small entrepreneurs of back-yard size who made their first efforts at expansion through sales without the guidance of experience or the advice of marketing experts and surveys, and they did very well for themselves mainly because of their ingenuity and perseverance. In Poughkeepsie, New York, a traveler passing through the town in 1847 dined at James Smith's restaurant and gave him a recipe for what he said was a tasty and effective cough remedy. Smith whipped up a batch of the stuff in his kitchen and offered his cough drops to his patrons, who suffered from coughing and hacking during the blustery winter months. James's two sons, William and Andrew, were more aggressive in exploiting the market for the first cough drops made in America. When New York-Albany stagecoaches stopped at Poughkeepsie, the brothers climbed aboard and, in the manner of later-day train butchers, sold cough drops to the passengers. In addition, both brothers traveled up and down the Hudson River Valley and into the Catskills installing large jars of their father's cough drops in country drugstores.

In 1866 the Smith brothers inherited the cough-drop business along with several new problems. The success of what were then sold as Smith Brothers' Cough Drops inspired a host of imitators to make cough drops and try to capitalize on the Smiths' reputation by using names that could easily confuse the customer. One competitor came right out and

labeled his product "Smith Brothers." Others used such names as "Schmitt Brothers" or "Smith & Bros." One outfit, applying a new twist, called itself the "Smythe Sisters." To protect their interests, the Smith brothers designed the distinctive trademark of a picture of each man with the word *Trade* appearing under the picture of William and *Mark* under Andrew. This now famous trademark, by which the two brothers became known to millions of people as Trade and Mark, appeared on all the glass jars in which their cough drops were displayed on drugstore counters.

The trademark was some protection, but there was nothing to prevent a druggist or a rival manufacturer's salesman from filling a Smith Brothers' jar with cough drops of some other make. To prevent such deception, the Smiths in 1872 packaged their product in paper boxes, thereby becoming the first concern to introduce "factory-filled" packages. Thus the Smith brothers were among the first manufacturers to perceive the sales value of a brand name

TRADE
(William)

MARK
(Andrew)

43

and modern packaging methods. The results were phenomenal. Production of cough drops at the Smiths' Poughkeepsie plant jumped from five pounds a day to five tons.

There was another important reason for the booming sale of the Smith brothers' cough drops. In an age when concoctions of every kind were ballyhooed as positive cures for every conceivable ailment, James and his sons never resorted to outrageous claims for the therapeutic powers of their product. A cough drop was no cure for bunions or rheumatism, and the Smiths wisely refrained from alleging that it might be. No customer of theirs could ever grumble that he had been, to use the popular idiom of the time, bamboozled or humbugged.

THE FREE SAMPLE MAKES A SALE

Some years after the Smiths had discovered the sales power of a respected brand name and good packaging, Perley G. Gerrish discovered the value of market-testing. Gerrish, a distributor of Squirrel Brand assorted nuts, had worked out a recipe for a confectionery item he called a peanut bar. Carrying a shoebox filled with samples, he called on a number of his regular customers. They refused to stock the peanut bar; children, they said, would never go for it.

Gerrish was not so sure that retailers were right. To find out for himself, he loaded a wagon with nut bars and made a trip from Boston to Providence. Along the way he stopped whenever he came upon a school building and handed out free samples to the children. A few weeks later he retraced his route and called on the retailers. This time they bought. Youngsters by the dozen had trooped into their stores with pennies and nickels, asking for the new peanut bar.

Sampling is an old device for testing a market or a product, but until Gerrish came along with his openhanded largesse, samples had been doled out in such a miserly fashion that nothing much could be proved one way or another. Gerrish established that sample-testing a product is worthwhile provided the sampling is done on a scale large enough to make the test conclusive. One penny's worth of demand for a peanut bar would have made no impression on a retailer. Many pennies proffered over his counter made a deep impression and one that was not forgotten when the salesman came around for an order.

LAMBERT HITCHCOCK HITS THE ROAD

As in the case of James Benedict with his shoes, Lambert Hitchcock of Barkhamsted, Connecticut, had to decide whether to wait in his small shop for people to come to him and order the chairs he made or to go out and look for customers. He chose the second of these alternatives. A diary kept by his wife, Eunice, indicates that that good lady spent much time alone while Hitchcock traveled widely throughout New England and made frequent trips to New York ("My dear husband has this day started for New York. He expects to be absent some time") and to the South.

Hitchcock was no man to hit only the high spots and pass up orders in the smaller cities and towns that lay along his route. In 1835 he wrote: "Thursday morning last I arrived in Chicago from Detroit, after a journey (by horseback) of thirteen days, not on the most direct route to this place, but winding throughout the territory from one point to another at which I wished to stop. . . . I expect to return home by way of Cincinnati, Pittsburgh and Philadelphia."

During the forty-three years that Hitchcock was in business he saw a great deal of the country and sold many thousands of chairs. It would have been considerably easier and possibly more to his liking to remain at home, making chairs for occasional local customers. Had he done so, antique collectors a century later would not have unearthed so many prized Hitchcock chairs in far-flung parts of the country.

THE START OF THE FIFTY-SEVEN VARIETIES

The business that Henry J. Heinz established was in every sense of the word a back-yard industry. When Heinz was a small boy, he lived with his family in Sharpsburg, near Pittsburgh, Pennsylvania. His mother was a woman with a green thumb, which Henry inherited, and together they cultivated a large vegetable garden in their back yard. Their success in growing things was so great that

After considerable experimentation, beginning in 1844, Cyrus Wakefield found a way of stripping the hard cane surface from rattan and weaving it into cane seat covers. His back-yard industry developed rapidly. Through aggressive merchandising Wakefield built up such a thriving cane and rattan furniture business that he was able to purchase the clipper ship Hoogly to carry rattan from India to the plant he built in Boston.

In 1897 the Wakefield Company, which had made the first rattan furniture sold in this country, merged with the Heywood Brothers Company and became the Heywood-Wakefield Company.

each year there was a surplus of vegetables, which Henry loaded onto a wagon and took to Pittsburgh, where he sold the produce to retail grocers.

By the time Henry was sixteen he was making three deliveries a week and had developed a chain of customers. Late in the evening he would load his wagon, then go to bed until three in the morning, when he would start for Pittsburgh, an hour's journey away. In the course of his rounds, young Heinz began to wonder about the sense of delivering fresh produce to grocers at such an unearthly hour —not that he minded getting up at three, but there seemed little point in the grocers getting up at four or five in the morning to receive his deliveries. The vegetables were picked late the day before; why could he not deliver them that evening?

Henry suggested to his customers that he make his deliveries just before they closed shop at night. At first the grocers were against the idea, but when

Henry explained that they could sleep a few hours longer in the morning, they agreed to his plan. This was not a world-shaking idea, but it impressed the grocers as an indication of Heinz's consideration for his customers, and though they might not say so, they probably admired his spunk for breaking with an old tradition.

In later years Henry's good relations with his customers paid off. One of the crops in his large garden was horse-radish, which he sold in root form to the stores. Housewives who wanted horse-radish bought the roots and shredded them into sauce. It was a laborious task, and the pungent roots were as hard on the eyes as the strongest onions. As another special service for his grocers, one that would garner good will for them, Henry undertook to save the housewife both labor and tears by grating and bottling his own brand of horse-radish.

His customers readily agreed to stock the first Heinz-prepared food product; most of them, in fact, made an extra effort to push the sale of Henry's horse-radish. Later, when Henry added celery sauce and pickles to his line, these were stocked and pushed by his grocer friends.

Heinz, Crandall, Terry, Gerrish, and all the other men whose success is chronicled here began business in a small way at home. What made each of them prosper were the quality of their products and the imaginative and energetic ways they found to distribute, merchandise, and sell them. These men, and their contemporaries who sold ideas or products in this young and bustling country, were the progenitors of a giant industrial America.

From Yankee notions to nuclear reactors is a jump on a scale undreamed of by the early backyardsmen. No matter—the birth struggles of small and big business are similar and all find "voiges" of selling necessary.

In the rear of the handsome old house shown at the right Henry J. Heinz (left) and his mother raised vegetables, including horse-radish, which became the first of the famed "57 Varieties." Young Heinz's sensible break with tradition when selling vegetables to Pittsburgh grocers helped pave the way when he began merchandising his bottled goods.

46

Made in U.S.A.

Throughout the land factories were built, replacing home workshops, and the smoke from tall chimneys signaled the bestirring of American industry.

EVEN THOUGH MANY of our early back-yard industries were finding ways to increase production and sales, home manufacturing was quickly becoming inadequate to meet the market for various products. Besides, the men who came to this country seeking political and religious freedom were dedicated to economic freedom as well. They were dead-set against importing anything they could make for themselves—a line of thinking in sharp contrast with that of the people in other colonial possessions of the European powers. Thus, long before we had won our final battle for political freedom, small factories, equipped with crude machinery, began supplanting our cottage industries.

The roster of companies doing business today whose history spans a hundred years or more is long. In the records one can find a recurring pattern that set the stage for the success of these enterprises. In every case the founders recognized the importance of selling and knuckled down to mastering techniques in an age when salesmanship was an undeveloped art. For those old-timers, selling was very much a personal affair, executed by the physical act of getting out of the office and calling on prospects and customers. Large advertising cam-

Ashbil Griswold's beautiful pewterware and accurate accounts of 1824.

paigns to create a market or to act as a crutch for poor sales efforts were impossible. No mass-circulation media were available to an advertiser, and if there had been, these firms with their shoestring finances could not have afforded expensive campaigns. Direct-mail advertising was next to impossible—printing was crude and expensive, reliable mailing lists were nonexistent, and the mails were erratic, to put it mildly. Wholesalers and agents could be relied on to some extent to cover certain key marketing areas, but distribution by such subsidiary outlets was still in its infancy.

It was not enough for these young firms simply to make products that were a little better than their competitors' or those that could be imported, or even to come out with brand-new products for which there was an apparent market; thousands of failures attest to this. The firms that endured through the years were managed by men who were not lulled into a dangerous complacency by the now famous cliché that people will beat a path to the door of the man who makes a better mousetrap. As a matter of fact, Joseph Bostwick of Sharon, Connecticut, did design and make a vastly improved mousetrap, but he placed little credence in the old fable and hustled far and wide to explain to people why his trap was better. By doing so, he overcame the human aversion to change that acts as a strong drag on the sale of any new or improved product.

Some of our pioneer industrialists formulated the basic fundamentals of selling as it is practiced today. These men were not trained salesmen, and they had only an intuitive understanding of the fine points of closing a sale, but they succeeded because they were honest, sincere, and enthusiastic, and covered the ground for prospective buyers like a hound dog sniffing out a coon in hiding.

49

At the Philadelphia Centennial Exposition in 1876 this huge machine, reeling out an endless stream of brightly colored wallpaper, attracted great crowds of gaping spectators and symbolized the economic growth of America on its one-hundredth birthday as a republic.

Late in the afternoon of a sparkling day in October, 1799, a young man rode slowly up the deep valley that hems in the upper reaches of the Housatonic River. He was a lean, serious-minded man who had ridden west, as so many other men rode west at that stirring time in American history, with a very definite purpose in mind. Although Zenas Crane was only twenty-two years old, he was reconnoitering for a suitable site on which to establish a paper mill, the first in Massachusetts west of the Connecticut River. Zenas had examined and rejected a number of locations, none of which quite satisfied him, and it was not until he trotted into the western Massachusetts farming community of Dalton in the Berkshires that he discovered a place that met with all his exacting requirements. The swift-flowing Housatonic would provide an ample supply of the clear water so necessary for the manufacture of rag paper, as well as power to operate the mill's machinery. From the town's nine hundred-odd industrious citizens he could readily muster his working staff.

A few years later—in the spring of the year 1806 —there occurred a second burst of activity on the banks of the upper Housatonic. This event, accompanied by a considerable amount of noisy hammering, sawing, and shouting and by the active comings and goings of a swarm of men and many teams of oxen, took place in South Lee, Massachusetts. Some months later, when the commotion subsided and the dust settled, Samuel Church had himself a paper mill, the second to be built in the Berkshires.

By any standard, the Crane and Church mills were no great shakes as far as size and equipment were concerned. Church's mill was hardly more than a large wooden shed housing two mixing vats, a room for sorting rags, and a drying loft. Crane's mill employed one engineer, a vat man, a coucher, two teen-age girls, and two boys. Crane occupied himself as general manager, superintendent, salesman, bookkeeper, and all-round handyman, a versatility not at all uncommon in those days before efficiency experts and platoons of vice-presidents. Production, when everything went smoothly, averaged between one hundred and one hundred and twenty pounds of finished paper a day.

Except to the people of Dalton and South Lee, the construction of these two paper mills was not particularly noteworthy; many entrepreneurs had struck out on their own and opened shops or offices and built paper mills to make paper, cloth, nails, tinware, and all the other products needed by the six million people, more or less, who made up the population of the young American republic. It is noteworthy now because the Hurlbut Paper Company, which Church founded, and Crane and Company, begun by Zenas, are still going strong more than one hundred and fifty years after the first paper was proudly hung in their drying lofts.

What was the secret of the survival of these firms during that era when business mortality was shockingly high? Were these particular companies more favored by luck and happenstance than the thousands of other enterprises just as hopefully begun and now long since gone and forgotten? On the contrary, it appears from the musty records that both firms had their full share of vicissitude. The Housatonic rose up and flooded the mills with no less frequency than it poured into the hundreds of other establishments strung along its banks from the Berkshires to Long Island Sound. Fire gutted the plants just as fire razed so many of the ramshackle frame structures erected in New England during the 1800s, when lumber was cheap and bricks were expensive. Even the day-by-day routine operations were plagued by events that, if not unusual for the times, would be exasperating under any circumstances. It took many weeks for a new part for a broken-down machine to arrive from New York. Dealers failed to deliver rags when their wagons slithered off the muddy roads, and one or the other of the two mills was forced to close down for several days until rags finally arrived. And customers in Baltimore or Philadelphia, complaining that business was at a standstill because of an outbreak of cholera or yellow fever, asked for a six months' extension of their notes, then due, for paper delivered almost a year earlier.

Except for the fine supply of water, the Berkshires at the turn of the nineteenth century offered little to induce a manufacturer to locate his mills in that area. The population of the United States was still concentrated along the seaboard. The principal

Zenas Crane

Thomas Hurlbut

markets for paper—and for any other commodity, for that matter—were Boston, Hartford, New York, Philadelphia and Baltimore. The Erie Canal, which in later years led to the opening up of the West, was no more than a wild-eyed dream of a few farsighted men, and Albany, Pittsfield, Springfield, and other place-names bravely printed in boldface type on the maps of western New England were thinly populated and linked together by primitive rutted roads. The village of Lee and its environs, which included what is now South Lee, was hardly more than a settlement when Sam Church arrived there from East Hartford. His neighboring mercantile establishments included a grist mill, several small sawmills, a tannery, and a distillery that specialized in peach brandy. Among the tradesmen were a hatter, a wagonmaker, a blacksmith, a cabinetmaker, an innkeeper, and the owners of a general store. The entire population of the town was less than five hundred. By no stretch of the imagination was such a place, so typical of nearly all inland settlements, a local market for paper.

It definitely was neither luck nor chance that carried the Church and Crane enterprises through their early years. What established their success and reputations was a combination of close attention to management and manufacturing, and unrelenting sales efforts—at a time when getting around the countryside to sell was a real effort. Until his two sons grew up and could join him in the business, Zenas Crane carried the sales burden of his company alone. For long and weary weeks at a time, Crane spent hours in the saddle or in jolting stagecoaches, calling on old customers and ferreting out new ones. But the success of Zenas the salesman added to the woes of Zenas the harassed production manager. Each new order for paper accentuated the need to expand the plant's capacity and make far greater efforts to secure rags from housewives and local peddlers.

In 1822, when Charles M. Owen and Thomas Hurlbut took over the ownership and management of Church's mill, they were able to divide the tasks of management. Owen was a successful merchant from Windsor, Connecticut, well skilled in sales and merchandising. Hurlbut was a papermaker from

Winsted, Connecticut, with a professional's knowledge of papermaking and plant operations. The two men were a good team. Owen traveled constantly, calling on printers and stationers throughout the East. In Washington, D.C., he landed a sizable order for paper from the U. S. House of Representatives (good credit, but slow pay) and, in time, he established a chain of commission agents and merchants in all the principal markets along the East Coast. The Cranes were also on the move to increase their sales. Governor Strong in Boston used Crane paper for executive proclamations and state documents. Tiffany's elegant gaslit shop on Union Square in New York placed orders for Crane note papers, as did Bailey, Banks & Biddle in Philadelphia and Shreve, Crump & Low in Boston.

The slump in general business following the Civil War hurt both companies temporarily and called for redoubled sales efforts. The Cranes were able to turn a new wrinkle in men's wearing apparel to their advantage. Almost overnight the paper collar had become the rage, and the Cranes landed a whopping order from a collar manufacturer, which, during the short-lived fad, put their mills back on a six-day week. Several years later, young W. Murray Crane, grandson of Zenas, went to Washington and entered a successful bid to supply banknote paper to the Bureau of Engraving and Printing.

Meanwhile, Thomas Hurlbut's son, Thomas Otis Hurlbut, packed his bags and heavy trunks of samples and went traveling. From all evidence he was a good salesman. His days were spent calling on old customers and soliciting new ones; his evenings, writing up orders. He used hotel stationery for this purpose, and thus we are able to trace his routes and identify the hotels where he stayed—the Grand Pacific in Chicago, the Merchants in St. Paul, the Russell House in Detroit, the Nicollet in Minneapolis—all of them run in the grand manner with silver toothpick containers on the dining-room tables and a bath with hot and cold running water on *every floor*. (A man named Ellsworth M. Statler was thinking of building a hotel in which every room would have its own bath, but at the time Thomas Hurlbut was traveling, Statler's fine idea had not yet reached the architects' drawing boards.)

THE ESTERBROOKS HAVE A GO AT IT

In 1858 a young Englishman named Richard Esterbrook, Jr., came to America to find out firsthand if it was in truth the land of opportunity everyone said it was. He brought with him a stock of British-made steel pens, which he peddled until all were sold. He wrote home to his father, the owner of a successful stationery business in England: "I am presently in Camden, New Jersey. . . . American industry is stirring and the nationalistic pride the American people are taking in the phrase 'Made in U.S.A.' is having a great effect on the market place.

"With your help, I believe we can become America's first pen manufacturers. So, I suggest that you consider coming here and bringing with you a small crew of skilled pen makers so that we may have a go at this thing."

Before the coming of the steel pen.

53

Esterbrook Senior was a man getting on in years. He had a successful business in a part of the world which, to him, was home—in the fullest meaning of that word to an Englishman. There was no compelling reason for him to cut his ties and come to America, but come he did, bringing along to Camden five craftsmen to staff the steel-pen manufactory his son had recommended.

Selling the steel pen took quite a bit of effort. The quill had performed a fairly satisfactory service as a writing instrument for a long time and, as a prospective buyer was quick to mention, it cost less than the pen these men from England were trying to sell. Both Esterbrooks tramped the streets of Camden and Philadelphia. They journeyed to New York and Boston and south to Baltimore and Washington, calling on railroads, banks, insurance companies, government offices, and any other prospect they could think of who kept voluminous records and carried on a wide correspondence.

Eventually the steel pen replaced the quill, largely because the Esterbrooks refused to quit when a stodgy prospective buyer said, "We're satisfied with quills," or, "We may make a change sometime; come back a year from now." In later years, when the Esterbrook Pen Company sent representatives abroad to drum up export orders, the same dogged persistence in selling took one of these representatives far up the Amazon River in a canoe to Manaos, Brazil, to sell steel pens in a jungle area where shoes and the kerosene lamp were still something of a novelty.

THE MUSIC MAKER

If ever there was the antithesis of that mythical character known as a "born salesman," Dwight Hamilton Baldwin was it. He was a mild-mannered, soft-spoken man who for six days a week labored as a music teacher and on the seventh day taught Sunday school in Cincinnati. In 1862, at the age of forty-one, he suddenly decided to enter the world of commerce. For many years his pupils had sought his advice in the purchase of pianos and reed organs, and the thought occurred to Baldwin that he would earn more money selling the musical instruments he recommended than he did teaching people to play them. He was right. He did well as a dealer in

musical instruments. He made frequent sales trips, renting a spring wagon, loading it with six reed organs, and setting out from Cincinnati, not to return until he had sold the lot. He sold the instruments door to door and to agents and dealers in small towns, and so far as is known he never failed to return to his store with an empty wagon in time to teach his Sunday-school classes. A religious man, Dwight Baldwin believed that no one should do a lick of work on the Sabbath. He even went so far as to refuse to mail letters on Saturday because he did not wish them to travel on Sunday. However, if a friend or pupil called on him on a Sunday and indicated an interest in purchasing a piano or an organ, Baldwin opened his shop, either before or after Sunday school, and closed a sale. Before many years had passed, Baldwin had opened branch stores in Louisville and Indianapolis, and in 1890 he began manufacturing the Baldwin piano.

Dwight Hamilton Baldwin was a good teacher of music and, as it turned out, an even better salesman of musical instruments.

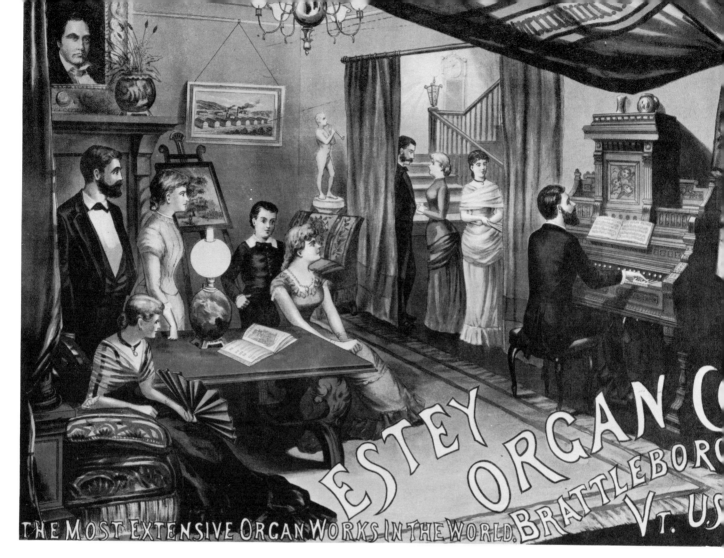

The artist who painted the Estey Organ Company advertising poster shown above managed to include a picture of the Estey factory, artfully hung on the wall of a mid-Victorian drawing room. In a less subtle manner the editor of an Estey catalogue lashed out at the price policies and humbug practiced by some of Estey's competitors. His heated words are reprinted below.

ABOUT PRICES

There is a certain fascination about the fallacy known as "cheapness" which deludes very many people. In articles of luxury, as well as those of necessity, it is well always to bear in mind that *cheapness in price* very often means *cheapness in quality*. To advertise anything as cheap is too often to stigmatize it as worthless.

It is undeniable that the market is flooded with cheap Organs that may be had at temptingly low prices. Unscrupulous makers apparently do not hesitate to put inferior instruments into flimsy but showy cases, that they may offer enticingly large discounts to agents, enabling them in turn to give confidential discounts to buyers. The age of humbug is not past, and this is one of the most arrant humbugs of all. Such a policy carried to the end can only result in ruin and disgrace. "My reputation, Iago, my reputation!" cried the repentent Cassio. . . .

Messrs. ESTEY & CO. value the reputation of the ESTEY ORGAN as they do their own. They have earned an honorable name, and their great success has been achieved by honest, plain, straightforward dealings with patrons, agents and all concerned. NONE BUT FIRST CLASS INSTRUMENTS IN EVERY RESPECT are allowed to leave their establishment, and their prices are uniformly fixed at a point which makes them moderate and reasonable for the purchaser, and leaves legitimate margin for a fair profit.

A PEDDLER EARNS A SILVER-PLATED FORTUNE

When Horace C. Wilcox, age twenty-one, became a peddler in 1845, he found himself in a highly competitive business. On every road leading from Meriden, Hartford, Berlin, and other Connecticut towns there was a heavy traffic of peddlers carrying a stock of tin and pewterware, ivory combs, buttons, and a wide variety of Yankee notions made by Connecticut's thriving industry. Peddling had reached the point where a man had to travel a long distance to find a territory not already thoroughly canvassed by other peddlers; it was becoming increasingly difficult to find prospective buyers in the New England area who had not already exhausted their budgets for pewter mugs, fancy laces, and ribbons.

This situation set young Wilcox thinking. He had chosen peddling as a career because he believed that no other line of work would be as stimulating or rewarding, providing he became proficient at salesmanship and sold honest goods at fair prices. And all things considered, he had not done badly. In two years he had, with the help of his brother Dennis, earned enough profit to buy a team and wagon and had established a reputation as an industrious and honest peddler. But he was not satisfied. The time had come, he decided, to find a manufacturer with a new and salable product and con-

The silversmiths of Meriden, Connecticut, were master craftsmen who could turn out some mighty fancy pieces of silverware when they put their minds to it. In the 1890s a silver fruit dish was just the thing to choose as a wedding present or an anniversary gift, or to impress the wife on Christmas morning.

centrate on the development of the market for that one line. The question was, where would he find the manufacturer and product he was looking for?

The answer came more quickly than Wilcox had hoped. In Meriden he heard that three brothers named Rogers, in Hartford, had perfected a new process for electroplating silverware. It was worth looking into. Wilcox went to Hartford and entered the small shop where the Rogers brothers displayed the ware they manufactured in the back room.

The three brothers—William, Asa, and Simeon—were young men of about the same age as Wilcox. They were artisans, proud and enthusiastic about their products, but with little idea how to sell them. Wilcox was taken into the workroom, and he watched while the Rogerses silver-plated a cup and explained their process. The finished cup was a beautiful thing, bright as solid silver but only one quarter as costly, and the plating would not flake or peel off as on hand-plated hollow ware.

The four young men took stock of one another,

the artisans weighing in their minds if this was the man to handle sales for them, and Wilcox deciding if the three brothers might be the supplier he was ready to represent. Finally, they got down to business. Wilcox said he was leaving on a selling trip and might take along a few samples to test the market for Rogers Brothers silverware. In reply the Rogerses said they had ample stock on hand and Wilcox could take his choice of any samples he wanted. A selection of spoons, forks, cups, and candlesticks was put together and stowed in Wilcox's wagon.

It did not take Wilcox long to learn that the market for Rogers silverware was a big one. To-

gether with his younger brother Dennis, he set up H. C. Wilcox & Company, which became sales agent for Rogers silverware. The Wilcoxes gave up peddling from door to door and farm to farm and concentrated on selling to retailers in New England and along the Atlantic seaboard. To offer its customers a complete line of silverware, Wilcox & Com-

Horace Wilcox started business by peddling tinware. Later he switched to pewterware, some fine examples of which are shown below. When plated silverware came on the market, he acted as selling agent for a firm that eventually became the International Silver Company.

Meriden Britannia Co's Work

Horace C. Wilcox

pany took on the sales representation of other Connecticut silversmiths who made items not produced by the Rogers brothers.

Horace Wilcox was a good organizer as well as a fine salesman. He hired other salesmen, trained them, and assigned territories. To give dealers in New York City better service and catch out-of-town merchants who visited New York once or twice a year to do their buying, Dennis was sent to the city to open a sumptuous showroom on lower Broadway. A few years later a showroom was opened in Chicago, which was becoming an important buying center in the Midwest. In 1852 Horace was instrumental in merging a number of small companies into the Meriden Britannia Company (which later became the International Silver Company), for which Wilcox & Company became sole sales agent.

In less than a quarter-century Horace Wilcox had risen from a peddler of notions to a leader in the sale of silverware. His early wise decision to become a specialist and expert in the sale of one line earned him a silver-plated fortune. The Rogers brothers and the other silversmiths he represented prospered by selecting the right man to do their selling and backing him with quality products, fairly priced.

To bring about the building of this manufactory for the Meriden Britannia Company, the Rogers brothers and other Connecticut silversmiths contributed their craftsmanship and artistry, and Horace Wilcox contributed his energies and talent for selling.

59

These crude tools were all a farmer had to work with in the late 1700s.

GOOD SELLING SPARKS A REVOLUTION IN AGRICULTURE

Until comparatively recently, the United States was primarily an agricultural nation. During all of the last century more people lived and worked on farms than in towns and cities. Millions of acres of land had been given away free, or sold at very low prices on long-term loans, and the majority of our people, along with their horses and mules and oxen, were straining and struggling at the muscular tasks of plowing, harrowing, reaping, threshing, and in other ways tending the soil and its crops. It is not surprising, therefore, that many men occupied themselves with designing and making a variety of implements and tools that would lighten the farmers' work and increase his land's yield per acre. These men had a lot of catching up to do. Settlers moving into the West and Midwest took with them

farm implements very little different from those used centuries before in the valleys of the Nile and Euphrates. Such tools were only slightly better than nothing in this new land; a German emigrant with a flail that had served him well enough to thresh six acres of wheat in Bavaria found this implement hopelessly inadequate on his six hundred acres in Iowa or Minnesota.

And so, for whatever it was worth to them personally and to men everywhere, John Deere, Jerome I. Case, James Oliver, Cyrus McCormick, and hundreds more set to work to raise the standards of American agriculture.

It is one of the curiosities of history that this stupendous revolution in agriculture, which these men touched off, took place in America centuries later than it might have occurred in Asia or Europe with their big areas of rich land and masses of poorly fed people. To say that America was a new land offering greater opportunities to its farmers and the industries that served them is to pronounce a shopworn misconception. There was no built-in,

Land promoters boasted that corn would grow higher than a house in Kaw Valley, Kansas. Maybe it would, but the couple shown in the picture above would have been content with a crop of less prodigious height. When improved implements were available to the farmers in the West and Midwest, this land in Custer County, Nebraska, produced fabulous crops, and corn in Kansas did grow almost as high as a house.

come-easy opportunity for a man moving into the Dakota Territory, where winter temperatures plummeted to sixty degrees below zero and a drift of snow might pile up to eighteen feet or more; and the first men who looked out on the wide wastes of Kansas (which now produces more wheat per acre than any other area its size in the world) must have turned away in dismay at the forlorn vista they beheld. But Americans were candidly frank about their desire to eat well and were perfectly willing to work hard to coax a bountiful harvest from the soil, and there were men with inventive genius and flair for salesmanship who were more than eager to contribute their talents to this goal of plenty.

CORN IN THE KAW VALLEY, KANSAS.

61

McCORMICK'S
PATENT
VIRGINIA REAPER.

The above cut represents one of M'CORMICK'S PATENT VIRGINIA REAPERS, as built for the harvest of 1848. It has been greatly improved since that time, by the addition of a seat for the driver ; by a change in the position of the crank, so as to effect a direct connection between it and the sickle, (thereby very much lessening the friction and wear of the machinery, by dispensing altogether with the lever and its fixtures ;) by board ribs on the reel, (which operates more gently on the grain than the round ones;) by a sheet of zinc on the platform, (which very much lessens the labor of raking ;) by an increase of the size, weight and strength of the wheels of the machine, and by improvement made on the cutting apparatus.

D. W. BROWN,
OF ASHLAND, OHIO,

Having been duly appointed Agent for the sale of the above valuable labor-saving machine (manufactured by C. H. McCormick & Co., in Chicago, Ill.,) for the Counties of Seneca, Sandusky, Erie, Huron, Richland, Ashland and Wayne, would respectfully inform the farmers of those counties, that he is prepared to furnish them with the above Reapers on very liberal terms.

The Wheat portions of the above territory will be visited, and the Agent will be ready to give any information relative to said Reaper, by addressing him at Ashland, Ashland County, Ohio.

Ashland, March, 1850.

When Cyrus Hall McCormick moved to Chicago in 1847 to manufacture an improved model of the reaper he had invented and publicly demonstrated sixteen years earlier in Walnut Grove, Virginia, some thirty other manufacturers were busy cracking out similar machines, all of them brazen infringements of McCormick's earlier patents. There was little McCormick could do about this piracy; in court he lost one appeal after another. To salvage anything from his long lean years of experimenting with new designs, his only course was to outbuild and outsell the competition—which he set out to do. A cousin, J. B. McCormick, went into the Ohio River Valley to appoint and supervise sales agents. Other men, given the title of territorial supervisor, were sent off on long roving assignments.

McCormick was shooting for a live-wire agency organization that would be the biggest in the country. Nothing would satisfy him short of knowing that a McCormick reaper was on display and for sale in every town and at every crossroad. Blanketing the United States with an agency organization was important to McCormick's plans, but the caliber of the agents appointed was even more important. To do the sales job that McCormick insisted be done, an agent had to keep a sample machine on hand, diligently canvass his territory for prospective buyers, give buyers complete instructions in the operation and maintenance of the machine, do necessary repair work promptly and at a fair price, stock a complete line of spare parts, collect money from customers, and distribute advertising literature. Above all else the agent was expected to *demonstrate* the machines. All of this was nothing more than an agent worth his salt should do, but in those days when agreements between manufacturers and agents were casually entered into, the explicit duties of the agent set forth by McCormick were considered a radical departure from the normal order of things.

To boost sales, D. W. Brown advertised his agency for McCormick's reaper with handbills such as the one shown at the left and posted them throughout northern Ohio.

The first McCormick factory built in Chicago in 1847 employed thirty-three men and turned out five hundred reapers for the 1848 harvest season.

The twin battering rams in the McCormick sales campaign were a written guarantee to the purchaser that the machine would perform as claimed and a demonstration by the agent in a farmer's fields. Woe to the McCormick agent who missed an opportunity to demonstrate his machine alongside those of his competitors or who failed to put life and drama into his demonstration. A farmer was never too busy to drop his work to attend a field demonstration of competing reapers on a neighbor's farm. Loud-voiced claims and counterclaims were hurled back and forth; ridicule was heaped on competing machines. Enthusiasm for his own reaper spurred an agent to harangue the crowd with a spell of sparkling oratory. With a great show of expertise, expectoration, and perspiration on the agent's part, the machines were put through their paces so that all attending the demonstration could judge for themselves which was best.

After what must have been a real sockdolager of a demonstration, D. R. Burt, the McCormick agent in Waterloo, Iowa, wrote in triumph to McCormick in Chicago:

"I found in the neighborhood supplied from Cassville quite early in the season one of Manny's agents with a fancyfully painted machine cutting the old prairie grass to the no small delight of the witnesses, making sweeping and bold declarations about what his machine could do and how it could beat yours, etc., etc. Well, he had the start of me, so I must head him somehow. I began by breaking down on his fancy machine, pointed out every objection that I could see and all that I had learned last year . . . gave the statements of those that had seen the one work in my grass . . . all of which I could prove. And then stated to all my opinion of what would be the result should they purchase from Manny. You pay one half money and give your note for the balance, are prosecuted for the last note and the cheapest way to get out of the scrape is to pay the note, keep the poor machine and in a short time purchase one from McCormick. . . . Now gentlemen I am an old settler, have shared all the hardships of this new country with you, and taken it Rough and Smooth . . . have often been imposed on in the way I allmost know you would be by purchasing the machine offered to you to-day. I would say to all, try your machine before you [pay] one half or any except the

freight. I can offer you one on such terms, warrant it against this machine or any other you can produce, and if after a fair trial . . . any other proved superior and you prefer it to mine, keep [it]. I will take mine back, say not a word, refund the freight, all is right again. No Gentlemen this man dare not do this.

"The Result you have seen. He sold not one. I sold 20. About the same circumstances occurred in Lafayette County."

That was selling with a punch. In recent years sales presentations have been polished up and whittled down, but there are few now that could score better than Burt's combination of earthy bluster and uninhibited enthusiasm. Despite a constantly increasing number of companies manufacturing reapers, Burt and the rest of McCormick's hard-working agents outsold the combined output of all these firms.

By the time he was twenty-three years old, Jerome Increase Case had threshed enough wheat in Oswego County, New York, and suffered enough backaches to be convinced that an improved threshing machine was very much needed by the farmers of America. In 1842 he left home for the wheat fields of the Midwest, taking with him six of the best machines then on the market. Five of these he sold to cover his traveling expenses; the sixth he retained to custom-thresh wheat when he arrived in Wisconsin. He would use the income thus earned to design and construct an improved thresher.

Within a year Case had built a thresher that far outperformed any other. Local farmers who drifted into his shop to kibitz and keep tabs on his progress bought a few and put them to work in their fields with extraordinary results.

Young Case had a bear by the tail, in a manner of speaking. He had a superior product for which there was a market that extended from the Hudson River in the East to the Rocky Mountains in the West. He had very little capital and not much business experience, and there was no sales organization to which he could turn to get his machine marketed. He had to make a choice of two alternatives. He could settle for the prospect of a lifetime of being a small-time machinist selling to the easily reached local market, or he could shoot for the big time—the national market, and, possibly, fame and fortune.

Case chose the second of these alternatives. For the next few years he traveled for months at a time, selling to farmers, appointing agents, and building up a sales organization. He got leads from small advertisements he inserted in farm papers: "If you know of anyone in your vicinity who wishes to purchase a threshing machine, you will confer a favor on him, his neighbor and myself, by inducing him to examine my machines before purchasing elsewhere."

High-pressure artists of the time may have smiled at Case's soft sell in his advertisement and

A farm boy operating an 1871 model of "The Advance" reaper. Farmers bought thousands of these machines after agents had demonstrated them in the fields.

Jerome Increase Case

considered it slightly naíve, but the farmers did not. Perhaps they were fed up with being slickered with fast double-talk. At any rate, they looked into this new thresher, and when Case showed up to talk sense about threshing and machinery, the farmers placed their orders with him.

In this way Case made his sales and put together a sales organization. It was not easy. He once wrote: ". . . Tomorrow I start on foot for Dubuque, forty miles distant." On another occasion: "I am heartily sick of this way of getting about." But by getting about, and selling, Case eventually made the big time.

One farmer up in Rice County, Minnesota, hit the roof when a Case thresher failed at harvest time. The local agent quickly went out to see what was wrong. When he couldn't get the machine running properly, he wired the home office in Racine, Wisconsin, for a factory service man. The service man arrived, and did everything he could think of to set

65

things right—and failed. He finally recommended that the machine be taken back and the farmer be given a new one. Somehow the Big Boss got wind of the goings on and, to the utter amazement of everybody concerned, J. I. Case, by that time a multimillionaire, the world's largest manufacturer of threshers, and a man past his sixtieth birthday, packed his valise and took a train to Minnesota.

What happened was humiliating. Case arrived, worked on the thresher for five hours, and did no better than his agent and his factory trouble-shooter. Finally Case asked for a can of kerosene, which he poured liberally over the thresher. Then, after putting a match to the machine, Case instructed his agent to deliver to the dumbfounded farmer a new thresher the next morning, and went back to Racine. This highly tellable story about Case and his bonfire made a deep impression everywhere. Farmers had a new respect for a man and a company that could be depended upon not to argue or blame, but to make restitution when equipment failed.

JOHN DEERE BUILDS A BETTER PLOW

John Deere of Moline, Illinois, designed and manufactured a plow made of cast steel and shaped so that it dug deep and true into the rich, heavy soil of the West and Midwest. It was exactly the kind of plow that was needed, and Deere was the kind of man to make a success of his new product. He was a hustler for sales. Teamsters were hired, some at a dollar and a half a day, to load their wagons with Deere's plows and scour the countryside for sales. "The teamsters would stop at farms along the way, and if the farmer was in need of a plow the deal would be closed on the spot. Should there be any plows left over at the end of the route the teamster was to move further west to arrange with some storekeeper to keep the plows in stock and sell them on commission. *None of the plows was supposed to be brought back to the factory.*" In other words, anyone who sold for Deere was to keep going until he had sold his stock. And Deere was not above loading a wagon himself and going out on a sales trip. "Even the bookkeeper, when he was not busy, was out with a wagon load of plows which he had to peddle until all were sold. When he returned to the factory, if

John Deere

another load of plows was not ready, he posted the books."

No stone was left unturned in Deere's pursuit of sales. One of his partners made a trip to Iowa City, where the state legislators were in session. Each of the lawmakers was asked for the names of the leading merchants among his constituents. These merchants were then approached to act as sales agents for Deere's plows. "Business was done by leaving plows to be sold on commission, taking a receipt for the number of plows and the price to be paid when sold. In rating these merchants for possible business relations, a book was kept which classified them as either 'honest' or 'appears to be honest.'" (In the middle 1800s, when Deere was starting his

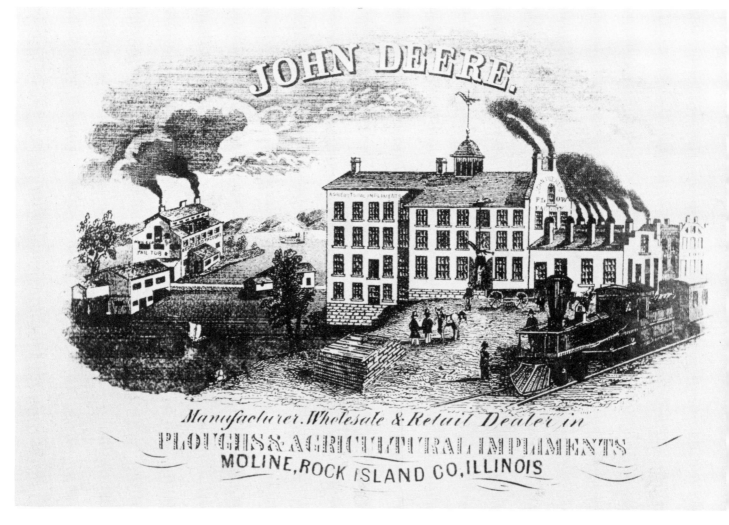

John Deere's offices and factory in 1856. When the bookkeepers were not busy with paperwork, they went on the road to sell plows from wagons.

business, about the only credit information a supplier could get on a merchant or an agent was that he was known to be honest or "appeared" to be so.)

Old records show that Deere's first salesman was George W. Vinton, who joined the company in 1855 and "traveled from ocean to ocean establishing agencies and doing general business for the great plow works." In 1868 Vinton was named general sales manager, and a few years later the Moline *Review* referred to his distant travels: "George W. Vinton, who for the past 15 years has carried the name of Deere & Company to every hamlet from the Mexican border to the line of eternal snows, started for the east on Thursday. Mr. V. will visit the principal eastern cities, mingling pleasure with business in about equal parts."

As with all manufacturers of farm equipment, a catalogue was important to Deere's sales, and like everyone else who used catalogues in those days, he had a devil of a time locating lists of farmers to mail them to. One method that worked rather well was to advertise in newspapers for people to send Deere the names of farmers in their communities. "On receipt of the names and post office address plainly written of fifty good farmers, we will send you free a box of Dominoes" was the way Deere worded one advertisement that got results. Many a farmer spent his winter evenings playing dominoes and poring over a catalogue from Deere & Company during this period.

PLOWING AND HARVESTING BY STEAM
A SUCCESS.

I am now manufacturing the Celebrated **REMINGTON TRACTION ENGINE OR STEAM PLOW**, adapted to all kinds of heavy work usually done by mules or horses. A number of these Engines are now in use, giving entire satisfaction, for plowing and pulling Combined Harvesters. I have also patented and put into the field a successful **STEAM HARVESTER**, which the above cut represents, and can be seen on the ranch of Mr. J. H. Kester, St. Johns, Colusa county, harvesting 65 to 100 acres per day. Note what the owners say in testimonial:

St. Johns, Cala., August 1, 1889.

DANIEL BEST—*Dear Sir:* You ask us to report how we like the Traction Engine and Steam Harvester purchased of you this season. We can only say that we are delighted with the purchase, and it is giving entire satisfaction. In other words, the whole outfit is a success. We never had better work done with any machine than we are doing with the Steam Harvester. We are using our 25-foot Header, traveling three miles per hour, cutting and threshing 65 to 100 acres per day. You can put us down for another rig for next season. Very truly yours,

KESTER & PETERS.

If you are interested in Steam Plowing and Steam Harvesting, go and investigate for yourself and be convinced. The following parties are using my Traction Engines and Harvesters, who will take pleasure in showing them up: J. S. Butler, W. Fennell, Tehama, Tehama county; Henry Best, Yuba City, Sutter county; and Kester & Peters, St. Johns, Colusa county. These last parties are running a complete steam outfit, consisting of Traction Engine and Steam Harvester. For further description, prices, etc., address

Daniel Best Agricultural Works,
SAN LEANDRO, CAL.

Mechanization of agriculture began when steam replaced horsepower. The early steam traction engines (left) ranged from four to ten horsepower. They were cumbersome and expensive, costing from $625 to $1,275. Daniel Best's steam harvester (above) was capable of harvesting sixty-five to one hundred acres a day and was popular with farmers in California.

It took real salesmanship to get farmers to change from centuries-old simple hand tools to awesome monsters like the one shown above. They were understandably hesitant to sign orders for such equipment until thoroughly convinced that they could operate it and that the machine would not break down frequently or explode and blow the operator into the next county. An agent who relied on talk did not get very far. Sales were made only after a demonstration, which the salesman here, wearing a derby hat and bow tie, is giving. He is putting one of the first gasoline-powered Caterpillars through its paces. The year was 1908.

ENGRAVED BY J. A. BOGERT

DRAWN BY A. R. WAUD

READE ST.

CHAMBERS ST.

BROADWAY, N.Y.

A. T. STEWART DRY GOODS STORE

70

The Seaboard Merchants

Only the hardy, enterprising merchants could survive to become the "merchant princes" of America.

THE SEA CAPTAINS, the peddlers, and the journeymen making things in their chickabiddy shops all were salesmen. They traveled across the risky oceans and up and down the dangerous trails; they made things, bought things, traded and bartered things, to the end that they could sell or barter something to someone at a profit. Because of their persistence, the strength of their muscles, and the sharpness of their wits, they flourished and increased in numbers. But in many cases the firm foundation for their success rested upon still another group of men whose interest in selling and merchandising transcended all others'. These were the merchants.

Merchants, in one guise or another, have been with us since the time when men came out of their caves. Long before the dawn of the Christian era there were merchants in Tyre and Sidon, Baghdad and Samarkand. Marco Polo, the Genoese merchant and master peddler, found merchants wherever he stopped during his long journey to Cathay and back. In their everlasting search for markets and profits the merchants of Europe contributed heavily to the cost of exploration to the far corners of the uncharted seas to the east. They came west, too, to North America.

A century ago A. T. Stewart's at Broadway and Chambers Street was the largest dry-goods store in America.

They came here out of curiosity and with a determination not to overlook any bets, and it was the fur trade that kept them here. They brought in case lots of junk jewelry, trinkets, sleazy cloth, knives, guns, and powder, and kegs of raw liquor, which they traded to the Indians for boatloads of valuable furs and skins. By 1629 the Dutch fur traders were firmly established on a pleasantly wooded island, now known as Manhattan, and were sending to Holland furs valued at fifty thousand guilders a year. The French poked their way up the St. Lawrence Valley and into the mid-continent along the shores of the Great Lakes and beyond. It was a rich territory. In 1660 sixty large canoes loaded with furs arrived at Montreal. The French trading center at Green Bay, Wisconsin, each year imported about eighteen thousand dollars' worth of goods to be traded for furs, and the post at Grand Portage sent 106,000 beaver pelts to France.

The British, with characteristic energy, were all over the place and causing all sorts of mischief—plying the Indians with strong drink to weaken their bargaining powers and furnishing them with firearms. Although most of the fur traders headed west, the British went as far south as Augusta, Georgia. From there, by 1740, they were sending five hundred pack horses a year with trading goods into Indian territory.

For a lucky few, such as the proprietors of the Hudson's Bay Company, the Company of the Hundred Associates created by Richelieu to monopolize the French fur trade, and John Jacob Astor's American Fur Company, the fur trade was a fabulously lucrative business. But in the final analysis the less adventurous merchants who set up shop in the seaboard settlements and catered to the trade of the

colonists arriving from Europe made out better—
the Indians and the fur-bearing animals were
quickly decimated, whereas the number of colonists
increased rapidly.

In the early days—up to sometime in the early
1800s, before the age of specialization—the term
"merchant" covered a much wider field of activity
than it does today. A man who proclaimed himself
to be a merchant was usually a Jack-of-all-trades
and functioned as a jobber, wholesaler, retailer,
commission agent, distributor, trader, broker, importer. Shipowners became merchants when they
bought and sold cargoes, and conversely, merchants
frequently became shipowners if, in their judgment,
they could increase their trade or reduce their expenses by moving their goods in their own ships
rather than in ships owned by others.

Robert Oliver, a Baltimore merchant, operated
his own vessels to facilitate his trade along the coast
and overseas. Thus he was a merchant-shipowner.
To fill his ships on outward voyages, Oliver bought
domestic goods, such as furs, skins, tobacco, lumber, cotton, flour, and so on. He sold these commodi-

72

Fur-trapping and trading was an adventurous life for merchants who had no fear of the wilderness or Indians. It was a profitable business while it lasted, but in less than a century the trappers had exterminated most of the fur-bearing animals in the nation.

ties abroad—which made him an exporter. Abroad, his agents or the supercargoes aboard his ships purchased dry goods, hardware, rum, sugar, coffee, and spices, depending upon where the ship was loading, all of which Oliver sold domestically upon the arrival of the cargo at Baltimore. Thus he was an importer. Some of these imports Oliver sold at wholesale and some at retail, so he was both a wholesaler and a retailer. On occasion he sold goods from overseas to other merchants, charging them a commission, thereby serving as a commission agent or factor. Quite often goods were stored in Oliver's warehouses until they could be sold; it might be said, therefore, that he was a warehouser, and since most goods were sold on long-term credit, he was a banker. If he exchanged one product for another on a barter basis, he was a trader.

RATE OF EXCHANGE FOR FURS

During the early days of the Hudson's Bay Company, Indians and trappers received trade goods in exchange for their beaver skins. The following is the rate of exchange in the middle 1700s:

NUMBER OF BEAVER SKINS	GOODS IN EXCHANGE
4	1 pound of gunpowder
7	7 fathoms of tobacco
1	1 pound of shot
15	an ell of coarse cloth
12	1 blanket
1	2 fishhooks or 3 flints
25	1 gun
10	1 pistol
7	1 common hat
4	1 ax
4	1 gallon of brandy
7	1 checkered shirt

William Russell Grace

THE GRACE LINES

The great potato famine of 1846 in Ireland was the indirect cause of events that led to the founding of one of the largest international shipping and trading firms in the United States. Among the thousands of Irishmen who left their hungry country in that year was a thirteen-year-old boy named William Russell Grace. He emigrated to Callao, Peru, where he got work as a clerk with Bryce & Company, dealers in ships' supplies and goods.

Callao was a busy port in those days. Hundreds of square riggers that had loaded guano at the offshore Chincha Islands called at Callao for supplies before beginning their long voyages home around Cape Horn. Competition among the ship chandlers was keen, and the arrival of a guano ship brought them scurrying aboard to bargain with the captain or his agent. The pushing and elbowing among the chandlers on the quarterdeck or in the captain's crowded cabin gave young Grace an idea. Instead of waiting for the ships to come to Callao to buy supplies, why not get a jump on the competition by taking supplies to the ships at the Chincha Islands?

He got an old barge, stocked it with supplies, built a small shack for living quarters, and had the barge towed to the anchorage where guano was loaded. The increase in business which resulted brought a change in Grace's fortunes: he was made a partner in the company in 1854.

From then on, with his ideas, energy, and imagination, Grace guided the firm into prosperity. Profits were invested in agricultural and manufacturing properties in Peru after Grace had traveled through the interior of the country appraising its prospects for future growth. He studied the Peruvian market for cloth, lumber, and other types of merchandise, and began importing. As the volume of imports increased, Grace traveled up the coast to Guayaquil, Ecuador, establishing agencies to sell goods he transhipped to them from Callao. In 1865, leaving his younger brother in charge of the business in Peru, William Russell Grace shifted his

Merchant Grace built a fleet of large ships to carry the goods he bought and sold in Latin America. The W. R. Grace (right) was one of the fleet.

74

headquarters to New York, where he began a triangular trade between Peru, Europe, and the United States. He bought ships, and to fill them he bought cargoes that included "everything from pins to locomotives."

Years later, speaking in New York, J. Peter Grace, Jr., said this of his grandfather, William Russell:

"He became, without knowledge of the business jargon of our time, an expert in what we call market studies, a pioneer in what we call diversification, a practitioner of the technique we now term integration." To which it should be added that W. R. Grace was also an able student of the art of salesmanship and merchandising.

There was an intriguing amount of versatility in such a business. A man could be a wholesaler of West Indian rum, a retailer of calicoes from India, a sales agent for a London silversmith, a jobber of tea from China, an exporter of beaver skins or Virginia tobacco, an operator of ships and warehouses, and a buyer and seller of just about everything people had for sale or wanted to purchase. We are inclined to think of such old merchants comfortably ensconced in their counting houses sipping tea or hot buttered rum while writing letters of instruction and advice to their captains and agents or lifting a spyglass to scan the outer harbor for the topsails of a ship due in from the Azores or China. But it was not quite so easy. In an interesting article about the trials and tribulations of operating a mercantile business a century and a half ago, a writer had the following to say about qualifications for success:

"A merchant was expected to have an extensive knowledge of business, strict probity, good faith, an understanding of bookkeeping and arithmetic, and a mastery of making out invoices, bills of lading, bills of exchange, and insurance policies. Further, he was expected to know the best sources of supply for goods in which he traded, and [the] most satisfactory transportation for them, the best markets for them, and how they were weighed, measured, or numbered. He had to know how the seasons or war or peace would affect their prices, and he should have been familiar with duties, customs, or other

Merchants who engaged in overseas trade called their transactions "ventures," an apt description. It was a very hazardous business. The number of ships and crewmen and the tonnage of cargo lost year after year were staggering. The crew of the storm-battered ship shown in this dramatic scene was lucky. They were rescued amid a winter gale by a passing vessel, but the ship and her cargo, valued at upward of $150,000, were lost. A run of bad luck with the loss of two or three cargoes in quick succession might bankrupt a merchant. Fortunes were lost with stunning rapidity, just as fortunes were quickly amassed when all went well with a number of ventures.

When a wooden ship carrying a combustible cargo caught fire, destruction was swift and complete. Prudent merchants insured themselves against such losses, but insurance rarely covered the full amount.

regulations pertinent to their exportation or importation. Some knowledge of foreign languages . . . was useful to the merchant. It was essential he be familiar with the qualities of goods he bought and sold. The laws, customs, usages, and consular jurisdictions of different countries should have been parts of his knowledge.

"Merchants were expected to keep themselves informed of the skills and activities of their competition and had to pay constant attention to price fluctuations affecting their trade. They were advised to be clear and concise in making their bargains, in order that they might avoid lawsuits that cost time and money. They were to extend credit with cau-

tion, but with no mistrust. It was recommended that toward negligent debtors they extend 'indulgence without negligence' and 'firmness without rigor.'"

We may feel that the merchant's task is even more complex today, and perhaps it is. But there is no denying that the pioneer merchant had to wrestle with problems that must often have seemed insurmountable. And in most cases the merchant had to play it by ear. There were very few experts to advise him and very few books and other publications to refer to. No one had as yet written a sales-training manual or a course on salesmanship. A man was almost completely on his own, and his degree of success depended largely upon how much he applied himself toward careful, competent, and farsighted management of his business. Above all, these merchants had to be constantly on the alert for new markets and customers. They were masters of the art of prospecting for new business.

As American commerce expanded, many seaboard merchants who had traded in a somewhat hit-or-miss fashion to all parts of the world tended more toward specialization in certain trades or particular types of goods and commodities. Thus the firm of N. L. & G. Griswold limited most of its efforts to the China trade and became an importer of tea, which was packed for the retail trade and sold in such enormous quantities that one writer of the times hazarded a guess that Griswold's tea was sold "in every country store, however insignificant, in the United States." A man with the unlikely name of Preserved Fish, a whaling captain of New Bedford, decided to give up the sea and, along with a partner named Joseph Grinnell, moved to New York and set up business as a commission agent for whale oil. In New York the firm of Suydam, Sage & Company became the leading flour exporter, and a John Wood piled up a fortune estimated at two hundred thousand dollars exporting ice, the trade that Frederic Tudor had pioneered some years earlier.

One specialized trade that paid off very handsomely was the importation of wines and spirits. Many early American fortunes were built upon the liquid base of strong drink; in 1844 there were no less than eighty-nine importers of wines and liquors in New York City alone. In Massachusetts the consumption of rum was estimated to be four gallons a year per capita—which was more than ample to warm the cockles of the hearts of the citizens of that hardy state.

THREE DEPARTMENT-STORE GIANTS

Among the many hundreds of seaboard merchants who specialized in selling dry goods was a man named A. T. Stewart, who had come to New York in 1825 from Northern Ireland. With him he brought a stock of linens and laces worth three thousand dollars, a lively imagination, and an instinctive sense of good salesmanship. A few years after he opened his dry-goods store, he was well on his way toward amassing a fortune, in the process of which he almost singlehandedly revolutionized the retail trade's practices of pricing. For all prac-

Even in the best shop with the highest quality merchandise, no sale was closed without a polite and often lengthy haggle over price.

tical purposes there was no systematic method of pricing when Stewart opened his business; prices were established by the primitive method of prolonged haggling. Manufacturers and importers bargained for the highest amounts they could get from wholesalers and jobbers. Wholesalers and jobbers put the squeeze on retailers for the last possible dime, and retailers in turn charged their customers as much as they felt the traffic would bear. A prosperous customer was quoted one price—subject, of course, to considerable negotiation—while a less affluent customer was quoted a lower price, also subject to adjustment if the customer had the time and stamina to negotiate. Price lists, if they existed at all, were mere scraps of paper. Customers who were

Macy's bold attempt to sell for cash resulted in the failure of this store in Haverhill, Massachusetts.

interested in saving money made it a point to wear old coats with frayed sleeves and dilapidated hats when they went shopping.

To Stewart's way of thinking, this rough-and-tumble in-fighting over prices between buyer and seller made no sense at all. After observing such goings-on in his own shop he concluded that the amount of time his clerks spent dickering for the highest price cost him more than the extra profit they might realize. In addition, haggling was no way to build customer loyalty and good will. So, in a bold move, Stewart established a one-price policy, put price tags for all to see on his goods, and placed advertisements in the newspapers to publicize his plan. His competitors thought it was a publicity gag; either that or the man had lost his senses and would soon go broke. But very quickly, Stewart's became the largest department store in the country and nearly all other merchants adopted his price system, as did most wholesalers and manufacturers.

Sanity in pricing brought about a profound change in salesmanship. Selling became more of a positive science. The emphasis was shifted from heated bargaining over price to persuasive eloquence about the quality or utility of the article being offered for sale. Thus, about a century ago, a long step forward was made toward what today is known as creative selling. The buyer was still very much on his own when it came to judging whether the quality of an article was all that it was said to be, but at least he could take some comfort in knowing that the price he paid would be no greater than that asked of the next buyer.

Another early advocate of the one-price policy was a young man named Rowland Hussey Macy, who opened a small retail dry-goods store in Haverhill, Massachusetts, in 1851. Not only was Macy a staunch supporter of a one-price policy; he went a radical step farther and sold for *cash only!* At that time almost all merchants offered to sell merchandise "cheap for cash," but they placed very slight emphasis on that end of their business, probably on the assumption that very few of their customers would by choice, or could afford to, forego the convenience of buying on easy credit and settling their accounts at any time from six months to a year later.

Macy contended that by selling for cash he could

The first of the great department stores was owned by Alexander T. Stewart, who established a one-price policy and thereby brought about a much needed reform in retail pricing.

Rowland H. Macy

81

Macy's business grew so rapidly in New York that he moved into a large store uptown on Fourteenth Street at Sixth Avenue. The new store featured big display windows, one of which was filled with dolls for the Christmas season.

afford to operate on a margin of profit so small that he would be able to sell goods cheaper than any of his competitors. To explain the advantages of his cash-only policy to the people of Haverhill, Macy instituted an aggressive, often flamboyant newspaper advertising campaign. In sharp contrast to the small, unimaginative advertisements of his competitors, one of Macy's first ads made quite a splash in the staid columns of the Haverhill *Gazette.*

"1. We buy exclusively FOR CASH!!!

"2. We sell Exclusively FOR CASH.

"3. We have but one price, and never deviate, except for imperfections!

"These are the three great principles upon which we base our business. Buying *exclusively* for cash, we keep our stock in constant motion and are having new goods from New York, Philadelphia and Boston *every day*. It also enables us to procure many of our goods under the market price, and our customers have the advantage of these bargains for this reason, viz:—selling exclusively for cash, we have no bad debts on our books, consequently our good customers do not have to pay them in the shape of extra profits.

"By adopting one price and never deviating, a child can trade with us as cheap as the shrewdest buyer in the country. Following out these three great principles as we do, to the letter, we return the public many thanks for the generous manner in which you have sustained us, and it shall be our endeavor, as it ever has been, to merit your most liberal patronage.

"Taking 'Onward and Upward' for our motto, we challenge any competition—confident that we can not be undersold—and with a larger and better stock (bought exclusively for cash) and with a constantly increasing patronage, we govern ourselves accordingly."

For a time business was fairly brisk, but Haverhill, a one-industry manufacturing town with a population of only eight thousand, did not offer the large volume of business Macy needed to make a decent profit on his very small markups. Many people still preferred to buy on credit, and when the town's industry slowed down, Macy's customers, who bought his bargains for cash, were short of money. The store failed in 1854, and undoubtedly the other merchants of Haverhill were very much relieved when Macy, the maverick merchant, departed from their midst.

Fundamentally, Macy's policies of buying for cash, selling for cash, underselling his competitors, and aggressively advertising were all sound, and in New York City, three years after clearing out of Haverhill, he proved them to be so. The small store he opened in the city was an immediate success, and Macy kept adding new lines of merchandise until his was one of the largest retail stores in the city. It was, in fact, along with A. T. Stewart's imposing emporium, one of the two first department stores in the country. As such, these two stores, and the enlightened policies of their founders, brought about a much-needed reform in pricing and merchandising techniques. The policies of Stewart and Macy were adopted in varying degrees by merchants throughout the country.

MACY'S WEEKLY DISPATCH
Received this Week

WEDNESDAY MORNING, Oct. 11, 1854
Great Bargains at Macy's this week!

Although we are proverbially modest, we cannot but feel flattered when we look back upon our four years' experience in the Dry Goods business in this town, and notice how closely our every act and motion has been followed by others in the trade. When we came here four years ago, the Dry Goods business was done under what is called the "old fogy" system. Dealers bought their Goods of regular Jobbers in Boston, at a profit of from 25 to 50 per cent and sold them to their customers in this vicinity at enormous profits, taking pay in due bills, orders, &c. &c. There was no regular price for anything, and the most ignorant were the most imposed upon. We claim to have broken down this *cut throat* business, and by *selling goods at one price—selling them cheap*—serving all alike, buying where we could buy cheapest (being perfectly independent in that respect) we claim to have made the business here *respectable*. Then there was a monopoly in the business. It was in the hands of two or three parties, who took the ground that interlopers were not wanted, and had no right here. We think we have been instrumental in proving to these gentlemen that "some things can be done as well as others," and we think we are willing this day that in *this*, as in every other improvement of the age, it is an inevitable law that the whole community must share its blessings.

We have received many new goods this week— New Thibets, Lyonese, Low Priced Prints, Plaids, Black Silks &c., which we are selling very cheap — Do not fail to look in at MACY'S this week, for we have some GREAT BARGAINS, and no mistake.

Lowest Prices always named First.

R. H. MACY

A short time before his business in Haverhill failed, an R. H. Macy advertisement in the Gazette *took a hefty swipe at the merchandising system of the time. This unorthodoxy probably riled his competitors, but it failed to bolster his sagging business.*

John Wanamaker

RETAILING COMES OF AGE

Another merchant who figured prominently in changing the slipshod retailing methods of his time was a Philadelphian named John Wanamaker. At the time of his death in 1922 at the age of eighty-four, *Printer's Ink* called Wanamaker "The Super Merchant of America." Reviewing his career, the publication went on to say: "In several elements of his character, essential to business success, John Wanamaker has rarely known an equal. In conception, initiative and courage, he was supreme. He was the greatest dramatist of dry goods that the trade has ever developed."

Enthusiasm and ambition can usually be counted upon to prod a man into producing ideas that will speed him along the road he has set for himself. This was certainly so with Wanamaker. When, at the age of twenty-three, he opened a small dry-goods store, he was bubbling with ideas, most of which were new to retailing and startling to his competitors.

For one thing, young Wanamaker had well-conceived ideas about improving the seedy quality of ready-to-wear clothing sold in the lower price brackets. A man's suit retailing at eight or ten dol-

lars was no bargain at any price, and the merchant who sold the suit did so hoping the customer was a sailor bound for some distant port or a Milktoast lacking the temerity to return with well-justified complaints that he had been gypped. For understandable reasons, such clothes carried no labels identifying the manufacturer or the retailer.

As a small merchant, there was little Wanamaker could do about this situation except buy the best of the unsatisfactory clothing available and refrain from gross exaggerations in describing it. Very early in his career he adopted as one of his mottoes "Accuracy in Word and Print." But all the while, Wanamaker was formulating an idea, and when his orders to manufacturers became large enough to be of considerable importance to them, he laid down, in emphatic terms, his standards of quality. Anguished cries that suits could not be made to Wanamaker's specifications at the prices he was willing to pay were to no avail. Clothing manufacturers interested only in a quick buck took their cheap goods elsewhere. Other manufacturers went along with Wanamaker's unbending contention that it was a merchant's duty to supply a customer with honest goods rather than the customer's responsibility not to be hoodwinked.

To complete his break with tradition, Wanamaker put his label in every garment he sold, and with this label went his warranty that "the quality of goods is as represented on the printed labels" and "the full amount of cash paid will be refunded, if customers find the articles unsatisfactory, and return them unworn and unimpaired within ten days."

The reaction in the trade was similar to that which had greeted A. T. Stewart's one-price policy (which Wanamaker had adopted when he began his business). The privilege of returning merchandise for a cash refund could only lead to ruin. It was a preposterous idea designed to gain publicity. Wanamaker was sarcastically referred to as the "P. T. Barnum of the retail business" by some merchants. Others, and probably the majority, rather admired him and welcomed his energetic leadership in improving the ethics and procedures of merchandising.

The allusion to Wanamaker as another Barnum was an error on all counts except one—showmanship. He was a showman without bluster and bombast when he displayed housewares and furnishings in attractively arranged model rooms he had instructed the architects to include in their plans for his new building. He was a showman, with absolute adherence to the truth, in his advertising. His advertising copy was clear and crisp; the layouts were smart and eye-catching. He used plenty of space and distinguished himself as the first person ever to buy a full page in a newspaper. A newspaper page may not be a distinction now, but at the time when most advertisers thought they were shooting the works with a single column, Wanamaker's space-buying splurge had a dramatic effect on readers, publishers, competitors—and his sales volume.

The sea captains and nabobs of New York who bought their clothes at the Brooks Brothers' store on Catherine Street in 1845 got quality, which was notably lacking in clothing sold by other merchants to ordinary seamen and clerks.

The big names, the Macys and Wanamakers and others who erected enormous "palaces of trade," are the ones we are most familiar with and look upon as the leaders in merchandising. There were thousands of other merchants whose names are less well known but who, in their own ways, were developing successful sales techniques in retailing. Their goal, in more circumscribed dimensions, was the same as that of the great "merchant princes" in the big cities. Forty-seven merchants advertised their wares in the July 26, 1837, issue of the Worcester (Massachusetts) *Republican*. There was not much "sell" in the ads and only three of them were illustrated, with crude woodcuts, but almost without exception each merchant let it be known that he was carrying a "wide selection" of the "latest goods" at the "lowest prices." Chester Dickenson, who dealt in musical instruments and umbrellas of all kinds, promised that "All orders will be gratefully received,

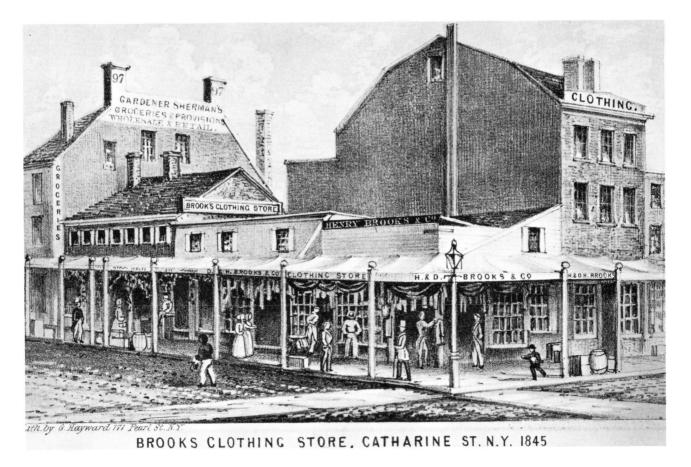

BROOKS CLOTHING STORE, CATHARINE ST. N.Y. 1845

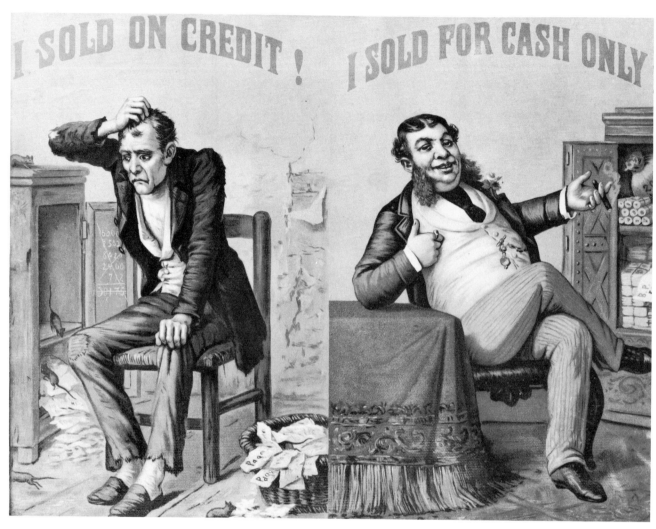

A well-known cartoon, which needs no explaining. It was naturally a fine subject for R. H. Macy and Company to use for promotion of their policy. Neither extreme was really needed—people eventually paid up.

and promptly attended to." Customers were invited to call and see for themselves the furniture on hand at Bancrofts' Furniture Ware Rooms, opposite the American Temperance House. Francis Blake announced that he had been appointed agent in Worcester for Farnum's Celebrated Loco Foco, or friction matches.

In Durham, New Hampshire, George Frost wrestled with the problems of a tidewater merchant catering to a village trade as well as many back-country customers. Frost bought his merchandise from wholesalers and commission houses in Ports-

mouth, Portland, and Boston, and much of his business was with small country merchants who brought wagonloads of timber and farm produce to exchange for flour, molasses, rice, and general merchandise. One merchant from Epsom paid for ten quintals of dried fish with a load of boards. Another merchant ordered salt, plaster of Paris, and bar iron in exchange for lumber. As did so many merchants in those days, Frost sold goods wholesale as well as retail.

Late in the 1700s William Douglas of New Haven had conducted a general merchandising business and occasionally invested in part shares of ships trading to the West Indies. His account books show that he sold two quarts of rum to a Stephen Hunnawell and accepted two bushels of oysters in exchange. He received sixty pounds of beef from

E. Lines for one parasol, and Solomon Tuttle agreed to deliver wood in payment for one gallon of rum. Another man paid for molasses with two watermelons and some fresh vegetables. A few of New Haven's more affluent citizens, including Benedict Arnold, paid for their rum, groceries, hardware, and walking sticks with cash.

R. H. Macy had his troubles getting his cash-only business started, but collecting overdue accounts was not one of them, as it was with most merchants, including Joseph F. & E. M. White, general merchants of Danbury, Connecticut, who inserted the following notice in the newspaper:

"DELAYS ARE DANGEROUS

"Those indebted to the subscribers, on Book or Note (now due by agreement), may have an opportunity of cancelling the same, by payment in Walnut, Oak or Maple Wood, Wheat, Rye, Corn, Oats, Buckwheat, Flax Seed, Hats, Saddles, or Shoes, at their full value, if delivered soon, but if delayed Cash will be the only substitute which will be received."

The Whites might have been able to dispose of a part of this produce and merchandise to local customers, but it is likely that they resold the wood to dealers who carried it by ship to New York City and the flaxseed to some sea captain bound for Europe, where a good market existed for this item. The hats, saddles, and shoes more than likely were turned over for sale by peddlers. At any rate, collecting overdue accounts was frequently a troublesome affair. A Montgomery, Alabama, merchant who advertised that he wanted payments made on overdue accounts exhorted his customers: "Pay up! Pay up! You rascals. . . ."

Life was not easy for those early merchants. A few of them were unscrupulous masters of the art of sharp practices, which did not endear them to their fellow townsmen. But most were fair and honest, ambitious and resourceful and, above all else, hardworking. The merchants of Biddeford, Maine, worked so hard and such long hours that at one point they got together and drew up this resolution: "*Resolved*: That the present manner of conducting business, which requires the constant and unremitting attention of the merchants and their clerks from daylight until 9 o'clock in the evening [averaging about fifteen hours a day throughout the year] is unnecessary and injurious to both body and mind, leaving no time either for social intercourse or mental improvement, and calls loudly for reform."

Not much came of these fine words, however, except to close shop earlier on Wednesday nights, thereby reducing the working time for the merchants and their clerks from ninety hours a week to about eighty-eight.

Clerks in the big-city department stores and the crossroads country stores put in long hours of hard work for small pay. Proprietors worked even longer. After closing time they toiled far into the night on their account books and other paper work.

Brother, Can You Spare a Dime?

Not all merchants were successful all the time. The number of failures was appalling, especially during the periods of hard times and financial panic that flickered over the land like sporadic lightning. One merchant-shipowner who went bankrupt was John A. Scoville. He eked out a bare subsistence after his failure by writing his memoirs in a rambling five volume work entitled *The Old Merchants of New York*. Scoville had amassed a considerable fortune, then lost every penny of it after a series of disasters at sea to five of his ships. Lamenting on his fate, Scoville wrote bitterly:

"Woe to the great merchant who comes down! He has hardly a resource left, if poor and unprovided for; those who knew him when well off, will see him starve before they would give him a five dollar a-week clerkship. It is hard, very hard, and very cruel in a community as wealthy as New York.

"There should be a home founded for the broken-down merchant in New York. Frequently the most deserving, the most energetic, and the most honest, are the most unfortunate. Refuges are provided for all classes. The old captains have a Sailors' Snug Harbor to go to. The merchant who has failed has no place to go except the poor house. This is not right. It ought to be remedied. No merchant is beyond the reach of poverty. To be an Odd Fellow or Mason is an advantage when poverty comes, but how rarely does the merchant, who signs his check for $5,000 or a million, ever dream that $5 will be a perfect God-send to him! Yet it is so. I hope yet to see towering aloft the tower of 'A Home for the Unfortunate Merchant.'"

Nothing came of Scoville's impassioned plea. Such a home for unfortunate merchants, had it been built, would of necessity have been of Pentagon proportions to accommodate all the merchants who might have applied for temporary or permanent refuge. In New York during the years prior to the Civil War, it was estimated that more than 50 per cent of the merchants failed. Some estimates run as high as nine out of every ten. However, these melancholy figures are somewhat misleading. In those days big risks and long-shot gambles were accepted as part of the ordinary hazards of doing business. Financial embarrassment was not uncommon, and it was seldom fatal. Many a merchant who went broke one day was back in business, usually at the same address, a few days later, rebuilding his fortune.

Colonial Advertising

One hundred years or so before R. H. Macy wrote his fiery advertisements and John Wanamaker jacked up his advertising budget to buy full pages in Philadelphia newspapers, three merchants in Boston exercised their skill at copywriting, with results that no doubt delighted the readers of the Boston *Gazette*.

"Leather Breeches. Philip Freeman, lately from London, makes and sells super-fine black Leather Breeches and Jackets, not to be discerned from the best super-fine Cloth; likewise makes Buff and Cloth Colour after the neetest manner, also makes all sorts of Gloves by wholesale or retale. The said Freeman lives in Prison Lane, near the Town House in Boston." —Boston *Gazette*, June 21, 1743.

"This is to give Notice, That Richard Fry, Stationer, bookseller, Paper-Maker, and Rag Merchant, from the City of London, keeps at Mr. Thomas Fleet's Printer at the Heart and Crown in Cornhill, Boston: where the said Fry is ready to accommodate all Gentlemen, Merchants, and Tradesmen, with sets of Accompt-Books, after the neatest manner; and whereas, it has been the common Method of the most curious merchants in Boston, to Procure their Books from London, this is to acquaint those Gentlemen, that I the said Fry, will sell all sorts of Accompt-Books, done after the most accurate Manner, for 20 per cent cheaper than they can have them from London.

"I return the Publick Thanks for following the Directions of my former advertisement for gathering of Rags, and hope they will continue the like Method; having received seven thousand weight and upwards already.

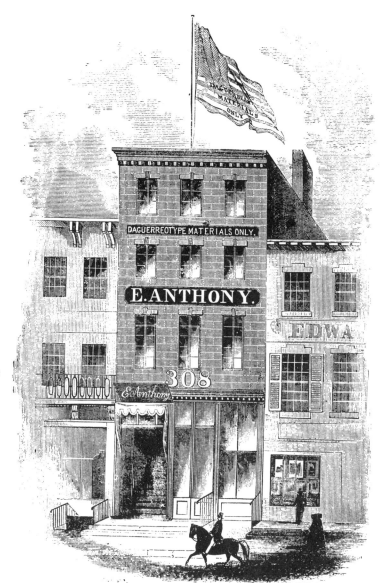

Illustrated advertising eventually broke the solid blocks of type, finely printed, usual in early American newspapers. E. Anthony not only displayed his shop front in his ad—he repeated his offering on the flag atop the building.

"For the pleasing entertainment of the Polite part of Mankind, I have Printed the most Beautiful Poems of Mr. Stephen Duck, the famous Wiltshire Poet; It is a full demonstration to me that the People of New England, have a fine taste for Good Sense and Polite Learning, having already sold 1200 of the Poems, Richard Fry." —Boston *Gazette*, May 1-8, 1732.

"John Ingram, the Original Flower of Mustard Maker, from Lisbon, now living at the house of Messrs. Townsend, near Oliver's-Dock, Boston, Prepares Flower of Mustard to such Perfection, by a method unknown to any person but himself, that it retains its Strength, Flavor and Color Seven Years; being mix'd with hot or cold waters, in a Minute's Time it makes the strongest Mustard ever eat, not in the least Bitter, yet of a delicate and delightful Flavour, and gives a most surprizing grateful Taste to Beef, Pork, Lamb, Fish, Sallad, or other Sauces. It is approved of by divers eminent Physicians as the only Remedy in the Universe in all nervous Disorders, sweetens all the Juices, and rectifies the whole Mass of Blood to Admiration. If close stopt it will keep its Strength and Virtue Seven years in any Climate. Merchants & Captains of Ships shall have good allowance to sell again." —Boston *Gazette*, September 19, 1752.

Adventure in the West and Midwest

A restless people were moving westward, and the merchants and traders went with them.

FOR SOME REASON that defies logical explanation, millions of men have for centuries turned toward the west with an aching belief that somewhere in that direction lies a promise of fulfillment of their dreams and aspirations. This phenomenon was not unknown to the early Americans. They had come to this land with the sunset in their eyes, and they were squinting into the west and wondering what they would find beyond the mountains.

The explorers were the first to succumb to the witchery of the sunset. After the explorers went the trappers and an assortment of oddballs and misfits constantly on the prowl for a pot of gold at the distant arc of a rainbow. Then followed the greatest migration of humans in history when the first settlers gathered up their scanty possessions and disappeared into the wilderness. And with the settlers went the merchants and traders, to face even more problems than plagued their counterparts on the Eastern seaboard.

It was a mighty big land in which to wander about searching for a place to settle and do business, and its immensity was accentuated by the complete lack of transportation between the East Coast and the prairies. There were the mountains—especially the raw-ridged Alleghenies that lay athwart Pennsylvania and West Virginia. The Alleghenies were to give men trouble until well into our own times, when the airplane finally conquered them.

Eventually the settlers and merchants developed the trails and lanes hacked through the forests by the explorers and trappers into roads linking east and west. But roads were not easily built over the mountains; it was often said with salty frontier sarcasm, but no great exaggeration, that a completed section of a road fell into disrepair and became practically impassable before further extension of the road was completed. Poor as they were, these roads made possible the movement of people and their commerce over the mountains. Without these roads, those who moved into Ohio and West Virginia and Kentucky would have been virtually excommunicated from the Eastern seaboard, and even with them the development of a two-way exchange of goods was a task of nightmarish proportions.

Seldom, before or since that time, has the ingenuity or perseverance of merchants and traders been put to such a test. It is a wonder they bothered to march westward at all. There was more risk than profit in being a pioneer merchant, but, as a Frenchman traveling through Ohio in the late 1700s remarked with some amazement, wherever there was a settlement, even though it might be only a half-dozen or so crude buildings, a merchant provided a brave display of goods for sale or barter. There were even cases of merchants setting up shop in lonely isolation at places where there were no settlers at all, in the expectation that such stores in the middle of nowhere would encourage settlers to move in, clear farmlands, and build a town. Such schemes often worked, and paid the merchant an extra dividend if he had been foresighted enough to buy land to sell to the people attracted to his wilderness store.

In central New York State, William Cooper, father of James Fenimore Cooper and founder of

A settler builds a log cabin in the clearing and soon a merchant will open a small store where a town will grow.

Cooperstown, acquired some forty thousand acres of land in 1785 and established a store to serve people who moved in and bought his land. Cooper's store at first was a lost cause. "For the ensuing four years," Cooper later described things, "the scarcity of provisions was a serious calamity; the country was mountainous, and there were no roads nor bridges. I erected a storehouse, and during each winter filled it with large quantities of grain, purchased at distant places. I procured from my friend, Henry Drinker, a credit for large quantities of sugar kettles; he also lent me some potash kettles, which we conveyed, as best we could, sometimes by partial

roads on sleighs, and sometimes over the ice. By this means I established potash works among the settlers. . . . I also gave them credit for their maple sugar and potash, at prices which would bear transportation, and the first year after the adoption of this plan I collected in one mass 43 hogsheads of sugar and 300 barrels of pot and pearl worth about $9000."

Things were a little better in 1789 when Richard R. Smith opened another store in Cooperstown; the population of the settlement had increased to one hundred.

A traveler who visited Pittsburgh, Pennsylvania, in 1785 reported that most of the people were engaged in merchandising and tavern-keeping, a statement that gave a somewhat exaggerated picture of the town. Pittsburgh at the time did not amount

92

to much; in fact, a year later, when John Scull lugged in a printing press and began publishing a newspaper west of the Alleghenies, Pittsburgh consisted of six stores and a population of around three hundred. Farther south, Ebenezer Zane operated a prosperous store at Wheeling, West Virginia. He bought land in southern Ohio and later transferred his business to what is now Zanesville, which he developed into an important way station on the Great National Road that was reaching out through Ohio, Indiana, Illinois, and eventually to St. Louis, Missouri.

THE WATER ROADS

Once over the mountains, the westbound settlers found their problems eased considerably by the long-armed tributaries of the Mississippi River. Notable among these was the Ohio, with headwaters reaching into western Pennsylvania and New York. Pittsburgh and Wheeling became important transfer points between land and river transport. Not that the rivers of mid-America were ideally suited for navigation: during the dead of winter they froze over tight for three or four months; in the spring they ran full with flood waters; in midsummer, during the season of low water, there was the constant menace of rocks, snags, and sandbars. At all seasons their currents were so swift that it was almost physically impossible to pole a keelboat upstream. And, of course, not all the horde of people moving westward were able to settle alongside or near the rivers; there were millions of acres of tillable land many miles away from the nearest navigable waterway.

This problem of transportation for those who settled far from the waterways was serious. The rich earth yielded an abundance of foodstuffs; yet, paradoxically, the people were beggar-poor. They had

Trade boomed and freight rates went down to two dollars a ton when the Erie Canal was opened for traffic between the Hudson River and Buffalo in 1825. The canal enabled farmers in New York State to get their produce to seaboard markets.

The isolated communities of upper New York State were drawn together by the water traffic on the Erie Canal, and the rural landscape along its banks gave way to cities.

arrived in the new land with barely more than the clothes on their backs, a few tools, a pathetic collection of household articles, and practically no money. Now they had a crop and a cornucopian abundance of products to sell, but the market for these products was far away.

Freight rates by road wagons to the eastern markets were staggering and all but closed the door to any large volume of commerce. On the turnpikes running west from Albany the rate for freight was $100 a ton for each one hundred miles. By road from Philadelphia to Pittsburgh it cost $125 to ship a ton of goods the three hundred-odd miles between those two cities. John Hopkins, a prosperous Baltimore merchant, paid Daniel Barcus $352 to haul eighty-three hundred pounds of merchandise to Mount Vernon, Ohio, and on the return trip Barcus picked up seventy-two hundred pounds of Ohio tobacco and $178 for freight. A commission merchant in Wheeling received 1,081 wagonloads of goods from the East in 1822. His freight bill was $90,000. A farmer in Pennsylvania loaded his wagon with grain and hauled it to the nearest grist mill. In doing so, he crossed Pine Creek eighty times going and eighty times coming home. The trip took eighteen days, and during that time a wheel came off his wagon in the creek, two axletrees broke, and the wagon upset twice. He might better have stayed home and distilled his grain into whisky; shipping bulky grain or flour more than a hundred and fifty miles by road was a losing proposition.

The problem of finding a way to move products in and out of the West was dumped into the laps of the merchants and traders. To these men the farmers brought their produce, and the operators of grist mills and sawmills their flour and lumber. Getting this glut out of the country was the merchants' job, just as it was their job to bring in supplies of nails from Wheeling, household goods from Connecticut, dry goods from the Eastern-seaboard cities, and coffee, sugar, drugs, and medicines from wherever they could find them. The fragile dream of the settlers was in their safekeeping, and they had no choice but to get commerce moving and fulfill their needs, or go broke. It was a magnificent challenge to ingenuity, salesmanship, and daring.

The best, and often the only, financially successful method of getting produce to market was to float it out. One man who did very well for himself afloat was a trader named Nathan Brown, who hailed from Jamestown in the northwest corner of New York State. Brown built a big flatboat, seventy-five feet long and sixteen feet wide, with a capacity of fifty tons. He painted the boat bright yellow with white trim, and in big red letters on the sides put the words "Yankee Notions." Into this cumbersome boat, Brown stowed eight hundred dozen scythe snaths, three hundred dozen hoes, one hundred and fifty dozen rakes, thousands of patent window sashes, and a large quantity of wooden buckets. These he took downriver to Pittsburgh and points south, where he sold them to wholesalers, retailers, and individual farmers along the river. Before many years had passed, Brown had a fleet of five boats in service, and the Jamestown *Journal* had this to say about his flourishing business:

"Jamestown Exports—On Wednesday last, Mr. Nathan Brown, the enterprising River Trader, started a fleet of five Flat Boats from the mouth of the Cassadaga for the Southern market. . . .

"The five boats contain 350 doz. grain-cradles, and 50 dozen Scythe Snaths, manufactured by Mr. N. Breed, and valued at $3,350; 500 doz. Scythe Snaths manufactured by Messrs. Cobb & Broadhead, valued at $1,800; 1000 doz. hay rakes manufactured by Messrs. Shaver & Willard, valued at $1,200; 125 grain-measures manufactured by Mr. I. Benedict, valued at $700; 250 Scythe Snaths, manufactured by Messrs. Garfield & Son, valued at $900; 40,000 lights of window sash and 500 panel doors, and 350 pair window blinds, manufactured by Messrs. Scott & Barrows, valued at $3,000; 20,000 lights window sash, 250 panel doors, manufactured by Mr. Albert Smith, valued at $800; 20,000 lights window sash, 250 panel doors and 75 pairs window blinds, manufactured by Messrs. Merriam & Fox, valued at $1,000; 19 lumber wagons and 19 buggies, manufactured by Messrs. Pitts, Cobb & Broadhead, valued at $2,000. The lading also embraces a lot of harnesses, manufactured by S. Shearman & Co. valued at $600; and scythes, forks, hoes, locofoco matches, &c. &c. manufactured at other places to the value

Poling a keelboat upstream with a load of goods for country merchants was slow going. From New Orleans to Cincinnati took four or five months.

of about $17,000. Mr. Brown has been engaged in the River Trade about 12 years. When he first entered upon it, each manufacturer of wooden wares in the village was in the habit of fitting out a boat and making his own sales in a Southern market; but latterly Mr. B. has purchased the wares at the manufactories, and made most of the exportations himself. He is now well known in the valley of the Ohio as a successful Trader, and very much through his enterprise, our fabrics, wrought away inland among the hills of Chautauque, and high up among the sources of the Allegheny, have also become favorably known."

Brown spent forty-four profitable years trading out of Jamestown, during which time, he estimated, his boats made one hundred and fifty-four trips downriver and carried about a half-million dollars' worth of goods. He built up a steady business with regular customers, who watched for the arrival of his boats each spring. These had been merchants, commission houses, and wholesalers, who resold the Jamestown products to smaller merchants inland and quite often to peddlers. In a sense Brown acted as a sort of floating wholesaler for dozens of manufacturers in Jamestown who found it more economical and practical to turn their downriver sales over to him than to send their own boats on such trips.

Colonel Henry F. Blount of Evansville, Indiana, also used the river to advantage. Blount operated a blacksmith shop and was the owner of a small plow factory. Each spring he loaded a quantity of plows on a large barge and drifted down the Ohio and Mississippi, stopping at dozens of landings along the way. Blount had fitted his barge with a forge and other accouterments, so that it was something

A merchant with business to transact in New Orleans, or a salesman on his way to St. Louis, traveled in luxury aboard Mississippi River steamboats. Travel by flatboats was more primitive, but the young in spirit enjoyed it.

96

During the 1860s the sutler's store furnished needed provisions and gear. Indians, army men, and ranchers crowd this store at Fort Dodge, Kansas, to buy goods brought in by wagon from St. Louis or Kansas City.

of a floating blacksmith shop. Wherever he stopped, he invited farmers to come aboard to buy new plows and get their old ones repaired. Floating down the broad rivers of America, stopping along the way at small towns or at lone farms that bordered the water, must have been a wonderful way to make a sales trip, providing a man did not daydream too much of the time. Blount must have enjoyed moments of peace and idle drifting, but he must also have been a good, hard-working salesman, for the Blount Plow Works he founded in 1867 soon became one of the largest producers of horse-drawn plows in the world.

For more than a half-century, transportation on the Ohio River was a booming business. In the spring, as soon as the ice broke up, a weird armada of keelboats, bateaus, skiffs, scows, arks, barges, pirogues, rafts, canoes and, after 1811, steamboats cast off for long voyages south. Some of these traded

locally, others went on to St. Louis, and many went down to New Orleans via the Mississippi. Getting under way as early as possible was important. The first boats to arrive at the downriver cities with merchandise and farm produce received the best prices for their cargoes. There were other potent reasons for an early start. Western produce arriving in the South after the beginning of summer was considerably damaged by heat: tobacco sweated, grain swelled and softened, pork and other meats spoiled beyond salvaging. But the prime reason for haste was that the Northern merchants and traders wanted their money. All winter long they had been doling out stocks of merchandise to farmers in exchange for farm produce, and until this produce was sold the merchants had precious little cash with which to rebuild their inventories of goods.

Produce arriving at New Orleans was sold for cash, preferably, and bills of exchange were sent to traders in the East, from whom the Western merchants bought their goods. If cash sales were unobtainable, which was often the case, produce was exchanged for cotton, which was shipped to Boston,

New York, Philadelphia, and other cities of the East.

The pioneer merchant in the West and Midwest (like many a merchant in New England) operated a general-store type of business. Regardless of whether it was a makeshift log cabin on the prairie or an elegant emporium in the county seat, his store stocked a varied line of general merchandise that included everything from calicoes to coffee beans and from sensational elixirs guaranteeing eternal youth to a wide assortment of coffin handles. From its shelves and storage sheds the people drew their sustenance according to their needs and ability to pay. In the warm glow of its potbellied stove in winter or the cool shade of its porch in summer men debated political issues, related the latest news and jokes, and remarked eternally about the weather.

The storekeeper knew everyone in the community intimately. In times of economic distress he listened to heartbreak tales when wheat dropped to twenty cents a bushel and corn went begging at a dime. And then, taking a long, hard look at the future of the West and finding it good, he extended

In Custer County, Nebraska, a homesteader and his family pose before their sodhouse home, circa 1888. Local merchants extended credit to such pioneer farmers until they had the land plowed and had earned a cash income for their crops.

long-term credit. In many a crisis, local or nationwide, the courageous merchant underwrote the future while others held back. In the late 1830s John Beauchamp Jones published a book, *The Western Merchant.* Jones, himself a successful merchant in Arrow Rock, Missouri, had this to say about his fellow merchants and traders:

"The merchants of the West, and particularly in the Far West, constitute a distinct class of society. This class is not only important from its numbers, but powerful and influential from its intelligence, enterprise, and wealth. . . . [The merchant] is a general locum tenens, the agent of everybody! And familiar with every transaction in his neighborhood. He is a counselor without license, and yet invariably consulted, not only in matters of business, but in domestic affairs. Parents ask his opinion before giving their consent to their daughters' marriages; and he is always invited to the weddings. He furnishes the nuptial garments for both bride and groom, and his taste is both consulted and adopted. Every item of news, not only local, but from a distance—as he is frequently the postmaster, and the only subscriber to the newspaper—has general dissemination from his establishment, as from a common center; and thither all resort, at least once a week, both for goods and for intelligence."

The following excerpt from John Beauchamp Jones's book *The Western Merchant* tells the story of his youthful experiences when he and his brother Joseph opened a store at Franklin, Missouri:

"In due course of time we arrived at the *new* town of Franklin, situated in the woods, some two miles from the river. The *old* town, which had been once the largest village above St. Louis, was rapidly undergoing one of the saddest processes incident to western villages on the great streams. The capricious and rightly-termed 'Mad Missouri,' was undermining and washing away the original town. More than two-thirds of it had already disappeared and the inhabitants were then bestirring themselves to save what wrecks they could of their property. They were removing the buildings themselves [mostly frame] back to the hills; and the new village in the woods presented the grotesque appearance of a new town built in a measure of old materials.

"My brother [Joseph] gave me a hearty welcome. . . . And now began my career as a WESTERN MERCHANT. . . . I soon perceived that the merchant was an important individual in society. His standing took precedence even of that of the professional gentlemen, who, at that day, at least, were rarely in affluent circumstances. . . .

"One of the partners in the establishment . . . was

daily expected to arrive on his return with the goods from Philadelphia. Letters had been received from him, announcing his arrival at St. Louis, a few days after my departure from that port. He stated that he would come up the river with his goods on the steamboat Ioway, and might be looked for at Franklin, by the 15th. Boats were 'few and far between' then, and some of them consumed two weeks . . . in ascending the river.

"About this time my brother and myself set off on horseback up the river, to see that the building for our new store should be completed and in readiness to receive the goods. Towards noon, we arrived opposite the famous new town of Pike Bluff, and after some delay in consequence of the great number of emigrants' wagons which were waiting to get across, we were ferried over the turbulent stream in a flat, rickety, open boat. We ascended the hill and beheld the town. It consisted alone of the new storehouse, in a half finished condition. It was composed of hewed logs, the chinks betwixt them not being yet plastered up. It had a roof on, however, and afforded a shelter. The workmen were that day just sawing out openings for the doors. We prevailed on them to concentrate all their forces on one of the rooms [there were to be just two, each about twenty feet square] so that it might be shelved, and in some degree of completion, provided the goods should happen to arrive a few days before the time appointed. They cheerfully complied, and exerted themselves to the utmost of their ability. The ugly interstices between the huge logs, were soon filled with clay and lime, and whitewashed on the inside. A counter was erected, and shelves put up.

"I remained with the workmen while my brother returned to Franklin, with the understanding that he would come up on the boat with the goods. All

A harassed clerk encounters a party "made up" to visit the store of the neighborhood—a barnlike place, with drugs and dress goods, hardware and groceries, all in one room. "Hats?"—no hats. "Shoe buttons?"—alas, these were never kept. "Ribbons?"—not in stock. "Writing paper?" . . . and the clerk began to have a horror of the chorus, and wondered if he should slip out the back door and let his inquisitors find out his stock for themselves, or simply laugh it off.

was bustle and curiosity. The people for miles around came in every day to inquire when the goods would arrive. There was but one store in the whole county, which was situated a considerable distance in the interior, and the beginning of a new town on the river, by means of the establishment of a store there, made a considerable noise in the community. I soon became acquainted with everybody; and after the first sight a mutual familiarity exists in new countries. I must own that I felt flattered by the novel importance of my position, being a sort of centre of attraction; and as I was not deficient in personal address, made the most of my advantage for the interest of the concern. Without the slightest knowledge of the value of merchandise, it was yet no difficult matter for me to produce the impression that *our* goods would be sold under the prices the good people had been in the habit of paying for similar articles; and, in consequence, the anxiety grew more intense on their part for them to arrive. . . .

"By the 15th April, we had the room, originally designed for the counting room, shelved round, and prepared for the reception of the goods. The cash drawer was ready, and I had cut a hole through the counter to slip the money into it. We postponed making a desk, until we could empty one of the shoe or hat boxes for that purpose. The last thing we did on the memorable morning of the 15th, was to put a lock on the door, and a bolt on the window shutter.

"About ten o'clock A.M., the people began to arrive. The first that came were from below, some eight miles down the river, who had distinctly heard the steamer puffing on her way up. At that day the steamboats puffed, and coughed, and wheezed immensely louder than they now do. These voluntary messengers had spread the news as they came along, and many others followed them to town to see the new goods landed. . . .

"Some six or seven boxes of dry-goods, and thirty or forty other packages of less size and value, piled up on the river bank, made the people stare; and my brother and myself were regarded as young merchant Croesuses. And some six thousand dollars worth of goods made a respectable pile. . . . There were other descriptions of merchandise besides dry-

"I may have a few left around here somewhere." The merchant who ordered stock for six months or a year in advance, with no chance of quick delivery or reorders, often was out of stock when he underestimated the demand. His dilemma was either to carry a very large inventory and take his chances on turning over the stock or lose sales when the shelves were bare.

goods. Hardware, queensware, shoes, hats, sugar, coffee, salt, spice, pepper, dye-stuffs, medicines [calomel and barks in enormous quantities] besides a long catalogue of other articles, made up the merchant's assortment in Missouri, eighteen years ago. And the beauty of the business was, no flaming advertisements or red-letter hand bills were required to make known the establishment of a new store in a new place. Every one took an interest in it, and lost no opportunity of spreading the news far and wide. . . .

"My first day as a merchant, or rather as a merchant's clerk, was a busy day. The opening and marking of goods, and placing them in order on the shelves, occupied the whole of the day, retarded and obstructed as we were continually by the re-

Purchasing power among the settlers in the West was low. Not even Governor Geary of Kansas Territory, who lived in this six-room mansion at Lecompton, had much money to spend at the local store for anything except necessities.

there was a trend toward specialization. Some merchants turned to wholesaling exclusively. Other merchants concentrated on wholesaling or retailing dry goods, hardware, or groceries. Dr. Daniel Drake of Cincinnati opened a drugstore and in 1816 caused quite a stir when he installed a soda fountain, said to be the first in the West. In Fayette, Missouri, two doctors named Crews and Benson not only took care of their patients but found time as well to operate a wholesale and retail drugstore. The store stocked drugs, surgical instruments, patent medicines and, of all things, ordinary paint. Many of Crews and Benson's customers were peddlers, usually referred to as "the saddle-bag trade," who, in their wanderings on the fringes of Western civilization, resold the drugs to small-town merchants or direct to farm families who prudently laid in a stock of castor oil, Seidlitz power, calomel, and quinine.

marks and inquiries of the eager crowd around us. Every piece of goods taken from the boxes was subjected to the inspection of the bystanders; and it would have been impolitic to have repulsed this interference. It was our policy to cultivate the good will of all. But there was a mark beyond which they could not go, or rather they could not go through it at all. Several of them had been either merchants or merchants' clerks themselves, in Virginia, or Kentucky; and had secretly conspired to ascertain our private mark, proposing to derive advantage from a knowledge of the cost of the goods. One of them had the following letters pencilled on a slip of paper: BLACKSMITH; another CLEANSHIRT; hoping by comparison with the letters placed on the tickets, to find that we made use of the same letters so long used by other merchants. But they were mistaken; and their countenances exhibited unequivocal signs of disappointment when they began to inspect our letters, which were as follows: SUABDTHRVZ. They gave it up in despair, and relied upon our generosity not to impose upon them.

"Towards night all our inquisitive company left us, many of them promising to bring in their wives and daughters the next day, or in a few days, when we should be in readiness to wait upon them."

As settlements grew into towns and small cities,

BEYOND THE WIDE MISSOURI

It has been only a little more than a century, though it seems longer, since the Santa Fe Trail was the highroad between the outpost towns of Independence and Westport on the Missouri River and Santa Fe in Spanish New Mexico. Long trains of Conestoga wagons, sometimes as many as fifty to a hundred of them, loaded with four to seven thousand pounds of freight each, lumbered over the Trail. On good days they average fifteen miles of travel between sunup and sundown. "Uncle" Dick Wooten's rapid-transit stagecoach line was faster, taking only fourteen days for the eight-hundred-mile journey. The one-way fare on the stage line was three hundred and fifty dollars (payable in gold), a princely sum that included three daily servings of pork and beans and strong black coffee.

William Becknell, a trader, is credited with being

Far-wandering traders were the first to map the Santa Fe Trail that ran west from Independence, Missouri. The picture above shows a trader's wagon train arriving at Santa Fe. Each wagon would earn about six thousand dollars' profit for the trip. One settler in a hurry is said to have rigged his wagon with a sail, hoping the wind would propel him west. It didn't. Below: a sentimental portrayal of wagons west.

the father of the Santa Fe Trail. A few men afoot had traveled the Trail before him, but Becknell, in 1822, was the first man to organize a wagon train for the trip. Becknell's train rolled into Santa Fe with fifteen thousand dollars' worth of goods, which were quickly sold at a substantial profit to the small vanguard that had journeyed this far west earlier.

In the beginning, traffic on the Santa Fe Trail was mostly freight. Homesteaders heading into the Far West generally took the Oregon Trail, which led to the promised lands farther to the north. No homesteader in his right mind would dream of taking the Santa Fe Trail and settling in the Kansas wastelands or the Great American Desert that lay beyond. Only the foolhardy among the traders dared make the trip during the winter months. One trader, riding the Santa Fe Trail on his first trip, wrote home that out there he could see farther but see less than a man would imagine possible. There was nothing, he reported, but the buffalo and an occasional clump of forlorn cottonwood trees.

But where settlers would not venture, traders did, and in increasing numbers each year as word spread of the profits to be made in the Santa Fe trade. Cheap calicoes sold for three to four dollars a yard. Hardware, firearms, and whisky were in great demand. At Santa Fe, skins, furs, silverware, blankets, robes, and horses and mules could be bought at low prices and sold in Kansas City at a good markup. Better yet, the merchants in Santa Fe often paid for Eastern goods in gold. A round trip by wagon, which took about three months, would net an average profit of between five and six hundred dollars. Josiah Gregg, whose book *Commerce of the Prairies* is one of the classics about the Old West, organized a train of nearly a hundred wagons laded with two hundred thousand dollars' worth of merchandise.

Merchants established along the Missouri River waxed rich on the Santa Fe trade and on selling supplies to settlers taking the Oregon Trail. River towns were jumping-off places from the fringe of civilization. Before pushing on, settlers who had come from Ohio or Kentucky or the Eastern-seaboard states stopped and made a final, worried inventory of their goods. Trail guides were hastily consulted: how much of this or that should a family carry with them? What had they overlooked that should be purchased here before the dawn take-off tomorrow? As each train came through, the stores in Independence and Westport were crowded with settlers making last-minute purchases.

Northrup & Company was one of the largest firms selling dry goods, hardware, and all manner of miscellaneous items to "traders who buy to sell again." Joseph Chick & Company specialized in groceries and sold millions of pounds of foodstuffs to traders and homesteaders headed west. There were dozens of such firms, acting as middlemen for the commerce between East and West, and many among those prospered through the years and became wholesalers who shipped tools and barbed wire, breakfast cereals and cough syrups, boots and bonnets to the children and grandchildren of the settlers who had stopped in their stores earlier on their way west. In 1880, when the Atchison, Topeka & Santa Fe Railway had completed laying track into New Mexico, the editor of the Las Vegas (New Mexico) *Gazette* wrote an epitaph to the old Trail:

"The Santa Fe trade increased from year to year, until at the time of the American Occupation it had reached enormous proportions, supplying not only New Mexico, the most northern province, with goods, but likewise extending into the departments of Durango, Zacatecas and to points 1,500 miles south of Santa Fe. It was truly a vast commerce transacted on these boundless plains. . . . The immense caravans which traversed this route have left a road worn deep in the surface of the prairie which will take many years of disuse to obliterate. But though the rains may wash it out and the grass of the prairies grow over it to a green sod, yet it will live in history. It was the line of an international commerce which has no counterpart in American history. Over it caravans of goods were transported, armies were marched, battles were fought and reputations made. It was the route for trappers and adventurers as well as for merchants. . . . Around it was thrown the glamour of romance and the coloring of the picturesque. . . . It has been the source of profit, history and fiction, and the iron trail will not entirely obliterate it, or destroy its prestige."

The history of the settling of the Far West is an extension of the pattern set in the Middle West.

The adventurers, the footloose, and the traders went there first. They trapped for furs, bartered with the Indians, and shot millions of buffalo, mostly for no good reason, though there was some trifling value to buffalo hides and bones. And later these men went almost berserk in a scramble to find the gold, silver, copper, and other minerals that were tucked away in the folds of this fabulous land.

Behind this vanguard of far-roving men came the settlers (or homesteaders) and the cattlemen, and along with these the merchants.

The pattern was the same as in the Midwest, but the country was different. It was big, so immense that it gobbled up groups of people and lost them from sight somewhere over the distant horizon. It was a rugged land, heaved and tossed about during the convulsions that attended the birth of the world. Transportation over this rough surface was a herculean task. There were few navigable rivers. With rare exceptions the only means of hauling goods was by pack mule or wagon. Nonetheless, people persisted in moving in and settling down and a trade of sorts between them was begun.

BIG DOINGS AT BISBEE

The history of the Goldwaters' department store in Arizona reads like a script for a television western. It has everything, including a gold rush, a hanging, and a robbery committed at gunpoint. The latter occurred on a Saturday night when five armed men sauntered into the Goldwater store at Bisbee and ordered Joseph Goldwater to open the safe. The gunplay started when a sixth member of the gang, standing watch, shot a passing citizen who had threatened to spread the alarm. The shot was heard by another citizen, who made the fatal mistake of rushing into the street to see what was going on. He got a bullet in his head for his indiscretion. The third person to die was a young woman who carelessly got into the line of fire. A fourth victim was plugged as he scampered for shelter.

Five days later a hard-riding sheriff and his posse caught up with the robbers, disarmed them, and brought them back to town. Five of the gang were

Goldwaters store in Prescott, built in 1878, one of the first brick buildings in the state of Arizona.

105

The interior of a Goldwater store.

sentenced to hang, and the sentence was carried out forthwith. The sixth member was committed to twenty years in prison, a sentence he did not live to serve. Fifty irate citizens of Bisbee took him from his cell and hanged him with a new length of rope they had purchased at the Goldwater store.

This episode took place twenty-three years after Michael Goldwater had arrived in the territory of Arizona with a stock of merchandise to sell to the men digging for gold at Gila City. Two years later, when the miners moved on to new diggings at La Paz, Michael and his brother Joseph had gone along also and opened a general store in a small adobe building with a dirt floor. In true frontier tradition the store sold everything a miner might ask for: gunpowder, shot, boots, clothing, foodstuffs (including oysters brought down from San Francisco

at no inconsiderable effort and expense), and a not bad brand of drinking whisky. In fact, the Goldwaters rather prided themselves on their wide selection of merchandise and its quality, which was better than that usually found in frontier stores.

The Goldwater store was moved from settlement to settlement as the gold ran out at one place and was discovered at another. By the time they opened at Prescott the Goldwaters had a reputation for good merchandise and fair dealing. The country was settling down. Ranchers and farmers had moved in, schools and churches were built, and the railroad came through on its way to California. As the country grew, the Goldwaters added more lines to meet the needs of their customers, some of whom got to town only once a month or even twice a year. The last move was to Phoenix and a swank new building—a sharp contrast to the dirt floor and oil lamps in the adobe store at Gila City, where Joseph and Michael learned the trade.

During the heyday of the California gold rush, men who turned to selling stood a better chance of making money than did those who grubbed about in the diggings. A sizable number of miners struck it rich, but for every man who hit the jackpot there were hundreds of dejected prospectors who returned from the fields with empty pockets.

The year prior to the discovery of gold at Sutter's Mill was a somnolent one in California. Only two small ships had bothered to call at the cluster of shacks which was San Francisco, and in all of California there were fewer than six thousand people. One of these was John Augustus Sutter, a Swiss soldier of fortune who built a combination fort, ranch, and trading post at the junction of the American and Sacramento rivers east of San Francisco. Here wagon trains bound for San Francisco stopped to rest and get supplies.

As the tempo of migration increased, Sutter decided to enlarge his operations. To build a new flour mill he needed lumber, and for lumber he needed a sawmill. He directed his foreman, James Wilson Marshall, to construct one. Ineptly, Marshall dropped the mill wheel too low. To deepen the mill-race, he let the water flow freely during the night. The next morning, January 24, 1848, Marshall diverted the stream, and when he bent over to examine the millrace to check its depth, he found gold. Within the next year and a half more than seven hundred ships brought one hundred thousand gold-seekers to San Francisco, and an equal number of men were on their way. They came by foot, horseback, oxcart, prairie schooner, and sailing ship from all over the world. They destroyed and built, built and destroyed, in a hysteria unmatched in modern times. The Spanish land grants were ignored; Captain Sutter's eleven square leagues became townsites and he was driven up the valley toward the hills. His fort was overrun, his ranchhouse burned, his mill destroyed, and his cattle were stolen.

At San Francisco the hulks of abandoned ships were converted into hotels and stores during the peak of the gold rush.

Ship cards announced sailings for San Francisco in 1849. Many prospectors who joined the gold rush took goods with them which they hoped to sell at high prices in California.

The horde of gold-hungry immigrants needed food, clothing, tools, and other supplies above and beyond the small stocks they carried with them. For several years the clamor for goods far surpassed the meager supply. Prices in San Francisco, Stockton, and Sacramento shot through the roof: boots sold as high as seventy-five dollars a pair, an ax for ten dollars, a long-handled shovel for twelve. A Frenchman made a killing selling toothpicks at fifty cents a dozen. A farm boy from Iowa wrote to his father: "Trade and digging gold is the business here. . . . Provisions and labor is very high . . . flour $50 a barrel, pork $60 a barrel, lard 60¢ a lb., butter $1.50 a lb., other things in proportion."

To the people back east the prices charged for goods in San Francisco smacked of quick and easy profits. The Yankees were particularly impressed, and by 1849 hardly a man from New England started for California without a load of trade goods to sell when he got there. Advertisements similar to the following from the Boston *Evening Traveler* appeared in all newspapers:

"CALIFORNIA GOODS

"G. C. Holman, 15 & 17 Kilby Street, invites attention to his large assortment of Fancy and Staple Goods, adapted to the California and Pacific Trade, on which Shippers and Adventurers will be sure *to realize handsome profits*. The assortment embraces Beads, Jewelry, Mirrors, Soap, Colognes, Brushes, Combs, Cutlery, Purses, Cigar Cases, Tobacco and Snuff Boxes, Indian Bells &c."

In many cases New England merchants swept their shelves clear of old, flyspecked merchandise that was not moving, knocked down the price on the assumption that California miners would buy anything, and unloaded these goods on bargain-hunters who were headed west. Captain Octavius T. Howe was a victim of such an inventory clearance by the merchants of Beverly and Salem in Massachusetts. Howe loaded the ship *Tigress* with all sorts of odds and ends, most of which were ut-

terly worthless to the miners, and sailed for San Francisco, where he let it be known that his ship was a veritable floating department store. Captain Howe lost money in the venture and learned, to his cost, the age-old lesson that success in selling and merchandising rests on offering people, even miners, goods of some practical use or value to them.

Among those who searched for gold but found none was a man from Boston named James L. L. F. Warren. When Warren quit prospecting, he decided to stay in California. He liked the place and believed it offered a bright future to a man who got into trade or agriculture. He bought a stock of general merchandise and miners' hardware and began business as a merchant under ·a tent he erected at a place called Mormon Island. He knew from experience what goods the miners needed and would buy, and he concentrated on these items, which he sold at a moderate profit. Within two months his business had grown to such an extent that he had to put up a larger tent—"The Excelsior Tent" he proudly named it. He hired as an assistant a young man named Livingston L. Baker. Like

Livingston L. Baker and his partners failed to find their fortunes in the gold diggings, but they did very well for themselves later as honest merchants selling supplies to miners at fair prices.

A broadside describes the articles for sale in the Tent Store on Morman Island.

Warren before him, Baker had come west from Boston, looked for gold, found none, and decided he would do better in trade.

One of the customers who stopped at Warren's tent to purchase a miner's outfit was Robert M. Hamilton. When the news of the gold strike at Sutter's Mill had reached Scotland, young Bob Hamilton booked passage on the first ship he could find sailing for California. He paused at Warren's only long enough to make his purchase and pick up the latest rumors about where the next rich strike might be made. Then he hurried off. Several months later he was back and asked for a job—which he got. His luck in finding gold had been no better

than Warren's or Baker's, but his good fortune in getting a job with Warren was greater than he realized at the time.

In 1850 the tent at Mormon Island was folded and Warren & Company moved into a two-story building in Sacramento, which was becoming a place of importance in northern California. By that time Baker and Hamilton were junior partners in the firm, and Warren turned over the management of the business almost entirely to their capable young hands. This left Warren free to travel about, expounding on what had become his favorite subject—the importance of agriculture to the future of California. He promoted the first State Agricultural Fair, founded a State Agricultural Society, and began publishing a newspaper, the *California Farmer*. Finally, in 1853, Warren sold out to his junior partners and the firm became Baker & Hamilton. The new owners slept in the store to save money. They opened the doors at daybreak and did not lock up until after dark. At night they worked rearranging the stock, keeping the books, and getting out orders and letters. On Sundays, Bob Hamilton rented a horse and buggy and rode about the countryside calling on farmers and discussing the kind of equipment and implements that would work best in the California climate and soil.

The two young men had the vision to foresee a time when they would manufacture their own line of farm equipment, but they had enough good common sense not to neglect the opportunities immediately at hand. New lines were added to their stock in Sacramento, where business was booming. A branch store was opened in San Francisco, and a resident buyer was employed in New York to keep the firm informed on new merchandise. In 1868 Baker and Hamilton began manufacturing their own farm implements. By then they had become the largest and best-known retailers and wholesalers of hardware and farm equipment on the West Coast.

WESTERN COMMERCE SETTLES DOWN

From San Francisco in 1850 Bret Harte, who was writing such picturesque stories as "The Luck of Roaring Camp" and "The Outcasts of Poker Flat," wrote a letter to a friend in which he remarked,

110

"Three men from the East are unpacking a supply of drugs within a tent and I paid them $12.50 for a small quantity of quinine, a bottle of Lyon's insect powder, and an ounce of rhubarb." Harte was not complaining about the price and, all things considered, he was not overcharged.

Like all boom towns, San Francisco was a place for the gathering of the clan of the quacks. The city was infested with them, and more outrageous concoctions were peddled in San Francisco than in any other city in America. Thus it was a good place for a trio of honest men to establish an honest drug business. The three from whom Harte made his purchase were Dr. Augustus Hogge from Philadelphia, Charles Langley, a druggist from New York, and H. C. Kirk, a drug salesman from Boston. They had arrived at San Francisco with a stock of drugs bought from reputable houses in the East and an unswerving intention to establish a solid business and grow with the community. Prices were based on a fair markup—no more. No customer was ever gouged, even if he was three sheets to the wind and his pockets bulged with bags of gold nuggets, as was often the case.

The opportunists who mistook the golden opportunities in the West as a chance to make a killing seldom made it. But for Hogge, Langley and Kirk, the Goldwaters, Livingston Baker, Bob Hamilton, and hundreds of others, integrity paid solid dividends year after year. They created a law of ethics of their own in a country where there was little law of any kind for a long time. It might have taken them longer to acquire their wealth than it did for a gunman to snatch his from a Wells Fargo stage, but then they never had to worry about a posse taking away the money they had earned through hard work and honest trade.

Gold washing in the California mines.

111

James A. Orr (above) gave up gold prospecting to manufacture and sell Pantaloon Overalls. Below: the tug-o-war pants just won't rip.

When the California gold rush was at its peak, James A. Orr, a New Yorker who had worked as a tailor most of his life, put aside his needles and thread and went prospecting. Out in the diggings, when Orr leaned over one day to pan what he hopefully believed was gold-bearing dirt, he split the seam in the seat of his pants. The sorry condition of his pants gave Orr an idea that grew steadily as the gold he sought eluded him. Why not go home and manufacture good-fitting, sturdily made work clothes?

Returning to Wappingers Falls, New York, Orr discussed the idea with his two nephews, C. E. and S. W. Sweet, both of whom had a little money to invest. The men agreed to form a partnership and, with several hundred dollars capital, launched the Sweet-Orr Company, the first manufacturer of overalls.

Jim Orr was a happy man. He was back in a trade he knew and understood. He designed a line of work clothes, bought six early-model sewing machines, and hired six girls to work at them. In the plant, he superintended production, making sure that a size thirty-eight was a full-measure thirty-eight and that the seams were firmly sewed. In a very short time he had nine hundred pairs of overalls in stock.

Production was wonderful, but business was terrible: the company did not have a single order on its books. At a worried conference of the partners it was decided that someone had to get out and sell, and it was further decided that that someone would be Jim Orr, who had never sold anything before. Could he sell? He did not know whether he could or not. Did he want to go on the road? No, he would have preferred to manage the plant. But there was no getting around the necessity for one of the partners to sell their overalls, so Jim Orr went.

Success, like an invention, is often mothered by necessity. Everywhere Jim went, in the mill and coal-mining towns in New York and Pennsylvania, shopkeepers laughed at the idea that workingmen would pay seventy-five cents for a pair of store-bought pants. If Jim had let them, the merchants would have laughed him into failure. He might not

112

have known much about selling, but he was persuasive and convincing, and merchants who were skeptical at the beginning of his sales talk usually were persuaded to buy. He arrived home from his first sales trip with orders for three thousand pairs of overalls.

MORE PANTS

At about the same time Jim Orr's britches were coming apart, Levi Strauss arrived in San Francisco with a consignment of trade goods to sell as a grubstake. Levi, aged twenty, had selected his merchandise with care before leaving New York, and he had no trouble selling everything except one item—a roll of canvas cloth. When a minor customer inquired if Strauss had any heavy-duty pants in stock and expressed the universal complaint, "Can't get a pair strong enough to last no time," Strauss had an idea. He took the miner and the roll of canvas to a nearby tailor and had a pair of pants made.

The upshot was that the miner strode about town showing off "these pants of Levi's," and as the word spread, a steady stream of men applied at Strauss's California Street store asking for Levi's. Within a few years Levi Strauss & Company had a factory working full blast and Levi's had become standard garb for miners as well as for the men who rode the wagon trains and stages between California and the Southwest. The cowpokes on the ranges learned about Levi's from the men on the wagons. Orders came in from Texas, and Levi's brother Louis made a trip throughout the Southwest to call on dealers and solve the problem of distribution. At that time, before the railroads had come, this could be accomplished only by shipping Levi's via water to Panama, then to New Orleans or Galveston, and then overland to the cow town of the plains.

Thus, through the spirit of adventure of the pioneers, the homesteaders' desire for land in the wide-open spaces, the lure of the limitless natural resources west of the Alleghenies, did the United States become a coast-to-coast nation. Each factor contributed enormously to our country's growth, as did the westward migration of the merchants, tradesmen, and salesmen who saw and supplied the needs of the people wherever they roamed in the New World of Opportunity.

Levi Strauss

The Country Merchant Goes to Town

Before there were salesmen on the road, merchants went to town, spring and fall, to buy fresh stocks of goods.

MERCHANTS IN THE WEST and Midwest dreaded the days that came after the first of the year, but not because of a letdown in sales following the holiday season. Christmas trade in the 1880s was nothing to get excited about. The reason for the grumping among the Western merchants was that January and February was the time for a buying trip to market.

Most merchants made at least one buying trip a year; many made two, and some three. Generally speaking, merchants in the New England and Midwestern states did their buying in New York, Boston, Philadelphia, or Baltimore, though some of the smaller country merchants confined their trips to the wholesale districts of Portland, Maine, or Pittsburgh, Cincinnati, Louisville, Charleston, and other nearby places. Merchants in the Far West, which is to say those west of the Missouri River, came east to visit the wholesalers and jobbers in St. Louis, Kansas City, Chicago, and St. Paul, although a few made occasional forays into the Atlantic-seaboard markets.

During the first half of the last century, getting away from the old grind and leaving an assistant at home to mind the store was not an event to look forward to with happy anticipation. Travel by stagecoach, canal boat, and river steamer was an exhausting ordeal, and there was no rest for the weary during overnight stops at inns and taverns. Clean

The hazards of travel.

sheets, if sheets were provided at all, were a rarity encountered only by the traveler who was fortunate enough to arrive at an overnight stop on the one day a week when the proprietor's wife had done the laundry. According to an account in *Valentine's Manual*, experienced travelers going by boat not infrequently carried their own bedding with them: "Merchants residing a hundred miles or more from New York, and distant from the Hudson River ten or fifteen miles, sent their bedding to the landing from which they were to sail for the city, by team, and themselves followed on horseback. At the landing, their bed & etc. was placed on board the sloop that conveyed their produce to market, and by it they took passage for the city. The horse was put to pasture, or in the stable, until their return, when the owner rode him home; and by the team that went for the merchandise [which the merchant had bought in New York] the bed and bedding were returned."

The proprietors of a line of packet boats operating on the Wabash Canal appear to have been more solicitous of their passengers' comfort than the operators of Hudson River sloops. The packet-owners boasted that "the boats are new, fitted up with great neatness and taste, low fare, and commended by the cleverest fellows in the world. What more could a fastidious public require? It is well worth while to make a trip to Cincinnati or Toledo just to enjoy the luxury of a passage on these boats." The identity of the "cleverest fellows in the world" remains a matter for interesting speculation.

Traffic on the roads, canals and rivers attracted any number of entrepreneurs who were quick to see in the increasing comings and goings of so many people, wagons, stagecoaches, and boats golden opportunities for trade and services.

115

The text visible in the illustration includes:

RY GOODS.

CLEAR THE TRACK.

SILKS
POPLIN
HOSE
CHALLIS
LACE SHAWLS   AMOSKEAG
MERINO VESTS   ALPACA
MOURNING PRINTS   SILK SHAWLS
DE LAINES
SUP. EX. POPLIN   Manchester ROBES
Lancaster AA Ginghams   Plaid Poplin
HAMILTON ALL WOOL
ENGLISH KERSEYS   OPERA FLANNELS
SATINE   DRESS
QUAKER CLOAK
BB MERRIMACK FAST COLORS
CREPE SILK
PACIFIC MILLS
LONSDALE
HOPE MILLS

ENTERED ACCORDING TO ACT OF CONGRESS, IN THE YEAR 1870, BY GIBSON & CO. IN THE OFFICE OF THE LIBRARIAN OF CONGRESS AT WASHINGTON

Country merchants who visited New York did much of their buying in wholesalers' display rooms on Liberty Street (above, right). One of the more popular advertising cards of the 1870s (above) was intended to portray the wealth of goods the merchant had en route to his store after his trip to the big city market.

Right: On the way to the ferry. Across the river the stagecoach awaits passengers to New York City.

Left: On the roads over the Alleghenies some of the overnight stopping places were excellent, others just so-so. One inn is pictured here.

116

LIBERTY STREET,
Near BROADWAY NEW YORK.

Bufford's Lith 114 Nassau St. N.Y.

MORGAN, HOLKINS & CO.	RHOADES, WEED & CO.	WEED & LITTLE.	VANSCHAICK & NOYES	W.M. TILESTON & CO	R.H. OSGOOD & CO.	CLARK, SMITH & CO.	COMSTOCK & ANDREWS	WRIGHT, WINSTON & STEBBINS
Wholesale Dealers in Foreign & Domestic	Wholesale Dealers in Foreign & Domestic	Wholesale Dealers In	Wholesale Dealers in Staple & Fancy	Wholesale Dealers in Boots	Wholesale Clothing	Wholesale Dealers in French & India	European & India Silks Leghorn & Straw Bonnets	Importers and Dealers in Foreign and Domestic
DRY GOODS.	DRY GOODS. Cloths, Cassimeres and Vestings.	DRY GOODS.	DRY GOODS.	SHOES LEATHER &c.	STORE.	SILK GOODS.	PARASOLS & UMBRELLAS	DRY GOODS.
67.	65.	63.	61.	59.	59.	57.	55.	53.
FRANCIS MORGAN. JOEL HOLKINS. HOMER MORGAN.	LYMAN RHOADES, IRA WARD, N. THWEED.		A.D.VANSCHAICK, W. TWISTBROUGH NOYES.			RALPH CLARK, S. SMITH. E.P. CLARK.	D.A. COMSTOCK. B.W. ANDREWS.	CORNER OF NASSAU ST.

117

Hudson River landing—news, goods, and people congregated at infrequent intervals, lending zest to an otherwise bucolic life in the upper reaches of the valley.

OPPORTUNITIES SEIZED

In Wheeling, West Virginia, Mifflin M. Marsh twisted tobacco into slender stogies and sold them from a basket he carried about the streets and docks. Cheaper than hand-rolled cigars, stogies were an instant hit. Before long, Marsh moved to a small factory, where he turned out vast quantities of stogies to meet the demand from wagoners, boatmen, and commercial travelers, who purchased in quantities for resale throughout the South and West. The first stogies, however, were made by a tobacco retailer in Washington, Pennsylvania, who called his odd-shaped smoke a "Conestoga" after the huge freight wagons that rolled past his shop. In short order his customers chopped the name "Conestoga" down to "stoga" and finally to "stogie," in which form it has been immortalized.

In New Haven, Connecticut, two oyster dealers named Edmund Bradley and Jacob Goodsell expanded their markets and piled up modest fortunes in the early 1800s by packing oysters in saddlebags

and going upcountry with them, just as Eli Terry did with his clocks. Their best customers were the inns and taverns that catered to stagecoach travelers. As business and profits grew, some of the more enterprising dealers in oysters employed large wagons drawn by four or six horses and extended their sales to Hartford, Springfield, northern New York State, Vermont, and Canada. Another man with a connoisseur's taste for oysters and an eye for trade was Colonel Henry Orndorff, whose National Hotel in Zanesville, Ohio, was something of a Waldorf-Astoria of its time and place. Orndorff had oysters shipped to him from Baltimore. Some of these he served to his guests at the National Hotel; the balance he sold to proprietors of taverns and hotels throughout the Ohio River Valley. His business in oysters prospered to such an extent that special wagons carrying oysters only, and dubbed the Oyster Line, traveled at a breakneck clip along the Great National Road from Baltimore to Zanesville on mail-stage schedules.

Travelers in America during the 1800s either ate too well, putting away prodigious quantities of rich and heavy food, washed down with strong drink and potent coffee, or they ate a fare barely fit for human consumption, depending upon where they stopped

118

and the unpredictable table of their lodging places. In either case the result was a national plague of gastronomic disorders and an insatiable demand for pills or powders that promised relief. Drake's Plantation Bitters was one of the most popular remedies and one of the most widely advertised. Whoever it was who promoted Drake's Plantation Bitters did himself proud. He gave the product the mystical brand symbol STI860X and, in an early version of "Kilroy was here," painted the symbol on the sides of taverns and barns, the trunks of trees, big rocks along the highways, and surfaces that must have seemed inaccessible to an astonished traveler.

When all went well, which was not often the case, a buying trip by a Western merchant consumed an average of six weeks, two of which were spent getting to market, two buying, and two getting home. Upon arrival at the market the merchant called first

on the firms with whom he had been doing business in the past. He carried with him a list of the merchandise he was open to buy from these established suppliers—usually replacements of staples and assorted wares for which the merchant had a steady demand. This business over with, the merchant spent the balance of his time in town poking around for new products, specialties, and odds and ends that might appeal to his customers and provide a note of wonder and excitement when he got home and unpacked his goods.

Wholesalers, manufacturers, and agents treated their out-of-town customers with time-honored so-

The opulent St. Nicholas Hotel on lower Broadway. Confederate Army officers set this famed hostelry afire in 1864 in an unsuccessful attempt to burn the city of New York.

119

licitude and courtesy, and they did everything possible to restrain the visitor from wandering too far afield where he might fall into the arms of a competitor. In New York City many firms maintained comfortable rooms above their stores to rent to their customers at reasonable rates, the hope being that this would tend to keep a visitor on their premises during most of his stay in town.

The temptations of the big city were by no means confined to the hours after nightfall. A merchant casually walking along William Street or Pearl Street, or registered at a hotel, was constantly accosted by a flying squad of "drummers" employed by wholesalers and jobbers to entice out-of-town buyers to visit the showrooms of the firms that employed them. A drummer was a persuasive talker, quick to stand a round of drinks and well supplied with good Havana cigars. He hung on with the persistence of a head cold until the prospect agreed to accompany him to his firm. There the merchant might be bamboozled into buying second-rate goods or be happily surprised to run across a fine selection that he was glad to add to his purchases. There was a riffraff element among the drummers just as there was among the peddlers, and it was the wheedlers and the uncouth among them who were responsible for their fall into ill-repute in society. These were the minority; most drummers were decent men and served well as outside salesmen and solicitors for reputable houses.

UP FOR AUCTION

For many years a large volume of goods was sold at auction in New York and other wholesale markets. Imported dry goods predominated at these auctions, although nearly every conceivable article of commerce passed under the auctioneer's hammer. Prices at auctions were generally lower than those charged by importers and wholesalers, and they fluctuated widely in a dramatic exposition of the sensitivity of the law of supply and demand. The unexpected arrival of a number of vessels from Europe with dry goods, or a falling-off of the number of buyers in the market, perhaps because of a severe snowstorm, caused prices to fall through the floor and enabled a visiting merchant to pick up real bargains. A Connecticut merchant made a trip to Boston and Salem, where he "purchased at auction an extra-fine piece of broadcloth, brought it home in the stages, and sold it to a merchant tailor beyond the expenses of my journey." Shortly afterward this merchant made another trip to Boston, where, he noted, "goods generally are greatly depressed . . . and staple dry goods often sold by auction from 25 to 50% loss for cash. I determined to commence purchasing. . . ."

WHAT TO BUY—WHAT TO SELL

The buying of merchandise on annual, semi-annual, or tri-annual shopping trips was done with infinite care and so was the selling by suppliers. It was a case of the merchant's estimating what his customers might need during the next six months or so and what he might prudently add in the way of novelties and semi-luxury items. He had to take into account the money his customers would have available to spend, basing his figure on the results of the previous year's harvests, the prices paid for farm produce, the outlook for the season ahead, the general level of business and prosperity in his area, and the growth of his community. He made his own economic forecast, there being none other available. If he guessed far wrong about the future price of wheat or hogs, or the full-time employment of the workers in his town's local industry, he was headed for serious trouble and, perhaps, final disaster. The risks were great and unpredictable; buying for a year or half-year or so ahead was an act of faith and courage.

The seller who extended as much as a year's credit to the merchant had more than a passing interest in the merchant's appraisal of his market. Little, if anything, would be salvaged should the merchant fail. There were no collection agencies and few banks, and a sheriff's sale rarely returned the creditors more than several cents on the dollar. The wholesaler, while he naturally wanted to make as good a sale as he could, rarely oversold a customer who might later find it difficult or impossible to pay. The better houses went out of their way to help

What a field day the writers of television commercials could have with Wigwam Tonic!

121

their customers strike a reasonably good balance between buying too little and buying too much. Then, as now and always, a supplier who displayed a genuine interest in his customer's needs and problems built up a clientele of loyal buyers. At the same time, the merchant and the supplier realized they had an obligation that transcended their own interests. The country was growing in population and industrial output. New wants were being created and a profusion of new products was coming on the market. The distribution of these goods was of prime importance to the economic and social welfare of the country and all the people in it, and there was no way to get these goods into circulation except to buy them and take a chance that they would be bought by the people back home.

If a merchant ordered too little and ran out of stock before his next buying trip, he could reorder by mail or, occasionally, pick up small stocks from peddlers who wandered into town. But the mails were erratic (it was reported in 1822 that the mails from Pittsburgh for the East were "lost or stolen" four times in less than two months), and peddlers' prices were fairly high. Ordering anything except staples by mail was further complicated because the merchant could seldom be sure exactly what merchandise his wholesale supplier would have in stock at the time his order was received. For example, the owner of an upstate New York general store received the following letter from the New York City wholesale firm of Hill & Ogden:

Henry W. Carter's splendid teams brought an impressive flourish to the last years of the era of peddling. This old billhead indicates the wide variety of items this "merchant prince" of New England managed to stow in his wagons.

IMPORTER AND WHOLESALE DEALER IN

British, French, German and American Fancy Goods,

Hosiery, Gloves, Watches, Silver Ware, Jewelry, &c.

Also, a great variety of Shell, Ivory and other Combs, Buttons of every description, Sewing Silk, Twist, Linen Thread, Spool Threads by the case, Suspenders, Brushes, Cutlery, Looking Glasses, &c.

TERMS, NET CASH.

Dec 21st 1868.

Bought of **H. W. CARTER.**

"Sir: We received your favor of the 20 May and have sent you such articles you requested as we had on hand as nearly to your directions as we could. Some articles you mentioned we had, but not of the Quality particularized, for instance Lawn, we have none but High price & our Velverets we were afraid were not fine enough. If you wish either a piece of the fine Lawn or of the Olive Velveret, we will send them. . . . We have two purple Cottons but not Calicoes and were afraid they would not suit, shou'd have sent a piece."

Hill & Ogden's letter was typical of the uncertainty of ordering by mail. It is, as well, a good illustration of the way in which a respectable supplier carefully considered his customers' best interests. At the same time, it apparently occurred to Messrs. Hill and Ogden that this was as good an occasion as any to dun their upstate customer for some money, for their letter, written in June, goes on: "We hope that it may be convenient to you soon to discharge the last Fall Bills of Goods to enable us to make our own remittances on the punctuality of which depends the existence of our Business."

Uncertainty regarding prices was another obstacle to reordering by mail. There were very few established brand names, and prices of all types of goods were subject to rapid and violent fluctuations. In the occasional catalogue or direct-mail solicitations received by merchants from wholesalers and manufacturers, there often occurred the tantalizing notation that the prices would be "the lowest in the market" or, as the New York wholesale firm of Douglas & Fitch remarked in a sales-solicitation letter they sent out in 1830: "We shall be able to supply dealers with Genuine Drugs & Medicines, at prices that may induce them to favor us with their orders." In a similar vein, D. Devlin & Company, New York, wholesalers and retailers of men's and boys' clothing, advised their prospects that "we guarantee the prices to be lower than those of Merchant Tailoring Establishments generally." Under these circumstances cautious merchants wrote to suppliers inquiring for firm prices before placing an order.

"THE MERCHANT PRINCE OF NEW ENGLAND"

Merchants in New Hampshire and Vermont who ran out of stock between buying trips relied on a wholesale peddler named Henry W. Carter for replenishments. Carter was an extraordinary man who got into trade at the age of eight when he persuaded his father to permit him to sell candy in the tavern his father owned. At fifteen Henry Carter branched out, peddling books, stationery, and candy from a wagon, a career that almost foundered when the door was slammed in his face at the first farm he visited. But at the next farm he was warmly received, and he sold a Bible and a hymnal. Within a few years Carter had established a wholesale business at Lebanon, New Hampshire, and he became known far and wide as the "Merchant Prince of New England."

Carter was not one to wait for his customers to come to him; he had too much get-up-and-go for that. To serve his customers and keep their shelves stocked, Carter kept four large wagons on the road. These were not just ordinary peddler wagons pulled by a scrawny nag or two. They were immense affairs, gaily painted, the side panels and tailboards decorated with large oil paintings showing Carter's store and factory, where he had begun manufacturing work shirts and overalls. Harness trimmings were of pure silver and polished daily. Each wagon was drawn by four perfectly matched black horses and carried upwards of two thousand dollars' worth of Yankee and imported notions, dry goods, cigars, and tobacco. They attracted attention wherever they went. Teachers in one-room country schools recessed classes so that the children could watch these splendid wagons come rolling down the road. In towns and villages crowds collected when a Carter wagon pulled up at a store and the driver climbed off his box to do business with the merchant.

This was good showmanship, which is important to selling in any trade and at any time. But Carter did not rely solely upon showmanship to build his business. He backed his advertising with fair prices, honest goods, and excellent service. And Carter saw to it that his cigars were of better than ordinary quality, for often his drivers could sell an innkeeper enough cigars to pay for a night's lodging.

Getting goods home from wholesale markets was fraught with danger. Disasters afloat, such as this steamboat crash on the Hudson River, were a common occurrence.

In other parts of the country where there were no reliable wholesale peddlers like Carter, the captain of a boat or the driver of a stage could be entrusted with the purchase of a small stock of goods. The owners of the New Haven & Albany Packet Line of Steamers advertised that its vessels "are commanded by experienced masters who will . . . attend to the purchasing of goods, when required, without any charge for commission." Such a service by the captains was all very well so long as it was not used by a local merchant's customers, which, apparently, was done by the people of Newfield, Connecticut. To discourage his customers from ordering goods from New York through steamboat captains, general merchant David C. DeForest, who had just replenished his stocks of dry goods, advised his customers: "Those ladies who can with convenience ride to Newfield will oftener be pleased in

choosing for themselves, than in leaving it to the choice of some tasteless captain of a packet boat."

GETTING BACK HOME

When they had completed their buying in the wholesale markets, country merchants preferred to accompany their goods home rather than have them shipped separately. Such an arrangement enabled the merchant to stand over the roustabouts who loaded and unloaded the goods en route and to plead with them to handle the boxes and bundles with some semblance of care. Goods unaccompanied by their owners were subjected to manhandling in transit that bordered on a maniacal attempt to see how much damage could be done. One merchant wrote to his suppliers, who had shipped his goods by boat: "The shoes and linen have arrived, but by the negligence of the vile Master they have come in very bad condition being stowed among the coal and suffered by downright carelessness to get wet." From St. Louis a paper wholesaler wrote to a manufacturer in New England who had forwarded a consignment of paper by sloop to New

124

Orleans, then by Mississippi steamboat to St. Louis: "The Boxes you put your paper in are not strong enough to come this distance. The Boxes are handled by ruffins in getting them on board of ship, and then off and many require cooperage at N. Orleans. This being done in a hurry and by some fellow who is not very particular, bad havoc is often made."

Of course, if a wagon tipped over, spilling the unlucky merchant and his goods into a stream, or a steamboat caught fire, there was little the merchant could do except thank his stars to be alive, collect whatever insurance he had, and head back to town to replace the goods lost or damaged beyond salvaging. The number of road accidents was appallingly high, and steamboat disasters were a frequent occurrence. A merchant whose goods suffered in these accidents was in a bad way, and often had nothing but bare shelves for the whole of a spring or summer season.

When a merchant in Salt Lake City departed on a buying trip to the wholesale markets of Kansas City or St. Louis, he reckoned on being away for eight to ten weeks at the very least.

Fresh goods and the expected return of a merchant from the city had a news value not to be overlooked by the editor of the local newspaper. Thus, the *Deseret News* in Salt Lake City, in its issue dated June 15, 1850, carried the following items concerning the expected arrival of the first merchandise shipped from the East in the spring of that year:

"Mr. Thomas S. Williams, who left the Missouri River on the 1 of May was the bearer of the mail mentioned in our last issue. Mr. Williams has a storehouse . . . in rapid progress of erection . . . for the reception of a large stock of goods, now on the way, which he expects in about a month.

"Mr. Holladay—Merchant of Missouri, left the river the same day. Some of his teams were failing, and he came forward, to procure assistance, which he readily obtained. . . . We understand he expects his dry goods in two or three days; his groceries are further in the rear. . . .

"We hear that Mr. Kinkead, of the firm of Livingston & Kinkead, is *en route* with goods. . . . We have no doubt the market will be substantially supplied in a few weeks."

The safe arrival of a consignment of merchandise was a great day for the merchants and the townspeople as well. Boxes and crates and bales were opened and their contents stowed on the shelves. More than likely there had to be a rearrangement of the space allocated to groceries or drugs or hardware to make room for some new types of goods the merchant had purchased. Display signs and placards advertising a brand of plug tobacco or cough medicine or, perhaps, Salada Tea were hung in the show windows or attached to the glass panels in the entrance door.

One of the first things to be done was to prepare advertising copy for insertion in the next issue of the local newspaper. How those old-timers must have struggled writing their copy, going over it time after time, packing as many words as possible into as small a space as possible. If the merchant had picked up bargains at auction, it was important that this fact be played up in boldface type. "Bought Cheap at Auction" appeared in many advertisements, the connotation being that the merchant was sharing the cost savings with his customers, which, in fact, he was.

In the city the merchant undoubtedly had performed a number of errands for his friends and customers. Upon his return he reported on these errands and delivered special items of merchandise not ordinarily stocked: books, perhaps, or a wedding gown, or an article imported from the Old Country and unobtainable except in the city. And, of course, the returning merchant was a fount of information. He was a man of authority on such matters as the state of the nation, the outlook for trade, the truth behind the rumor that a railroad was coming to town, and the latest fashions from Paris and London.

Trade was brisk following the arrival of fresh merchandise; sales boomed on Saturdays, when people from the country came to town to restock staples and look over the merchant's wares. In Franklin, Missouri, when the merchants arrived home from their spring buying trips, the weekly visit to the village stores by the country people took on a new enchantment. Among the goods brought

On his return home from market, the merchant planned his advertising copy for the local newspaper (above). The two advertising display cards (below and opposite page) are excellent examples of nineteenth-century lithography. They were proudly placed in show windows.

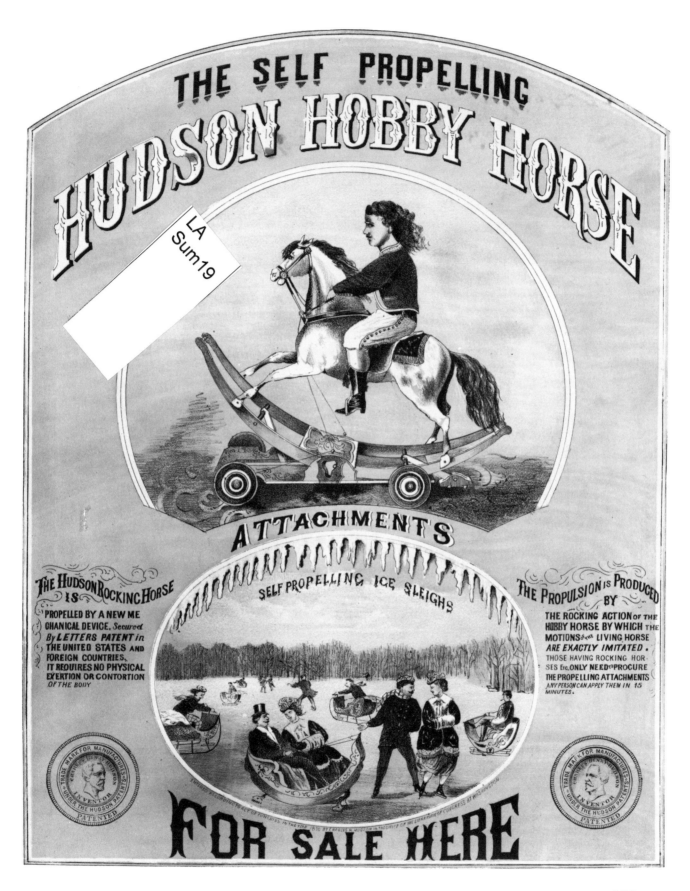

127

to Franklin were the latest spring bonnets. An old-timer in Missouri, remembering the annual "Bonnet Show" on the second Sunday of May at the Big Shoal Meeting House, when all the ladies appeared at church wearing their newly purchased hats, wrote:

"... After Lon's Expedition up the Missouri River in 1819 by steamboat, its navigation by steam began to develop. By 1826 it assumed something like regularity. Allen's landing three and one-half miles south of Liberty was established in 1825. At once on the

A well-stocked grocery store at Osborne, Kansas, in the 1890s.

beginning of steam navigation of the River, the merchants of Liberty began to purchase for local trade fine goods, bonnets and the like in Philadelphia and their fine groceries in Baltimore. This continued for a number of years. Merchants left Liberty for the east to make their spring and summer purchases early in February. Their purchases began to arrive in Liberty during the latter part of March, or the forepart of April. The stores in Liberty thus became centers of attraction for the ladies, old and young, in Clay and the surrounding country. The spring bonnets! The spring bonnets! It was a race with all the girls for the first pick of the new bonnets."

These merchants of another century, who opened their stores at seven in the morning and, dog-tired, bid their last customers "good night" at ten in the evening; who carried their neighbors through periods of financial adversity, which occurred with dismal frequency; who journeyed long distances to buy the merchandise their customers relied on them to supply and to dispose of the produce their customers raised for markets they could not themselves reach; who gambled on introducing new products and creating new markets—these were just ordinary men, entertaining no outsized notions that they were citizens of historic stature and each in his own way something of an empire-builder. Yet the buying and selling among thousands of obscure men, many of them long forgotten, wove together the commerce of a young nation. Their daily acts of individual courage and foresight nourished the growth of trade. Without them we would never have climbed to the pinnacle from which today some among us deliver sermons on the affluence of our age and the waste-makers in our midst. For the early merchants there were no such lofty towers, and there was very little national affluence to carp about.

A new Easter bonnet for the wife, and a chilly husband who made the buying trip.

129

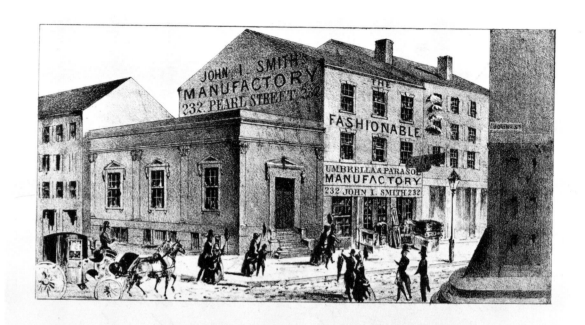

New York February 1st, 1847.—

Dear Sir

The time being near when our merchants will be in this city to purchase their spring stock. it is desirable they should know where to select the richest styles & best goods at the very lowest Market price.— — With regard to New York, all are aware that every kind of Manufactures & Imports may be bought at a lower price than any city in the Union. and far larger stocks to select from, the difficulty with many of our merchants on their arrival is to know where such houses may be found & therefore make their selection from limited & inferior stocks previously purchased either from the man ufacturer or Importer & not unfrequently very dear. Permit me therefore as a wholesale manufacturer of Umbrellas Parasols &c. to call your attention to this establishment, which I think you will allow is the most extensive in the United States. It would be useless to go into a detail of the variety of patterns & elegance of styles which I am daily manufacturing & upon which very much depends in order to insure ready sales at a good profit & would respectfully solicit you

Some manufacturers of long ago believed in direct-mail selling. Reproduced on these two pages is a facsimile of a letter written by a New York wholesaler, urging a

130

on your arrival to call & examine the manufactures before purchasing, which you will readily see is quite dissimilar to any in the city, and comprising hundreds of different sizes and kinds, and many of those kinds among the Parasols & Parasolettes, there is a vast variety of colors & figures, the patterns of which are very elegant, being selected by myself from the best manufactories of England, France, & Germany where I spent part of the last & former year, & made arrangement with those houses constantly to receive patterns of the newest styles, so that now my Customers will not only have the best materials & workmanship, but also the newest Parisian & Continental styles, & withal at far lower prices than has been offered in the United States, many being as low as those of London or Paris; for your guidance I beg to hand you on the other page an extract from the Catalogue of some of the kinds, with their numbers & prices which if you will put in your pocket-book when you arrive in the city you will find of service. All goods warranted in materials & workmanship. No deduction from Catalogue price, my rule is One price & no abatement; should you not come on this season if you will forward me your order by mail it shall have the same attention as if you were here to select it Hoping to receive your orders or the pleasure of seeing you the coming season   I Remain

Yours Respectfully

John J Smith

232 Pearl Street.

N B. Umbrellas & Parasols by the case adapted for Exportation to the Canadian, South American, West India & other Markets.

New Hampshire merchant to call at the wholesaler's
shop on his spring buying trip.

H. FINCH'S
Daily Line of Stages
FROM
KENSICO
TO
MILE SQUARE, NORTH CASTLE,
And A. DOWNES' STORE,

IN CONNECTION WITH THE
NEW YORK AND HARLEM RAILROAD.

On and after MONDAY, MAY 2d, 1853, a Stage
WILL LEAVE KENSICO

On the arrival of the 3.35 Afternoon Train from New York, passing by the way of Robbins'
Mills, Mile Square, Sands' Mills, to A. Downes' Store, North Castle.
LEAVE NORTH CASTLE

At $6\frac{1}{2}$ o'clock in the Morning, passing by the way of Sands' Mills, Mile Square, and Robbins'
Mills, arriving at Kensico Station in time to take the 8.22 Train to New York.

Passengers to the above places will find it to their advantage to secure Through Tickets at the Broome Street Office,
New York, where they can be obtained at reduced rates.

HIRAM FINCH, Proprietor.

132

"Itinerating" Expands

Customers were still few and far between, and getting out to see them wherever they were became increasingly necessary.

T RAVELING SALESMEN covering specific territories and carrying samples and order books were practically nonexistent prior to the Civil War. On the face of it this would appear to indicate that the sales profession was a late starter, slow to recognize its opportunities in the rapidly expanding American economy. By educated guess there were probably fewer than one thousand salesmen—or "drummers," as they were disparagingly called—on the road in 1860, and many of this small squad were not much more than glorified peddlers or office supernumeraries sent into the field to try their hand at collecting overdue accounts.

Management's approach to building a sales organization was haphazard. When business was good and profits were high enough to justify the expense of sending out a salesman, the owner might decide to "take a flyer" at such a manner of increasing his sales and developing new accounts. Thus, the Collins Company in Connecticut sent John Barlow on a trip through the Western and Southern states in 1830. His official title was "traveling agent." Prior to his trip Barlow had been employed by the company as a bookkeeper and office clerk, which would suggest he was better qualified to collect money due from delinquent merchants and wholesalers and prepare reports on their financial status than he was to sell them the Collins line of axes, adzes, hatchets, and other cutting tools. There are no records avail-

able of the results of Barlow's trip, and we can only surmise that it was not a spectacular success, for the trip was not repeated and Barlow settled down to a nonroving clerkship in the firm's New York offices.

The Scovill Manufacturing Company, producers of brassware in Waterbury, Connecticut, employed a young man named Merit Welton to make a sales trip through the West and South in 1832. Welton made a number of such trips for Scovill during the ensuing three years, after which no one seems to have been traveling for the company until 1852, when Samuel Holmes hit the road and made extended trips throughout the country. Other brass manufacturers apparently had men on the road, for both Welton and Holmes, in their reports to the home office, refer to crossing the paths of these competitors.

George K. Smith, who in 1841 established a wholesale-retail drugstore in Philadelphia (the forerunner of Smith, Kline & French Laboratories), did his own selling on sales trips throughout eastern Pennsylvania and New Jersey. It was not until after the Civil War that the firm was prosperous enough to employ salesmen to call on out-of-town physicians and druggists.

Two years after Eli Lilly began his business as a manufacturing pharmacist, his younger brother James Edward joined him as a one-man sales force. James worked without pay until he built up enough business to warrant drawing a salary. His customers were druggists and physicians, most of whom were located in the rural areas of Indiana.

Eli Lilly often said of his brother: "A better salesman than Jim Lilly never walked in shoe leather." Eli's selection of a verb was accurate. To cover the state, James traveled by buggy and on horseback, or by canal boat if he found one headed in the direc-

tion he wanted to go. But when no public transportation was available or when his funds were low—both often the case—James walked to see a customer. With him he carried Eli's elixirs, cordials, and pills in a sample case "about twice the size of a large valise," which, on many a hot, dusty trip, must have seemed to weigh close to a ton.

As business grew and Eli Lilly & Company began to show a profit, James broadened his travels to include Illinois, Missouri, Kansas, and Nebraska. A branch house was established at Kansas City to handle the Western trade. More men were added to the sales staff. Six years after James had made his first sales trip, eighteen salesmen were on the road for Eli Lilly & Company.

Waiting for the stage.

To get to their customers salesmen used every means available, resorting to foot when necessary.

The problem of reaching out-of-town prospects was a frustrating one for ambitious men who wanted to expand their sales beyond the local market. In the middle years of the last century there were few reliable trade directories from which names of prospects might be obtained. But if a man was really determined to increase his sales, he usually found a way to do it, as did James Moss Bemis, for example. Bemis had a small plant in St. Louis where he manufactured an improved type of cotton bag for the

James E. Lilly

The Indiana countryside was filled with spellbinders when James Lilly went on the road. Salesman Lilly prospered; the quacks faded into obscurity.

135

flour trade. Sales to the millers in St. Louis were fairly substantial, but earnings were not fat enough to enable Bemis to employ salesmen to travel about, calling on the hundreds of flour millers who were grinding grain from the newly settled Western states.

Bemis found the answer to his problems by **prowling** the levees. St. Louis was an important transshipment port on the Mississippi River, and tons of freight, including thousands of bags of flour, were constantly being transferred from one riverboat to another. Paper and pencil in hand, Bemis spent hours on the levee examining the cargo. Whenever

he found shipments of flour, he jotted down the name of the miller stenciled on the sacks. He then wrote a sales letter to the miller and sent him a sample of his flour bag. It was not an easy way to dig up the names of prospects, as anyone knows who has ever been on the St. Louis waterfront on a sultry summer day or a bleak winter afternoon. But Bemis got surprisingly good results from his name-gathering sales letters. Before long he had customers as far away as St. Paul, Kansas City, and the cities along the Ohio River.

There were valid reasons why there were so few salesmen stirring about the country. Travel was

Judson Moss Bemis was a man with imagination and energy. At left, the arrival of freight at St. Louis where Bemis compiled his direct-mail list.

expensive in relation to the value of the dollar. True, overnight lodgings cost only twenty-five to fifty cents at country inns, and good accommodations in the larger cities rarely exceeded a dollar. Two or three dollars a night for a room was a downright extravagance. Meals varied from twenty-five cents for a hearty breakfast to seventy-five cents for an adequate dinner. Transportation, however, was more expensive. Stage-line rates ran five to six cents a mile. Canal-boat fares were cheaper than those of the stage lines, but travel by water was slower. "A cent and a half a mile, a mile and a half an hour" summed up the cost and pace of canal travel.

Time was the most important factor of all in determining whether a sales trip would be worthwhile or not. Before the days of rapid transit, the time a man spent with a customer in relation to the inordinate amount spent getting to and from the customer's place of business was a real problem. The number of calls a salesman could make in a week could be counted on the fingers of one hand. A Boston traveler began his trip to St. Louis via a

137

schooner to Baltimore—a voyage of fifteen days. From Baltimore he rode the Baltimore & Ohio Railroad to the end of the track in the foothills of the Alleghenies. He then walked to the banks of the Monongahela River, where he caught a boat for Pittsburgh. At Pittsburgh he transferred to a steamboat for St. Louis. The entire trip took thirty-seven days, which was not an exceptionally long time. Merit Welton, on one of his trips for Scovill, boarded a stagecoach from Philadelphia at three o'clock on a Thursday afternoon and arrived at Pittsburgh at the ungodly hour of three o'clock Sunday morning. During winter months a journey from Chicago to St. Louis might take up to six or eight days over icy roads. In Iowa the *State Journal* was moved to editorialize in 1849 about the condition of the road between Des Moines and Iowa City, then the state capital. Said the *Journal*:

"A semi-weekly line of stagecoaches has been established from Des Moines to Iowa City, but the proprietors are unable to run coaches at present because of the badness of the roads.

"If the people would attend to bridging a few

The number of calls a salesman could make was small in relation to the time he was on the road. Even a short trip took a long time because of frequent delays. Travel in winter was particularly difficult.

Before the telegraph and reliable mail service a salesman might not learn that the city he was headed for had been gutted by fire or that a cholera epidemic was raging and all business had come to a standstill.

streams on the route, they would have the advantages resulting from the running of a line of stages, instead of the mail coming in on muleback and passengers being compelled to travel in some other direction."

In the spring, when the thaw came, roads were impassable for days at a time, and rivers ran amok, making travel by water a risky adventure—when such a mode of travel was possible at all.

Poor communications, as well as slow transportation, contributed to making a salesman's trip unrewarding. There was no telephoning ahead for an appointment, and there was little use in writing to announce an unpredictable arrival at some distant date. The only thing to do was to take a chance and make a cold call on a customer. And a big chance it was, too. After a tedious journey the salesman might find that the man he had come to see was off on a buying trip or had just come back from one and was fully stocked for the next six months with the kind of goods the salesman was selling. It was not unusual for a salesman to arrive in town to find that a disastrous fire had razed the business district

"Peaches, one cent."

a day or two before. This could be good or bad news for the traveler, depending upon whether or not his customer was covered by fire insurance (obtainable from Eastern companies, mostly in Philadelphia and New York) and could order new stock or was flat broke and could not afford anything. On the other hand, a town or city shut down tight because of a raging epidemic of cholera or yellow fever presented a hopeless proposition, and the best thing for a salesman to do was to get out of the place as quickly as he could.

Even when things went well and a sale was made, an order worth two or three hundred dollars was considered a fair-sized piece of business. A thousand-dollar order was cause for jubilation. Under these circumstances it was next to impossible for a salesman to write a volume of business great enough to cover his traveling expenses plus his salary, which could vary from five to thirty dollars a week. A trip was worth considering only if the salesman performed a number of other services besides selling for the company he represented. A capable man was expected to evaluate the market. He would report on competition, either local or from other firms sending men into the field. His evaluation of the business outlook, including crops and growth of local industries and population, would be of value to the home office. He was expected to recommend alterations in his company's products which might make them more suitable for certain markets and to suggest new products his company might profitably include in its line. Through his conduct, his integrity, and his enthusiasm, he built good will, to the end that when buyers went to market they would remember to visit the showrooms of his firm. A call on a customer that resulted in only a token order or no order at all, might be compensated by a large order placed when the customer made his buying trip to the wholesale market.

Two other functions were performed by these versatile traveling salesmen: they appointed local agents and representatives, and they collected past-due accounts and reported on the financial status of their firms' customers.

Working capital for American industry and commerce was in short supply until well after the Civil War, and the common practice was for manufacturers and merchants to accept notes due in six months or more. In 1842 a paper dealer in Boston wrote to the Hurlbut Paper Company: "Could readily dispose of a large amount of paper at fair market prices to good and safe customers *some of whom pay Cash.*" (The italics are ours.) Cash-and-carry customers were scarce prior to the Civil War, and most sales were on a credit or barter basis. Long-term credit sharpened the hazard of financial loss. A note accepted for payment six months later carried with it a fervent hope that the nation's economy would not be flat on its back at maturity date and that the debtor would not have succumbed to small-pox or overextended his own credit beyond reasonable limits.

Manufacturers of farm equipment had to carry their customers and agents until after the harvest season, which was the usual time for farmers, country merchants, and dealers to settle their accounts. And squaring accounts did not always mean payment with cash. John Deere, for example, found himself with such a great accumulation of butter, hams, wood, skins, and Lord knows what else that he had to rent a warehouse near his plow factory to store it. The company historian reports: "In connection with that warehouse, the contents of which represented a greater part of the company's income, Gould [an early associate of Deere's] made several trips to St. Louis. He sold what he could from the warehouse's miscellany and bought supplies for the factory." In 1875 H. E. Barber, who traveled throughout Nebraska Territory for John Deere, was paid for a shipment of plows with two hundred dollars' worth of postage stamps. In many communities the leading merchant was also the postmaster, who was paid a commission on the stamps he sold. By fobbing off stamps on Deere, the merchant made money coming and going—on the stamps and on the plows he sold for Deere.

Kilpatrick's Supply Store at Broken Bow, Custer County, Nebraska, circa 1886. Such an establishment would seem to be of small interest to a traveling salesman, yet he learned that all outlets, big and small, needed the service he could give.

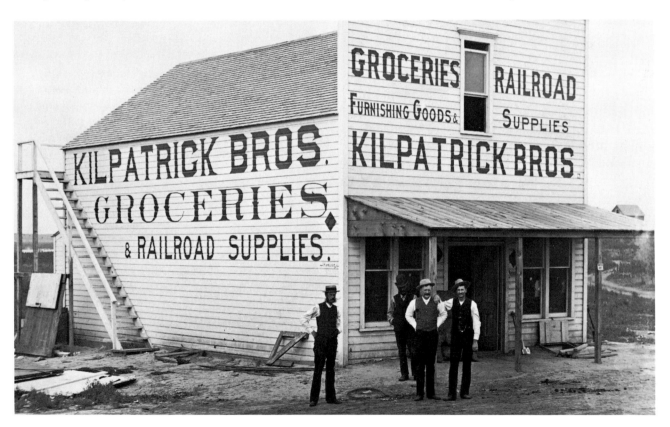

TRAVELING AGENTS

Jerome Case, who made almost as many trips into the field to collect money as he did to make sales, came home to Racine after one such trip with only a piffling fifty dollars in cash out of twenty-five hundred due. It was discouraging. When things got really bad and money was tighter than a clam, Case accepted horses, wagons, hogs, cattle, and anything else worth while in lieu of cash for his threshing machines. At one time he was the unhappy possessor of eight gold watches given him by debtor farmers unable to scrape up cash for their past-due notes. Case did not want gold watches any more than other sellers wanted produce or family possessions. Such goods were accepted because they were offered by honest men in payment for obligations they could not meet with cash. Cyrus McCormick, who also had his troubles collecting payments, once remarked that one could sell a reaper only if he was willing to wait for payment until the reaper had paid for itself.

A manufacturer's agent or a wholesaler's salesman whose territory included small towns and settlements in the West got few large orders from the merchants and dealers he called on. Often he came away with nothing more than a token order that did not even cover his expenses. However, these travelers did get large-sized meals at the local restaurants, where the victuals served were usually far better than the decor.

It was clearly impossible for the owner of a business to spend much of his time trying to collect payments, and so, for many years, this chore was of major importance for men who went on the road as combined salesmen and bill collectors.

As for the appointment of local agents or representatives, a chain of agencies throughout the country served as a stopgap expedient until such time as a permanent sales organization could be built on a profitable basis. The definition of what constituted an agent was very loosely applied. Dwight Baldwin served as the agent for a number of musical-instrument manufacturers in Cincinnati, Louisville, Indianapolis, and nearby areas. Actually, he was more of a merchant specializing in musical instruments. Julius Ward Butler moved from Vermont to St. Charles, Illinois, in 1841, where he opened a general store from which he sent peddlers throughout northern Illinois and southern Wisconsin. Butler acted as agent for a number of manufacturers of tinware, paper, dress goods, and hardware whose products he sold locally and through his peddlers.

Very understandably, agents preferred to remain as close as possible to their home base, leaving the task of getting around the countryside to peddlers who were going there anyway. The agents' reasons for not wandering far afield were the same as those that discouraged manufacturers from sending salesmen out on the road—hard, expensive travel, few calls on customers per day or week, and small orders which, when the agent deducted his commission, hardly paid the overhead.

One man who was an exception for those times prior to the Civil War was John Kirk, best described as a manufacturer's agent, who handled a number of lines, including iron and hardware.

Kirk was an inveterate traveler, and a copy of his letterbook reveals the problems and vicissitudes that beset a traveling man in the 1850s. In February 1853 he wrote from Lafayette, Indiana, to one of the firms for whom he sold iron:

"I called last evening at the office of Messrs. Reynold & Co. . . . Mr. Reynold says that Martin Kane are perfectly good and responsible and that Messrs. Hances & Potter are one of the richest firms in the place. I called on them today. Mr. Potter will pass through your city on his way east in a few days and has promised me that he would call and see you.

"This itinerating is a curious, as well as uncertain business. Last evening Mr. Lane called on me, and invited me to come up to their establishment today, and he would give me an order for ten tons of Waggon tin."

Had Kirk obtained the order "last evening," he would have been a happier man, for when he made his call the next day, Lane had changed his mind and ordered his tin from a local dealer. Kirk then goes on to say in his letter:

"Well here I was bound for another day, and nothing more to be done. I had rooted all around amongst the window glass dealers . . . and concluded to try them once more as a forlorn hope. I succeeded in getting a little order from one of them for $300, and a conditional order for more than twice that from the other."

Shortly after his disappointment in Lafayette, Kirk wrote in a more optimistic vein from Freeport, Indiana, where he had secured a trial order about which he wrote the manufacturer:

"This little sample nibble is from a firm of honest dutchmen. . . . I was selling them some goods for E. & S. and persuaded them to let me sell them a few kegs of nails and a ton of assorted iron, so that they could compare for themselves. They consented. Now, these 'Sour Krauters' are queer fellows, and if they should find your nails and iron any better than L. S. & Co., then you will have them salted away for permanent customers, and when a dutchman begins to trade they are the hardest class of customers to change. Not so are the Yankees. You are to assort the iron of the most saleable description, tin not to be over a half inch thick. . . . Yours for the next ten days, Kirk."

Kirk's success was not overly rewarding to him financially, but he was persistent and hard-working, and he performed a valuable service for the firms he represented. His letters show that he made conscientious reports about the finances and reputations of the firms he called upon. He mailed in a steady trickle of what he referred to as "little sample nibble" orders, which, while perhaps of insignificant dollar value, served the important purpose of introducing his lines to firms that later became steady customers and bought in larger volume. On one occasion, when Kirk forwarded a trial order for fifty dollars' worth of wagon springs from a new customer in Owasso, Michigan, he wrote: "You will doubtless say that this is small potatoes, and few in a hill at that. Well, it is even so. But I have often

144

made a good permanent and profitable customer out of parties by taking small orders to make a beginning. This is a firm well recommended, and I liked their appearance well."

There are ten thick volumes of copies of letters and accounts Kirk wrote while traveling as a manufacturer's agent. From them we learn that in one year between January 1 and April 16 his expenses totaled two hundred and ten dollars, including such items as dinner at Salem, twenty-five cents, bridge toll, six cents, apples (apparently, he continually munched on apples), six cents. During that period of time he traveled 171 miles by stagecoach, 1414 miles by steamboat, and 676 miles by the pioneer railroads then reaching into the Midwest. We also learn that by 1857 Kirk began "to feel old age and its accompanying infirmities creeping on apace." He added: "I do not feel willing to put the old Adam to such severe tests as I do by knocking around from pillar to post, by day and by night, by land and by sea. . . . I will try to spend the evening of my days with my wife and children instead of wandering to and fro, up and down. . . ." He quit traveling and took up farming. But Kirk was an old war horse. Five years later he was back on the road selling and collecting money for a number of firms who appointed him as their agent.

One of the most successful and colorful of all the men working as agents in America was Mason Locke Weems, who specialized in books and periodicals. This extraordinary man had studied medicine, had been ordained as a minister, and had written and published several books, including a *Life of Washington*, in which Weems invented the story of Washington's youthful indiscretion in chopping down a cherry tree on his father's estate. In 1796 Weems was a traveling agent for his good friend and book publisher, Matthew Carey of Philadelphia, and doing very well at it except financially.

It seems that Weems was allowed a 5 per cent commission on books sold in lots to dealers. It was about this low rate of payment that Weems wrote Carey:

An advertising handbill from E. F. Marshall, a pioneer paper merchant and bookseller in western New York State who represented the Allings & Cory line.

"I hope that by this time of day I hardly need assure you that I had much rather subscriptioneer and vend books for you than for any other man whatever. But I know that you are, like Brutus, an honorable man, and would not exact a bond of barren service from anyone, and least of all from a most devoted friend. Now that your allowance to me (in the store settling business, I mean) is rather of the lean and bobtailed kind, may, I hope, be easily demonstrated to your entire satisfaction. You allow me 5 per cent for books sold by commission. Well, I'll *suppose* that I am going down to Richmond to place in proper hands a box of books. . . . This box is . . . worth 300 Dol. The sum total of my profits on the box . . . is 15 Dol.

"Stage hire from Dumfries to Richmond, 5 Dol.
      do   back again, 5 Dol.
"Expenses on road for 3 days & 4 nights, 5 Dol.
                  ————
                  15 Dol.

"Here you see that without the help of drams for drivers, half bits for poor Negro waiters, or any of those countless petty larceny robberies to which flesh and blood on the highway is heir, I have fairly got to clear of all my five per cent for a trunk containing 300 Dollars. Thus after rolling & jolting, tumbling and tossing through a journey of 200 miles, rous'd from sweet sleep at one o'clock in the morning, coop'd up in a common stage for almost three days and nights together, my head aching from loss of rest, my ears startl'd with female screams or masculine imprecations and whole senses stun'd with rattling wheels, cracking whips, rushing water & clouds of dust I at length get home, not to exult like Buonaparte over his ducats and florins, but to mourn with old Naomi: 'Woe's me, for I went out full, but the Lord hath brought me back empty.'"

Weems was understandably dead serious about what was quite obviously a well-merited demand for a higher commission. For thirty years he went traveling about the country selling books to dealers, to passengers in stagecoaches, and to patrons in taverns, carrying his stock in a wagon and calling on rural families, all the while bemoaning the rigors of such a life and the impoverished condition of his finances.

Book agents, as well as ordinary peddlers who carried books as part of their stock of miscellaneous goods, were among the first commercial travelers in our nation. There was a good level of literacy in America, and the sale of reading material was exceedingly high on a per capita basis. Weems, for example, sold four thousand copies of *The Life of Washington* at ten dollars a copy—an amazing performance considering the small population of the country, the high price of the book, and the difficulties of distribution. In American cities, bookstores were among the first shops to open for business. But in villages and thinly populated rural areas bookstores were almost unknown. Thus the sale of books was dependent upon the peddler and the itinerant book agent. The latter often increased his sales and saved his sole leather by prevailing upon a general store or other local merchant to put in a stock of books. Drugstores were selling books a hundred years before the modern drugstores got around to installing a rack of pocket-sized paperbacks.

The subject matter of the books that sold best varied. Self-improvement and how-to-do-it books were always popular. The *New England Primer* went through dozens of printings and sold well over a million copies. *Webster's Blue Back Speller* sold sixty-five million copies in thirty-four years. Children's books sold well, as did those on homemaking

and care of the sick. The Bible was a perennial best seller.

History was another subject that went over big whenever an agent opened up a ponderous volume, flicked through pages of gory illustrations, and began his sales pitch. After 1865, histories of the Civil War poured off the printing presses and through subscription agents into practically every parlor and town library in the land. In those same years there was a boom in local histories. These books were usually sold on prepublication subscriptions. An agent would arrive in a flourishing town with the glad tidings that his publisher was about to bring out a handsome volume on the history of the place; if the town was too small to warrant a full-sized book, the projected work would be the history of the county. Naturally, such a history would not be complete without biographical sketches of the prominent, and near-prominent, citizens, which worthies were expected to buy one or more copies of the book. For a slight additional cost they could have their pictures included. Hundreds of subscription agents were employed on such projects by enterprising publishers. Some people regarded this business as a racket. On the other hand, most of the books have stood the test of time and serve as fairly accurate historical records of people and places.

Books sold to the gold miners at King's Book Store in Shasta City (left) were sent to California in clipper ships. Readers in other parts of the country bought their magazines and books from the thousands of men and women who answered advertisements such as the one shown on the right. Many publishers sold through subscription agents only.

ALL WHO WISH TO MAKE MONEY!

Male or Female
AGENTS!

NOW IS YOUR TIME!   READ EVERY WORD!

You can Make a Fortune at Home
BY TAKING SUBSCRIPTIONS FOR

THE FAMILY JOURNAL,

The Cheapest Literary, Art and Fashion Paper in America!

Mrs. B.—Oh, Henry! see what I made during one day, taking subscribers among my friends for THE FAMILY JOURNAL. It is warranted 18 carat gold, a good timekeeper, and worth $60.
Mr. B.—It is truly a beauty and a sensible gift; and any publisher giving such premiums should succeed.

The FAMILY JOURNAL is an 8 page paper, size of the New York Ledger, and each number contains 40 columns of the choicest reading matter, by the best writers of the day, besides one page of Illustrated Fashions in advance of all other publications, all for only $1.00 a year, postage-paid, with either of the following premiums:
The pair of "TWINS ASLEEP and TWINS AWAKE," size 9x11, mounted ready to frame, or the "UNWELCOME VISITOR," 16x20, "ANNA'S PETS," 16x20, "HEEL AND TOE," 20x24, and "GRANDPA'S WATCH," 20x24, or the Engraving of "HORACE GREELEY AND FAMILY," 22x28; or $1.50 yearly with the magnificent Chromo "CONSECRATION," 20x24, or the four beautiful Fruit Chromos—Basket of Strawberries, Peach and Pear, Peaches and Strawberries, Apple and Plum—printed in 16 colors, size 9x11, each mounted ready for framing. Or we will give a choice of any two of our chromos for $1.50. CONSECRATION is a large and magnificent chromo, printed in twenty-two colors. It is chaste and beautiful, and the skillful execution has done justice to the beautiful design. As a proof of the value of this new and superb premium, the Publishers may state that a leading dealer in chromos offered to purchase two thousand copies at $4.00 each, with a view to place it on the market at $10.00, a price its intrinsic worth and beauty would readily command.
We send all the above Chromos neatly arranged with oil cloth cover with samples of the JOURNAL, Blanks, Circulars, etc., including the FAMILY JOURNAL one year for $2.00. Each Outfit contains 12 Chromos that would retail for $25 at New York prices. Any Lady or Gentleman cannot fail in making from $100 to $200 monthly.
As an additional inducement, we give $50,000, in Cash, and other premiums to encourage our Agents and Subscribers to work in our interest and behalf. We are determined to make ours the leading paper of the United States, as regards circulation, value of contents, and the low price at which it is given to subscribers. For the first few years we intend all the profits of the paper to go to those who are helping us to build it up.
Many of our agents only devote their evenings or spare time in taking subscriptions to the JOURNAL. If you are so situated that you cannot devote your whole time to the business, take the Outfit and solicit subscriptions during your leisure hours. Those persons who have not all their time engaged can procure from 100 to 500 subscribers without interfering with their other duties, thus making many dollars, if not hundreds, in a very short space of time. We feel warranted in saying that ladies or gentlemen who may devote their whole time and attention to canvassing for the FAMILY JOURNAL are reasonably certain of a snug income, of from $1,000 to $2,500 a year. If you wish to make money you can become an agent where you reside.
Agents, remember that no paper in the United States gives such inducements. The paper is worth the money, and the chromos or engravings cannot be purchased for less than $1.00 to $10.00 each. And we pay, besides, the large commission of 40 per cent on each subscriber.
Send stamp for sample with 32 page Illustrated Catalogue, containing list of 85 new articles, fast selling Chromos, Novelties, etc., giving list of Gifts to Agents and Workers. What our Agents are doing. What Agents, Subscribers, and the Press say of the JOURNAL and its Chromos.
☞ For information to strangers we will give the following leading Houses as references: Pelletreau & Raynor, 35 and 37 Vesey St., Publishers; Warren & Howard, 39 Park Place, Paper Dealers; O. Bissell, 54 Gold St., Paper Dealer; Bromell & Roehner, 92 White St., Printers; R. Shugg, 1 Chambers St., Publisher.
We will send the JOURNAL six months on trial, postage paid, on receipt of 25 cents, to those who desire to know what the JOURNAL is before being regular subscribers. FAMILY JOURNAL, 300 Broadway, N.Y.

147

WHOLESALERS' SALESMEN

Good manufacturers' agents such as John Kirk were hard to find, and for most companies the best arrangement for the sale and distribution of their goods was through wholesalers. Throughout the country wholesalers were among the first businesses to employ outside salesmen calling on the local trade. William B. Belknap was a wholesale jobber in Cincinnati for iron products manufactured in Pittsburgh. Shortly after starting his business in 1840, Belknap printed a modest catalogue (three by five and a half inches, sixteen pages) listing iron bars, nails, heavy hardware, and blacksmith equipment. He hired several salesmen to carry these catalogues to customers and take orders. Although his men did much leg work, they were not traveling salesmen, since they stayed fairly close to the local trade in Cincinnati, crossing the Ohio River occasionally to call on customers in Jeffersonville and New Albany on the Indiana side.

In Toledo the firm of W. & C. B. Roff & Company advertised that they were wholesalers and retailers of hardware and farm implements and sole agents for Stearns & Marvin's fireproof safes. Toledo had a population of eighty-five hundred when the Roffs opened for business, but a few years later when they hired Oscar Alonzo Bostwick as their first outside salesman, the population was considerably larger. Like the men working for Belknap in Cincinnati, Bostwick did no long-distance traveling, finding as he did plenty of small retailers, farmers, and other prospects to call on in the booming area of Toledo. As so often happens to men who began their careers in selling and stayed with it, Bostwick became one of the principals in the firm.

When the wagon trains opened up the lucrative trade to Santa Fe and homesteaders by the million began spilling onto the plains, the business of wholesaling goods boomed in St. Louis. The city became the supply center for nearly two thirds of the nation, and through it funneled an immense tonnage of merchandise of every description.

Among those quick to recognize the opportunity St. Louis offered was C. F. G. Meyer. In 1847, at the age of seventeen, he left Germany and settled in Fort Wayne, Indiana, where he went to work as an apprentice to a retail druggist. Four years later he was the proud owner of the drugstore in which he had learned his trade. But Meyer had come to this country in search of opportunity, and he decided he would move to the place where opportunity seemed to be knocking the loudest. That place was St. Louis, and in 1852 he set up business there as a wholesaler of drugs.

At first most of Meyer's sales were to transients —physicians, druggists, merchants, and traders— who stopped off at St. Louis en route west. Once they were settled in the West, these customers replenished their supplies by mail. To keep them informed of new products coming on the market, Meyer printed a catalogue and mailed it to them. This was a fairly satisfactory way of doing business, but not good enough for young Meyer or for any other wholesale firm that was on its toes. The one sure way to get customers and keep them was to employ salesmen and send them into the field. Meyer, who with the help of his brother built his

148

business into one of the largest drug-wholesaling firms in the Midwest, had its first salesman traveling far afield for the firm within a few years after his arrival at St. Louis.

Another man who went to St. Louis to make his fortune, and did, was Samuel Cupples, who arrived by steamboat in 1851 with three hundred dollars of

The pharmacist was one of the first merchants to open up shop in a new settlement. He usually began with drugs and patent medicines, bought from wholesale drug houses, which were among the first firms to have salesmen on the road. To supplement his income, the pharmacist added a soda fountain in the 1870s and also carried a line of paints, glass, brushes, oils, varnishes, and wallpaper.

149

working capital tucked in his pants pockets and a small stock of wooden pails, kegs, well buckets, and brooms. Cupples was nineteen years old when he hung up his shingle: "S. Cupples & Co." Within a short time he had another youngster, Asa A. Wallace, working with him, and together they advertised themselves as "Manufacturers and Wholesale Dealers in Cordage, Twine, Wicking, Batting, Paper, Brooms, Brushes and Cigars, Wood, and Willow Ware, Mats, Matches, Blackening, Sieves,

St. Louis was the great wholesale center for the Western trade. Salesmen for St. Louis firms had a lot of territory to cover, and a swing through the West took four or five months of hard travel.

Bird Cages and French, English and German Fancy Goods." The management of the firm was rounded out in 1866 when two brothers were employed—twenty-year-old Harry and sixteen-year-old Robert Brookings, who had left their home in Virginia with a burning desire to "get out in the world and be doing something."

Robert Brookings in particular realized his craving to be "doing something" when he went to work for Cupples. He was hired as a clerk at twenty-five dollars a month. When he let it be known he knew a little about double-entry bookkeeping, he was offered an extra ten dollars monthly to work nights on the firm's books. To learn about selling, he got up early in the morning and waited on the customers who arrived at the store before the staff was on hand. In later years he would have the time and wealth to found the Brookings Institute, but for the moment he was mighty busy with the affairs of S. Cupples & Co. Even so, he and Harry and Cupples and Wallace, who were equally busy, found the time to get away on sales trips. To expand their business it was necessary to call on out-of-town customers.

Eventually, by economizing and taking practically no money out of the business, the partners accumulated enough working capital to support the cost of employing traveling salesmen nationwide.

Wholesalers and jobbers throughout the country served as the fulcrum that moved goods into the markets. Our system of distribution could not have developed without these firms. It was utterly impossible for manufacturers to cover the market on their own, and it was equally impossible for a merchant to attempt to buy direct from the thousands of manufacturing concerns sprouting like mushrooms throughout the land. No merchant could have kept track of the number of firms, products, and prices. There was one wholesaler who, with unabashed enthusiasm, advertised: "We sell everything," and it is not a great exaggeration to say that some wholesalers and jobbers did sell just about everything.

The men who traveled for the Midwestern wholesale firms were trail blazers. Their territories were high, wide, and handsome. Only by constant travel, with incredible difficulties, could they get about and see a customer more often than two or three times a year—which was about as often as they made it back to headquarters for a few days at home. They were traveling salesmen in the fullest sense, with heavy emphasis on traveling.

Another type of seller who performed an important service very early in our history was the commission agent. Many such agents, particularly in the textile industry, would contract to sell the entire output of a particular mill. How well the agent performed in drumming up sales was often the determining factor in the success or failure of the mill.

A case in point was the Pepperell Manufacturing Company, which was making slow progress in selling its output of textiles until the Boston commission house of Francis Skinner & Company was appointed sole sales agent in 1850. Skinner had initiative and imagination. He had begun his career as an errand boy for a Boston shop; at twenty-five he had been made a partner in a commission firm and, before he was thirty, he had established his own company. When he took over the Pepperell output, he was an experienced salesman with a well-formulated and proved belief that opportunities were greatest in the textile market for the firm that produced the best quality. He was not interested in competing with other commission houses through price concessions or favorable terms of payment. Pepperell, he declared, would compete in this highly competitive and cost-conscious market solely on the excellence of its cloth.

In America there were many men manufacturing various kinds of goods who were as much concerned about the quality of their products. They made the best product they could. These were men involved primarily in the manufacturing end of their businesses, and they were imbued with a professional pride in workmanship. By no means was Skinner alone in preaching the virtues of quality, in examining the goods with a hawkish eye for imperfections. What made him unique was that he was a salesman, and, unlike many salesmen, not concerned solely with price.

Within a year after he took over, Skinner had Pepperell standing steadily on its feet. Until his death fifteen years later the mill worked at capacity to fill the orders he drummed up in the American market and for the export trade. The records of the Pepperell Manufacturing Company for those years

151

reflect the constant preoccupation of its production department with meeting the exacting standards of quality insisted upon by Skinner. One memorandum notes: "This cotton is to be worked under the inspection of Mr. Skinner, and he complains of Quality easily," and another: "Mr. Skinner . . . pushes me hard for a high quality of Cotton. . . . Be therefore very careful as to quality."

In time Skinner established a branch office in New York and subagencies in other important cities. This was a sharp break with precedent in the commission-agency business. Eastern commission agents, particularly those in Boston, made no bones about expecting jobbers, wholesalers, exporters, and other customers to come to them to examine goods and place orders. Skinner and his agents did not do much traveling, but he did the next best thing by establishing a chain of agencies from which he could demand results, thereby covering a substantial territory for Pepperell.

A GOOD DAY FOR JOSEPH DAY

In the winter of 1892 a swirling blizzard descended upon New York City. An icy wind lashed at pedestrians, the thermometer tumbled to near zero, and snow drifted knee-deep in the streets. It was no time to go outdoors unless absolutely necessary, and very few people did so.

Among those who remained indoors were the salesmen employed by James Talcott & Company, one of the leading dry-goods commission merchants in New York. All day long the men sat around the big potbellied stove in Talcott's display rooms on Franklin Street, going over lists of prospects, planning calls for the day when the weather improved, and engaging in general conversation. It was the same throughout Manhattan's sprawling wholesale district. Men who earned their living by selling were holed up in their offices like a clutch of cats come in out of the rain.

The exception was Joseph P. Day, a young apprentice at James Talcott's who had recently been made a junior salesman. Day was gone from the office early in the morning, with his order book and samples, and he did not return until late in the afternoon. He came back tired and cold, and a place was made by the stove so that the young man could warm himself. Questions were asked. Were the elevated trains running on time? How about the streetcars on Broadway? Did the weather show signs of clearing? And finally, James Talcott asked a question: "How did your sales go?"

"Fine," Day said, and he went on to explain that he liked to sell when the weather was bad. On stormy days competing salesmen remained in their offices, and buyers therefore were unhurried and had plenty of time to examine samples and discuss merchandise. Furthermore, while his competitors hibernated, Day had time to get to know the buyers better, and they got to know him. On that stormy day he had sold forty-three cases of goods, a fine performance by any standard and especially so for a youngster just learning the trade. His salary was promptly raised to ten dollars a week.

When Day was twenty-one, he took his small savings and went into the real-estate and insurance business on his own. Within a few years Joseph Day was one of the up-and-coming brokers in the city. He became an expert appraiser of property and a prophet of the rapid development of neglected land in New York's then uncrowded midtown and uptown sections. Often he was called in to appraise the huge mansions on Fifth Avenue when the estates of their former multimillionaire owners were being settled. In 1910 he auctioned off the Third Avenue Railway for twenty-six million dollars, the biggest single auction in New York's history up to that time. Later, after World War I, he sold and auctioned off millions of dollars' worth of surplus government property.

Joseph P. Day made a fortune and a reputation as one of the country's largest and most progressive realtors because he never let circumstances of any kind, including blizzards, prevent him from getting out and selling.

The volume of sales and the number of orders written by the early salesmen in America were, as John Kirk expressed it, "small potatoes." These men did not always earn their keep. That their employers kept them on and that the salesmen stuck to their uphill task is a great tribute to them all. They were the forerunners of what has become one of the nation's largest and most vital professions.

*At about the same time of the year Joseph Day braved
the elements and went out to call on customers in
downtown Manhattan, young Alfred Stieglitz set up
his bulky camera, ducked under the hood flapping
wildly in the wind, and took this remarkable
photograph on upper Fifth Avenue in 1892.*

MOTHERS LOOK OUT FOR YOUR CHILDREN!

ARTISANS, MECHANICS, CITIZENS!

When you leave your family in health, must you be hurried home to mourn a

DREADFUL CASUALITY!

PHILADELPHIANS, your RIGHTS are being invaded! regardless of your interests, or the LIVES OF YOUR LITTLE ONES. THE CAMDEN AND AMBOY, with the assistance of other companies, without a Charter, and in VIOLATION OF LAW, as decreed by your Courts, are laying a

LOCOMOTIVE RAIL ROAD!

Through your most Beautiful Streets, to the RUIN of your TRADE, annihilation of your RIGHTS, and regardless of your PROSPERITY and COMFORT. Will you permit this? or do you consent to be a

SUBURB OF NEW YORK!!

Rails are now being laid on BROAD STREET to CONNECT the TRENTON RAIL ROAD with the WILMINGTON and BALTIMORE ROAD, under the pretence of constructing a City Passenger Railway from the Navy Yard to Fairmount!!! This is done under the auspices of the CAMDEN AND AMBOY MONOPOLY!

RALLY PEOPLE in the Majesty of your Strength and forbid THIS

OUTRAGE!

The Steam Cars Link the Nation

With the railroad-building boom after the Civil War, the nation became a happy hunting ground for an army of salesmen, and a coast-to-coast market for manufacturers.

IT BEGAN WITH A HUFFING and puffing of a ludicrous teakettle mounted on wheels, boiling along the thirteen miles of track of the Baltimore & Ohio Railroad, and while it was a nerve-tingling spectacle, most of the people who attended the event went to their beds that night in April 1837 unaware that they had been witnesses to a historic occasion. Admittedly, there was something to be said for a self-propelled steam engine pulling a string of two or three cars with passengers and freight at the reckless speed of fifteen miles an hour, which the proponents of the railroad said could ultimately be reached. But on sober second thought it was against nature to endure hurtling along at such a pace. The proprietors of stagecoach lines, canal-boat routes, and taverns on the post roads—all of whom had uneasy premonitions about the possible effects of the railroads on their businesses—warned that the steam engine was a dangerous thing to fool with, what with the possibilities of calamitous wrecks, fires started by sparks from the engine's chimney, and milk cows going dry from nerve shock caused by the noise of passing trains.

But something had to be done, and quickly, if the sprawling nation was not to be strangled by a lack of transportation. The steam locomotive was the first effective man-made machine to conquer time and distance. Until it sped over the tracks that linked settlements with villages and villages with cities, much of the vast empty space of the nation had no future, either political or economic. Wherever the railroads arrived, they created economic wealth and opportunity. The vaguest rumor of the coming of a railroad could send land values, offhandedly placed at a modest nickel an acre, soaring to a dollar or more. The arrival of a steam locomotive was, in many instances, the final arbiter of the destiny of many an American community.

Chicago is a case in point. In 1803, when Captain John Whistler, grandfather of the famous painter, marched in with a company of infantry and built Fort Dearborn where the Michigan Avenue bridge now spans the Chicago River, the place did not amount to much. For neighbors Captain Whistler had three French fur trappers with their half-breed wives and an indeterminable number of ragged children. For the next thirty years the squalid little settlement grew hardly at all. It could count only two hundred-odd citizens when it incorporated as a town in 1833.

Then one memorable day in April 1849 a locomotive, the old Chicago & Galena's Number 1, the *Pioneer*, came to town, the smoke from its fat stack drifting away on the chill wind of a Midwest spring. That, for Chicago, was the beginning. Within twenty years ten railroads had entered Chicago, and wherever a man gazed, except out over the lake, the plume of locomotive smoke marked the comings and goings of trains that ticked off the mushroom growth of the city.

It was much the same for Kansas City, a river town marked for oblivion as the number of people on the Missouri dwindled along with the traffic in furs and skins. But the steam engines came in the nick of time and nailed Kansas City permanently

155

This busy stretch of track, crowded with freight trains and fast limiteds equipped with drawing-room cars, was symbolic of the new era in American transportation ushered in by the railroad-building boom that came after the Civil War.

on the map. Soon it was almost as important a rail and packinghouse center as Chicago. Millions of homesteaders hurried west behind a galaxy of locomotive types—Americans, Atlantics, Ten Wheelers, and Prairies, among others. Kansas City printed their books, made their clothes, tools, wagons, and harness, stored their grain, and slaughtered their livestock.

Or consider Los Angeles. The dusty Spanish pueblo Nuestra Señora la Reina de Los Angeles slumbered peacefully through the years, its handful of citizens undisturbed except for the day in 1846 when Captain John Frémont, the Pathfinder, galloped into town to claim it for the United States. This event was soon forgotten, and Los Angeles dozed again for forty years until its soft siesta was ended for all time by the first string of steam cars that clattered in from the East. The coming of the steam engine to Los Angeles touched off one of the flashiest land booms in history. The first shipment of California oranges east by rail sent the professional land boomers into a frenzy of oratory and golden prophecy.

When railroad-building worked up a full head of steam in the years immediately after the close of the Civil War, land and harvest were no longer of mini-

Not all trains got through on time, as this horrendous scene indicates. Despite such accidents, rail travel was vastly superior to that by the old stagecoaches.

mal value. Lots in Emporia, Kansas, began selling for one thousand dollars when the Santa Fe railway track reached that settlement. It might well be said that the growth of the nation and the destiny of its people were determined by the number of railroad ties battened into the soil and the tons of cinders that fell along the rights of way. The railroads created national wealth by providing a grid for national distribution of the things that people grew and manufactured.

The railroads of the West also provided much of the exuberant advertising that sold the wonders of the West to the world. Every Western railroad had a staff of land agents whose combined efforts whipped up the greatest, and by far the most extraordinary, real-estate boom in history. The story of the railroad land grants is briefly this: In the unpopulated West a projected railroad that ran from nowhere to nowhere, with no immediate prospect of passenger or freight traffic, was of very little interest to the average investor and of only slight interest to the most avid speculator. To get railroads built, the federal government gave railroad companies land, usually alternate sections along the proposed right of way. The government had bought most of this land from Napoleon for an average price of six cents an acre, and had tried to sell it, with

little success, for $1.25 an acre to homesteaders. The land was given to the railroads in exchange for an agreement to carry government troops and supplies at reduced rates, and it served as an equity for the issuance of bonds to finance construction.

But the mere ownership of land was not enough. Millions of acres of real estate and thousands of miles of track were of no value unless there were passengers and freight to bring in operating revenue. So the railroads set about selling people on the idea of moving into the empty spaces served by their tracks. This job was entrusted to their land agents.

The first order of business for a promotion-minded land agent was to print bales of pamphlets and stacks of posters and pump them into circulation. Charles DuPuy, the land agent for the Illinois Central, which had over two and a half million acres for sale, mailed a hundred thousand posters to farmers in the East and South. He inserted advertisements in Eastern newspapers, and passengers riding the horsecars in New York City occupied their time, as they rode along Third Avenue, reading Illinois Central placards. Later, a crew of agents was hired. After being infused with enthusiasm, fiction, and some fact about the country served by the Illinois Central, they were turned loose to travel about the East.

The railroads' campaign to find people to ride their trains and buy their land did not stop at the shores of the Atlantic. The Atchison, Topeka & Santa Fe cranked out a stream of booklets printed in German, Dutch, Swedish, French, Danish, and Russian for distribution abroad. Carl B. Schmidt, a German who came to Kansas and built up a profitable agricultural-implement store in Topeka, was appointed general foreign colonization agent for the Santa Fe. The Illinois Central sent Carl Malmborg, an Illinoian of Swedish descent, to Scandinavia to distribute booklets, give lectures, and write descrip-

tive articles for newspapers and magazines. Kent K. Kennan, who represented the Wisconsin Central Railroad, distributed tons of pamphlets and pocket maps throughout Germany.

All these land agents were skilled practitioners of the "hard" sell and the dubious art of exaggeration. The land they sold was not always quite the milk and honey paradise they pictured it to be. But they got results. In somewhat less than a quarter-century, more than one hundred million acres of railroad land were sold to some ten million people who had been prodded into pulling up stakes and moving. In sheer size it was the greatest real-estate sales campaign of all time. Not since that wonderful era has America been so thoroughly and convincingly sold to the people of the world. The selling was done by men who were salesmen first and propagandists second, and they did their job without benefit of the highly complex and costly propaganda apparatus of our own times.

HERE, THERE, AND EVERYWHERE

The advent of a fluid, low-cost system of distribution by rail had a profound effect on selling and merchandising, although obviously not overnight. By the middle years of the 1800s the peddlers had come a long way from the primitive pack-on-the-back men they once had been. Many of them had become tradesmen of considerable stature in the existing system of distribution, and they would have laughed at anyone who suggested they were working on borrowed time. So, too, would the country storekeepers have been amused at a prophecy that the days of their kind of operation were numbered. But they were. Change was in the air throughout the nation.

Among those who fanned the change in commerce in America was George Huntington Hartford. In 1859 Hartford, who was twenty-six years old, bought a shipload of tea from China and sold it at retail on an uncovered dock in New York for about one third the retail price prevailing in the city. The idea of buying tea direct from the Orient, thereby bypassing the charges and commissions of the usual middlemen, and selling at a small markup, earned Hartford a profit, and he decided to get in out of the weather and open a store at 31 Vesey

This is one of the more restrained of the railroad land-grant posters. Some showed corn growing higher than a house, hogs too fat to walk, and cattle grazing on lush grass, whereas in fact, as it frequently turned out when the homesteaders moved in, there might not be any water within twenty miles.

159

160

Interior views of A & P stores after the company added a full line of groceries, including butter at seventeen cents a pound.

For some years A & P operated a fleet of route wagons selling tea and coffee house-to-house. Many of the drivers who learned selling and merchandising from these wagons moved up to top positions in the company.

Street. It was quite a place. The front and interior were painted Chinese vermilion flaked with gold. The cashier's cage was built in the shape of a Chinese pagoda; Japanese lanterns hung from the ceiling. On Saturday nights a band was engaged to play in front of the store, over which hung a sign: "The Great Atlantic Tea Company."

As Hartford's business increased, he opened more stores in New York City as well as in Boston and Philadelphia, and added coffee and spices to his line. His great leap forward to becoming a national chain (and adding "Pacific" to his corporate name) came in 1871, when, after the great Chicago fire, a call went out for emergency shipments of foodstuffs for the stricken city. Hartford sent tea and coffee by train and set up a temporary store amid the ruins of Chicago. When the city was rebuilt,

he decided to stay. By 1880 there were ninety-five A & P stores forming a chain from Boston to Milwaukee.

Without low-cost rail transportation it is doubtful that the chain-store type of operation, pioneered by Hartford, would have been workable. Nor would Frank W. Woolworth's brainstorm have worked before there were railroads. Woolworth's imagination turned a little idea into a big thing. He was clerking in a Watertown, New York, dry-goods store when, one day, the owner heaped a pile of odds and ends on a counter and offered them for sale at five cents each. This was nothing new. Country merchants frequently gathered an assortment of goods and sold them at bargain prices *for cash only*. Customers who ordinarily would have asked for the usual long-term credit dug up a surprising amount of hard money when confronted with such enticing bargains.

What impressed Woolworth was the speed and ease with which the goods were sold. He reasoned that a store stocked with goods priced at ten cents and under could be profitable, since it would have the advantages of cash on the barrelhead for each

162

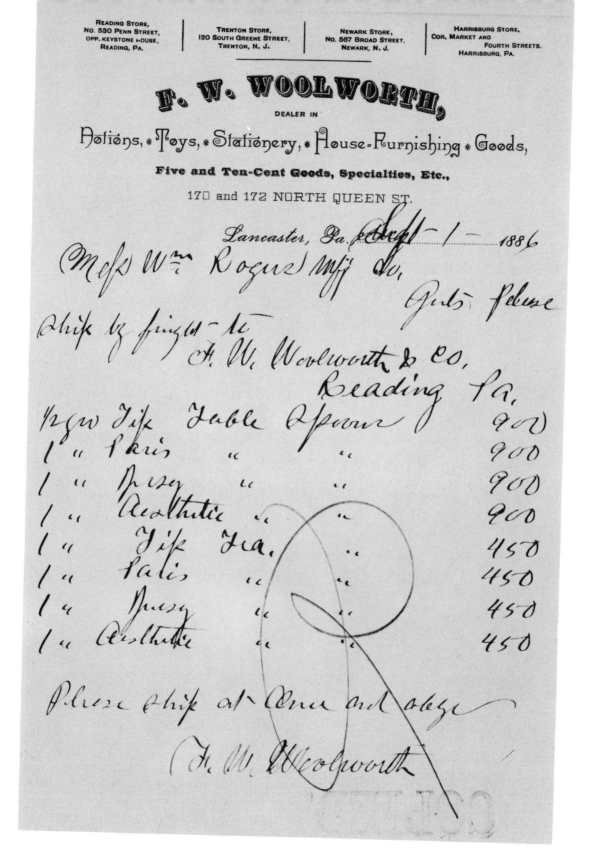

One of the essentials to good selling was not to overlook
small customers, such as F. W. Woolworth, whose
first orders to his suppliers were not large and were
placed only after careful selection of merchandise.

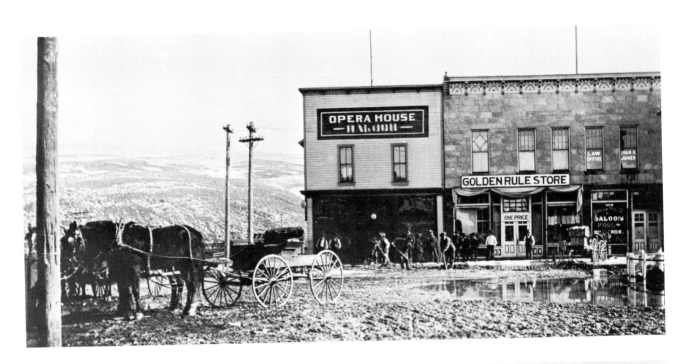

purchase and a quick turnover of stock. With three hundred dollars' worth of merchandise he opened a store in Utica. It failed. He then moved to Lancaster, Pennsylvania, and opened his second store. It did better. Later he opened three more stores in small Pennsylvania towns. All three failed. But Woolworth's sixth store, in Scranton, was a success, and he had a start on building his chain. Within five years he had seven stores going and, in 1895, with twenty-five stores, annual gross sales passed the million-dollar mark.

J. C. Penney Company, nationwide department-store chain, grew by a unique kind of proliferation that appalled practical businessmen. James Cash Penney's first store actually was one of a small chain known as The Golden Rule Stores. His two partners had developed the idea of helping to set up new stores with a third partner as manager. After Mr. Penney had been employed for a year in their Evanston, Wyoming, store, they agreed to share in the financing of a new store in Kemmerer, a small mining town. Each of the three invested two thousand dollars, but since Mr. Penney had been able to save only five hundred dollars, the balance of his share was borrowed.

The new Golden Rule store was a tiny thing, but as Opportunity it loomed large to Penney. "The opportunity to share in the ownership of the store," he said, "fired my soul with an ambition I cannot describe." There is little point in speculating whether ambition took precedence over his religious impulses, for he always kept them interlaced. "The Golden Rule principles," he once said, "are just as necessary to operating a business as money and men."

In Kemmerer he attacked the problem of selling only for cash in a community where the miners were paid in scrip and rarely had access to enough cash to buy outside the mine company's store. He knew

Salesmen who passed up as "small potatoes" the Golden Rule Store wedged between a saloon and the Opera House at Kemmerer, Wyoming, missed an opportunity. Owner J. C. Penney had dreams of operating a chain of stores. By the time he opened his forty-eighth store, below, in Cumberland, Wyoming, in 1907, he was an important buyer in any salesman's book.

it could be done only by the shrewdest kind of buying and close control of selling expense. The latter he accomplished by working seven days a week, from daybreak to late at night, as long as there was still a prospective customer to be seen coming down the street.

In its first year, the Golden Rule store grossed nearly twenty-nine thousand dollars and made enough profit so Mr. Penney could pay off his fifteen-hundred-dollar loan.

As an employer, he was so demanding that scores of men came and went, unable to meet his exacting standards. Smoking or drinking was cause for summary dismissal, first because he disapproved of them on moral grounds, but almost equally because they showed that an employee was not devoting all his time and energy to his work. With burning honesty, he described to applicants how they would have to work ninety to a hundred hours a week, often at less pay than they had been getting. But he also pointed out the opportunities, based on his own vision of the success that lay ahead.

In 1907, after an exhaustive and revealing exchange of letters with Earl C. Sams, who was then working in Kansas, he agreed to employ the unseen prospect. When Sams and his wife arrived with a small dog in tow, Penney had momentary doubts about the wisdom of his choice. Could a man who kept a dog Tend to Business? His doubts were promptly laid to rest the next Sunday morning when Penney arrived at the store at eight o'clock to find that Sams had been waiting since seven. Penney had forgotten to tell Sams that the store opened an hour later than usual on Sundays. Later, Sams would become board chairman.

If Jim Penney was hard on employees, he drove himself even harder. Sweep the sidewalk, dust the stock, sweep the floor ten, twenty times a day if there were no customers, save the twine from incoming shipments, draw nails carefully from packing cases, which could later be used as counters, eat lunch in ten minutes and eat it alone, for his wife kept the store while he ate. The habits of thrift established in the early days were deeply ingrained in Penney executives, who still pay close attention to expense control.

The saving grace in this harsh picture was Penney's "dream"—the word is his, and a favorite one. He felt sure that the Kemmerer store could produce enough profit to finance a second store, the first two a third, and so on. But how to develop the men? His insatiable demands upon his men were a kind of trial-by-fire, to see which could be developed into partner-managers. The capable ones would have an opportunity at the same part-ownership that had started Penney on his way in the original store. Once they had passed the ordeal, he would trust them to the ends of the earth. He was rarely disappointed. It is a matter of company pride that no employee— and there are now more than fifty thousand full-time —has ever been bonded.

The casual growth pattern of stores and partnerships continued on its autonomous way until 1913, when they were incorporated as the J. C. Penney Company in Utah. It was perhaps the most complicated incorporation ever devised. Stock was issued separately for each of the thirty-four stores. (Class 1, for example, was Kemmerer.) Each of the partners involved in a store received stock certificates specifying his particular interest. If Penney, Sams, and a third man were partners in a store capitalized at nine thousand dollars, ninety shares with a par value of one hundred dollars were issued, thirty to each. As profits accrued in a store, they were distributed to the holders of stock in that store. At the time of this first Utah incorporation, Mr. Penney was a partner in all but one of the thirty-four stores.

As the partners accumulated surpluses from their profits, and as suitable management men were developed, new stores were opened, usually with the new manager as the third shareholder. If the new man was a sound prospect, Mr. Penney or one of the others was quite prepared to lend him the money to finance his first venture into ownership. This gave many a good man an opportunity to go into business for himself which he might not otherwise have had.

Between 1917 and 1929, a succession of changes was made in the articles of incorporation, mainly to secure adequate credit for the rapid growth of the company. As various classes of stock were issued, more and more people not directly connected with the company could acquire an interest in it. In 1929, the Penney Company finally became a pub-licly owned corporation, listed on the New York Stock Exchange. Sales had risen from two million dollars at the end of 1912 to nearly two hundred and ten million, and stores had increased from 34 to 1,395.

THE FAST MAIL AND MAIL ORDERS

A favorite subject of writers of thrillers and producers of motion pictures a half century ago was the fast mail. All railroads of any importance had mail trains. They raced through the night in a shower of sparks and a hiss of steam, with the fastest engines and bravest engineers. What was in the mail cars that warranted this emphasis on speed? Occasionally there was a valuable shipment of gold or silver. There were a few business letters of alleged importance, a scattering of bureaucratic orders from Washington to commanders of distant outposts, and a fair number of personal letters. But the bulk of the letters and parcels contained orders for, or shipments of, such things as ax handles, clothing, housewares, sewing-machine needles, pump parts, and the latest edition of Ward's or Sears's mail-order catalogue. Speed was not always important. What really mattered was that nowhere in the country was there now a place so remote that a woman could not buy the latest corset or a man indulge in the luxury of waxing the handlebars of his mustache with the same brand of ointment used by the dandies on Broadway.

It was in 1872 when Aaron Montgomery Ward hit on the idea of putting the railroads and the U.S. Post Office to work for him. For many years Ward had been a traveling salesman in the West for a St. Louis dry-goods house. At the time he hatched his idea of selling direct by mail he was a dry-goods buyer for a Chicago firm. Thus he knew his line, he was an experienced salesman, and most important, he knew people and what prompted them to buy. His plan was a simple one: by skirting the usual channels of distribution he could reduce overhead and markups and pass the savings on to his customers.

Ward wisely chose the farm market for his target. Farmers generally did not get to town more than once a week. But they had time on their hands at night to browse through Ward's list of bargains,

The FLIGHT of the FAST MAIL on the LAKE SHORE and MICHIGAN SOUTHERN RY.
The Popular Passenger Route between the EAST and WEST.
UNION DEPOTS, NO FERRY TRANSFERS, NO DELAYS.

The fast mail was a stirring symbol of the hustle and bustle in America.

and, of timely importance to Ward, the farmers in the early seventies were grumbling about the high cost of things they bought and the low prices they received for their crops. They were in a mood to do business with a man who, like Ward, offered real bargains.

Montgomery Ward & Company's first catalogue, if it could be called that, was a single printed sheet listing some fifty dry-goods items, all priced at one dollar or less. It was not much so far as printing went—cheap paper, no pictures, ugly type faces—but none of these bothered the farmers, who sent in their orders and were pleased to find, when they received their merchandise, that they had received their money's worth. Mr. Ward was in business.

167

No. 15620. Our Own Folding Ironing Board, has a steel wire tension at the bottom, which acts as an automatic folder; when set upright it can be used as a step ladder; in operating it, all you have to do is to open up the legs, then press upon the large end of the board. Give it a trial and you will have no other, as it certainly is the most complete table in use; weight, 18 lbs. Price, each, $1.

No. 15621. The Champion Bosom Board and Stretcher; the most complete in the market. After you have once used this board you will never be without one. Price, 40c.

REKA ADJUSTABLE CLOTHES BAR.

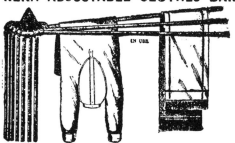

o. 15623. Eureka Adjustable Clothes Bar, intended asten to the wall. When not in use takes the space n ordinary broom. The bars are 3 feet in length, with tips; a very convenient household article; weight, 4 Each, 39c.
o. 15624. Same as No. 15623, with 6 bars, 2 feet long. h, 25c.

No. 15625. The Excelsior Clothes Dryer; is made of picked ash bars ½ of an inch thick, folds up snug against the wall when not in use, takes up less space and has more capacity than any other bar made; 10 bars, 36 inches long, each, 30c; 6 bars, 24 inches, each, 27c.

SCHMUCK'S MOP WRINGER.

No. 15626. Schmuck's Mop Wringers for simplicity, durability, dry wringing and adaptability have no equal. They are manufactured of wrought iron, the rollers made of hard maple chemically treated, and will fit any size pail. It is self-wringing, and while mopping

S., R. & CO. IMPROVED WESTERN STAR WASHING MACHINE. NO. 2 "FAMILY SIZE."

No. 15630. The Western Star Washer is acknowledged by all to be the best and most perfect machine on the market. No nails or iron of any kind are used in its construction which can come in contact with the clothes, causing iron rust on the linen, as is the case with other machines; this, together with other improvements, that have been made in this machine and not contained in any other, are of the greatest importance and must be seen to be appreciated. If you desire a more complete description of this machine send for descriptive circular, which will be mailed on application. Weight, 65 lbs. Price, $2.50.

ANTHONY WAYNE WASHER. NO. 2 "FAMILY SIZE."

No. 15633. The Anthony Wayne Washer, with corrugated stave and bottom. This is the best round washer made. Some prefer the round washer to the square; we have selected the Anthony Wayne as being the best on the market, and we offer it at a price which places it within the reach of all. Weight, 50 lbs. Price, $2.50.

CLINE'S IMPROVED STEAM WASHER.

No. 15635. Cline's Improved Steam Washer has several new features that others do not have. Has a corrugated cylinder, sliding cover and a faucet attached to the boiler for removing the water without lifting the boiler from the stove, which is a decided advantage. Weight, 32 lbs. Price, each, $6.

RACINE HOUSEHOLD MANGLES.

It is a well known fact that clothes are kept in a more healthful condition and will wear much longer when mangled than when hot irons are used.

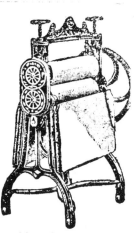

machine takes up a floor spa weight is 240 lbs. Price, $2

OUR HOTEL

Indispensable to the econ hotel or public institution.

more room than a sewing m with a handsome guard, pr any danger to the operator. with an automatic table ad manently attached to the m and marred or misplaced w only necessary to raise the te and this device automaticall position. In lowering them grees which releases the lock the side of the machine. Th ically treated, and measure takes up a floor space of 23x weight is 260 lbs. Price, $33

FOLDING WAS

W and rig that be

168

Richard W. Sears got into the mail-order business somewhat by accident. He was working as a railroad station agent at a place called Redwood Falls (population one hundred), Minnesota, when a shipment of watches arrived. Weeks later, when no one had called for the package, Sears offered to sell the watches for the shipper, which he did by writing letters to the agents at other stations up and down the railroad. In short order he had disposed of the lot and cleared twelve dollars profit. He ordered more watches, appointed station agents as his local sales representatives, and built up such a lucrative trade that he quit railroading and moved to Minneapolis, where he went into business trading as the R. W. Sears Watch Company.

Sears began selling direct to the consumer in 1887 through advertisements in weekly newspapers and farm journals. His first stab at direct-mail solicitation was made at about the same time. Sears had an uncanny knack for writing advertising copy that sold merchandise. On one occasion he mailed eight thousand ordinary postcards printed with a facsimile of a handwritten description of a watch he was offering at $9.95. He got back two thousand orders at a cost of four and half cents an order, which surely must stand as something of a record in the annals of direct-mail selling. By 1893 Sears had moved into the big time after teaming up with A. C. Roebuck and starting a mail-order business in direct competition with Montgomery Ward.

The biographies of Hartford, Woolworth, Penney, Ward, and Sears, and the histories of the businesses they founded, make fascinating reading. These men were extraordinary, and they capitalized on a sales opportunity made possible by the coming of the railroads. Each of them contributed to a whirlwind of change in our economic history, and their successes, rather than destroying the fabric of our system of distribution and selling, encouraged others to readjust their sights so that they, too, could capi-

The 1896 edition of the Sears, Roebuck catalogue was profusely illustrated with plain but accurate and easily understood drawings of the articles offered for sale. Nothing was exaggerated by extreme perspective to make a product appear larger or fancier than it really was.

talize on the opportunities available to them. The insistence of these five men on high-quality merchandise raised the standards for goods sold by others, and the rich variety of articles they offered forced independent retailers to expand their lines and lengthen their shelves. Likewise, the low prices charged by the chains and mail-order firms compelled other sellers to look to their efficiency and sharpen their methods of distribution and merchandising.

ADVERTISERS AND PUBLISHERS

The building of railroads and the subsequent coming of age of the Post Office Department brought two other interesting and important developments. Magazine publishers began to seek nationwide circulation, and advertisers awakened to the national market. Before 1860 only a few of the better magazines, such as *Harper's Illustrated Weekly* and the *Atlantic Monthly*, had a circulation that even came close to a national readership. A few copies of these wonderful old journals reached San Francisco via the slow and costly overland route. Such publications had a limited number of subscribers in the Midwest cities and throughout the South, but for the most part readership of general magazines, religious papers, farm journals, and the great number of what were referred to as the "fireside" papers (usually Saturday supplements published by newspapers) was restricted to the area close to the publishing headquarters. Advertising, too, was limited to the local market; there was not much point in shooting for national or even regional advertising coverage until broader distribution of an advertiser's product or service was possible.

The coming of the railroads changed all that. National circulation for publishers and national distribution of manufacturers' goods became a desirable possibility, and with this change came the need to make a fresh appraisal of the function of advertising.

The first advertisements in the pre-railroad era were inserted by local tradesmen in local newspapers. Such ads were more in the nature of notices—plain, unadorned announcements that a man made shoes or had tea for sale or operated a stage line up and down a turnpike. It was customary to contract

Bartering produce for a year's subscription to the weekly paper. Country editors ate well but rarely were paid in cash for subscriptions or advertising space.

for space in a newspaper for a year, prepare the meager copy that would run virtually unchanged during that time, and forget the whole matter.

Most newspaper publishers, who were also editors, were interested primarily in political crusading in their columns and job printing in their shops. Many accepted advertising "notices" more or less under sufferance as a community service, feeling that the unattractive displays cluttered up their pages and contributed little in income, which was true enough. Advertising copy was incredibly dull, and when money was scarce, publishers had to accept merchandise or services in lieu of cash from their advertisers. They were already receiving such payments in kind from their subscribers. The *Connecticut Courant*, for example, in the late 1700s was readily accepting such things as "One bushel and three pecks of Wheat" or "a half hundred of flour or a Load of Wood" as payment for a year's subscription. Wistful appeals for payment in any form were

published frequently in all newspapers, one publisher reminding his subscribers that some of them were as much as seven years in arrears.

Cash income in metropolitan areas was somewhat better than in rural areas, and very early in the 1800s newspaper publishers in New York, Philadelphia, Boston, and other cities began thinking of advertising as a possible source of substantial income. Sporadic efforts were made to sell space, usually by sending an employee out on the streets during a dull day in the office and letting him pound the pavements for new advertisers. But the advertisers' copy was still dull and remained so until the 1840s, when Benjamin Day, Horace Greeley, and James Gordon Bennett came out with their "penny" papers and engaged in a lively circulation battle. Until these mavericks appeared on the scene in New York, newspapers had sold for six cents, which, in

Richard Sears was no man to spend money for magazine advertising and waste part of it for white space. His ads were jam-packed with copy which, if not artistic in layout, had the virtue of describing the merchandise in detail. Another virtue: they sold goods.

170

171

Dr. D. JAYNE'S ALTERATIVE

This valuable preparation combines all the medicinal virtues of those articles, which long experience has proved to possess the most safe and efficient alterative and Deobstruent properties, for the cure of SCROFULA, KING'S EVIL, White Swellings, Ulcers, Scrofulous, Cancerous and Indolent TUMOURS, Mercurial and Syphilitic Affections, Rheumatism, Gout, Scurvy, Neuralgia or Tic-Douloureux, CANCER, GOITRE or Bronchocele, (Swelled Neck,) ENLARGEMENTS of the Bones, Joints, Glands or Ligaments or of the Ovaries, Liver, Spleen, Kidneys, etc. All the various Diseases of the SKIN, such as Tetter, Ringworm, Biles, Pimples, Carbuncles, etc., DYSPEPSIA and LIVER COMPLAINT, JAUNDICE and Nervous Diseases, Dropsical Swellings, Constitutional Disorders, and diseases originating from a depraved or IMPURE state of the BLOOD or other fluids of the body.

Prepared only by Dr. D. JAYNE, wholesale Druggist & Chemist, No. 8 South Third Street, Philadelphia

172

terms of money value, was the equivalent of twenty-five cents today. Circulation was small until the penny papers hit the streets. To keep his *Herald* lively and fresh, publisher Bennett created a ruckus by announcing that an advertiser would not be permitted to run the same copy for more than one insertion. Bennett acted on the sound belief that the same copy repeated over and over again discouraged people from buying his otherwise newsy, noisy, sexy paper. This scrappy, cross-eyed man forced his advertisers to spend more time on their copywriting and put life and *sell* into it.

ADVERTISING BECOMES A SALES TOOL

One of the first newspaper space salesmen was a Philadelphian named Volney B. Palmer, who in 1841 set up in business as an "Agent for Country Newspapers." Dressed in a greatcoat with brass buttons and carrying a goldheaded cane, Palmer was an imposing figure as he strode the streets of Philadelphia calling on advertisers. Less imposing during the first years was his income. Advertising was an intangible and there was very little proof of its effectiveness. Most of the businessmen Palmer called on agreed that publicizing their products in out-of-town markets was an idea worth considering, but it was not something to rush into. Perhaps a "square" or two, in a few papers at a dollar a square, might be bought as an experiment. To pay expenses while plugging away at putting across the idea of advertising as a modern sales tool, Palmer sold real estate and dealt in wood and coal on the side.

Palmer was a pioneer in a field where there was a tremendous opportunity for a hard-working middleman and the fortitude to call and call again on prospects. Even as early as the 1840s some fourteen hundred newspapers were being published. It would have been impossible for an advertiser to deal directly with all these papers, not to mention checking circulation figures and space rates and

Exactly what message the artist intended to convey when he made up this advertising card is not clear, except perhaps that Dr. D. Jayne's Alterative—which, it was claimed, cured almost everything—would calm the nerves of anyone who suffered from nightmares after viewing the artist's handiwork.

"Cheesecake" was not unknown to advertising men in the late 1890s. In this advertisement for the Howe Scale Company, Lillian Russell, who wowed the boys at the end of the century, is shown weighing in, at what appears to be an even one hundred and fifty pounds.

forwarding copy. Palmer did all these chores for the advertiser and charged the newspapers a commission of 25 per cent of the space rate. Within four years, after a discouragingly slow start, he had developed a volume of business in Philadelphia profitable enough to enable him to open branch offices in New York, Boston, and Baltimore.

In the publishing and advertising businesses there were many men of exceptional ability and vision who sold ideas and the intangible theory of advertising. One of these was Francis Wayland Ayer, a successful newspaper space representative who converted his business into one of the pioneer advertising agencies. Another was Cyrus H. K. Curtis, who nursed, and sold, a shaky magazine into a healthy, wealthy publication for women.

Ayer was a mere twenty years old and without a shred of experience when he went to work as an advertising space solicitor for the *National Baptist,* a weekly religious newspaper published in Philadelphia. Few business firms took the time to train salesmen in that year of 1868, least of all the pub-

lisher who hired Ayer. Casually pointing out the window, he remarked to Ayer that every one of the firms up and down the street should be advertising in the *National Baptist* and that Ayer would receive 25 per cent commission on any business he sold. Such methods of turning a man out on his own may not have been very scientific, but they were an acid test of a man's determination and self-reliance. Either he made it, largely through his own efforts, or he did not.

At the end of the first week it looked as though Ayer would not make it. He had not sold an inch of space. Probably, although we have no way of being certain, some of the firms Ayer called on promised to think about taking space in the *National Baptist* and give him an answer later. Procrastination, or letting a salesman down gently by holding out hope for a future order, was as prevalent a dodge then as it is today. But it might have been such thin straws of hope that encouraged Ayer not to give up. At any rate he was out making calls first thing the following Monday morning. He doggedly kept

Cyrus H. K. Curtis

Louisa Knapp Curtis

174

going from one office to another until finally, as will happen to all salesmen who make enough calls, he broke the ice and signed up an order for two hundred dollars' worth of space.

At the end of his first year of selling Ayer had earned twelve hundred dollars in commissions. He had also come to realize that the swift-paced upsurge of American industry, along with the development of communications, was creating a situation that offered an exciting and remunerative future to a man who made advertising his life work. He decided to go into business for himself.

While it is true that for the next dozen or so years Ayer was occupied chiefly with selling space for newspapers, just as Volney Palmer had done earlier, there was a good deal more to his work than appears on the surface. On many of the calls he made, Ayer had to sell a prospect on the *idea* of advertising before he could sell any space. This was creative selling rather than mere peddling of blank spaces in a list of newspapers. It was the first step, the selling of the *why* of advertising. Later, Ayer carried his creative talents a step further, to the *how* stage, when he began preparing advertisements and advertising campaigns for his clients.

When Ayer started his agency he asked his father, Nathan W. Ayer, to join him, and the firm began business under the name N. W. Ayer & Son. The "& Son" was the driving force behind the firm. Old N. W. was failing in health and could contribute little beyond encouragement and the high integrity of his principles. It was young Ayer who did the selling during the day and most of the paperwork in the office at night. As an aid to selling, he garnered facts at a time when circulation figures and space rates were more fiction than fact. To sell one important advertiser on the services of his agency, he had his staff prepare a market survey, one of the first market-research projects ever undertaken by an advertising agency.

CURTIS INVITES SUBSCRIPTIONS

When Cyrus H. K. Curtis was desperately attempting to keep alive his newly founded *Ladies' Home Journal*, he realized that if he could publish articles by well-known writers he would attract more subscribers—which he badly needed. The trouble

was that topnotch writers were doing very well contributing to established magazines and had neither the time nor the interest to prepare pieces for Curtis' unknown periodical.

Curtis prevailed upon Marion Harland to write an article for the *Journal*. It was a real feather in Curtis' cap, for Marion Harland had a large following among women readers; furthermore, she agreed to accept the modest sum of ninety dollars for her article. However, his wife, Louisa Knapp Curtis, who edited the *Journal*, was not as happy about the deal as was her husband. She reminded him that the *Journal* could not afford the luxury of big-name writers at ninety dollars a shot. The payroll had to be met, the printer and papermaker had to be paid, and the weekly cost of circulation-solicitation letters had to be taken care of. The total of these expenses, she pointed out, exceeded the magazine's financial resources.

These were harsh realities, and Curtis was realistic enough to understand that his wife was right. This left him with two alternatives. He could return Marion Harland's article and forego the prestige her name would give his magazine. Or he could put on his hat, go out, and walk the streets until he had sold enough advertising to pay for his editorial extravagance. He chose the latter and rounded up enough advertising to pay for the article.

All through the 1880s and 1890s, Curtis' business life was a daily round of plugging for circulation, hustling for advertising, wheedling articles out of famous authors, reassuring his printer about overdue bills, borrowing to pay for paper and, in general, performing a multitude of tasks to keep his magazine from folding. It was quite a juggling act, but Curtis managed to keep the *Ladies' Home Journal* going until it had turned the financial corner with soaring circulation and advertising revenue.

The problems that constantly harassed Curtis, and which would have overwhelmed many another man, were largely problems in selling, and the ultimate success of the Curtis Publishing Company is ample proof that Cyrus Curtis was a master salesman. During those days of early growth he had to do more than sell the *Ladies' Home Journal*. He had to sell himself and his integrity to his anxious creditors. In fact, Curtis the man was about all he had to sell, for his magazine was a frail thing, and people bet their money more on Curtis than they did the early issues of the *Journal*.

EDITORS SELL THE LAND

During the years when the railroads were opening up the country west of the Mississippi, the newspaper publisher was as sturdy and tenacious a pioneer as was the merchant. With his font of broken-face type and clumsy secondhand printing press he moseyed into a town that was only a timetable name on the nearly empty land and set to work to publicize the community with an enthusiasm equal to that of the railroad land agents. In lyrical prose and mile-long sentences the reader of his four-page paper was told that here would rise a thriving metropolis of the West, set amid a lush land destined to make the Garden of Eden seem barren by comparison. One editor boosting his community wrote that "the soil is the richest, the climate the most salubrious, the blizzards the warmest, the cyclones the mildest, the droughts the wettest, the hot winds the coolest, and the women the fairest in all the wide, wide world."

The editor of a pioneer paper such as the *Cherokee Cyclone*, the *Kincaid Knuckle*, the *Wano Rustler*, or the *Prairie Owl* was a self-appointed one-man Chamber of Commerce, Boosters' Club, and Development Commission. He was a good salesman, too. Subscribers to his newspaper sent copies to relatives and friends back home in the East or in Europe, where they were read with boggle-eyed wonder. Thousands of families in such widely sep-

The railroads enabled traveling salesmen to visit their customers more often. Merchants who had made only one or two buying trips a year went to the city more often when rail travel became available. The merchants in this Chicago & Northwestern coach are en route over the Bonesteel Branch to attend a convention.

arated places as Vermont, Wales, Bavaria, and the Ukraine laid aside these old newspapers, packed up their belongings, and went west.

THE EFFECT OF TRAVELING SALESMEN

Among the millions of people who climbed aboard the railroads' rickety coaches and sway-backed Pullmans were the drummers from the big cities. The drummers, or, to give them a more dignified title, the traveling men, took to the steam cars in great numbers. The railroads broadened their horizons. Instead of lounging in hotel lobbies and on street corners to waylay a passing out-of-town merchant, the traveling men went on the road to call on him.

To attempt to pick out one traveling salesman and portray him as "average" would be impossible as well as inaccurate. There was no average traveling man a century ago any more than there is today an average salesman or farmer or college professor or Madison Avenue advertising man (who might

well work on Third Avenue anyway). In vaudeville skits, folk tales, and some popular fiction the traveling salesman has been characterized as a smooth-talking sharp dealer, a hail-fellow-well-met who wore a diamond stickpin in his cravat, smoked long black cheroots, and had an infallible way with women. This picture belongs in the gallery of stereotypes that portray farmers as slow-witted yokels, merchants as crafty Shylocks, and bankers as the heartless foreclosers of mortgages. Undoubtedly there was, among the army of traveling men, a small percentage of slickers and humbugs who wowed a few of the country folk with their tall stories and

"The 9:45 Accommodation, Stratford, Connecticut." Edward Lamson Henry's oil painting of 1867 is considered by many people to rank among the finest of the early American railroad scenes. The railroads operated hundreds of locals such as this one, which delivered express shipments to country merchants and brought in salesmen.

177

hearty buffoonery. But most were intelligent, conscientious men working hard to make good in a profession that had been opened wide by the coming of the railroads. There was nothing very spectacular about them except their accomplishments in developing business.

The traveling salesman contributed to and accelerated the swift change that was occurring in the American economy. He had as much to do with altering the face and character of Main Street as any other influence on our economic life. The salesman who carried consumer products introduced new merchandise and styles much more effectively than had been possible when the merchant made his buying trips to the city. No matter how diligently a merchant called at manufacturers' and wholesalers' showrooms, he could not see and examine all the thousands of products that were coming on the market. Salesmen, arriving on the morning local with their trunks and valises of samples, brought the market to the merchant. They were, in fact, market-makers.

Equally important to the merchant was the salesman's role in helping him merchandise the goods he purchased. A salesman for a shoe manufacturer, for example, would not be apt to get much of an order from a general-store merchant who stocked a few pairs of shoes piled in a dark corner. To fatten orders, the shoe salesman had the job of convincing the merchant he would sell more shoes if he stocked more styles and sizes and displayed them in a manner that would attract more customers. Other salesmen gave the merchant advice and practical suggestions for buying and merchandising hats, ladies' wear, household items, hardware, and thousands of other items. There are innumerable records indicating that salesmen worked nights and Sundays helping merchants rearrange the layout of their stocks and make their window and case displays more eye-catching—in general, sprucing up the old place. The salesmen also rendered valuable service to merchants who decided to specialize in certain lines. They passed along to owners of specialty shops ideas that had been successful in other towns. And they warned against mistakes that others had made. Merchants who built up large businesses and competed successfully with the mail-order houses

and chain stores owed much to the legions of salesmen representing manufacturers and wholesalers.

"IT FLOATS"

Among the men who utilized rail travel to increase sales was Harley Procter. This man, who was 100 per cent salesman, took a product that was 99 44/100 per cent pure and made it the fastest-selling

Harley T. Procter

178

Well-known artists of the day drew illustrations for Ivory soap advertisements. These sketches are early examples.

soap in the country. In 1868 the old firm of Procter & Gamble, a Cincinnati manufacturer of soaps and candles, was doing a comfortable business. Mr. Procter ran the office and handled sales; Mr. Gamble attended to the manufacturing. To most people soap was soap and candles were candles, and although the P & G products were good, neither one had attracted great attention outside the local market in Cincinnati.

Then Procter's son Harley, aged twenty-one, came into the firm as sales manager. Harley coined a name for the soap—Ivory. He spread the word far and wide that it floated (most soaps didn't), and he advertised that Ivory tested only a fraction less than one per cent pure. Armed with this, Harley went on the road. He traveled so constantly that his friends wryly alleged he kept a standby pair of galoshes and an umbrella in every sleeping car operating out of Cincinnati by the Big Four Railroad. He was all over the country, calling on wholesalers and retailers, urging them to push Ivory and showing them how to feature it in their catalogues and display it on their shelves. In San Francisco he bagged an order from a wholesaler for seventeen carloads. On one occasion in Chicago when his attractive sample case was mislaid, Harley called on an important new prospect carrying his samples in a basket. It did not matter. He was selling soap, not sample kits, and he got the order.

When he was not traveling, Harley was busy dreaming up advertising campaigns, which, in a bold new concept of the use of advertising, established the brand name Ivory and the slogan "It Floats" in the mind of every housewife who could read.

Harley wrote the advertising copy himself, but he could not draw the illustrations. He surmounted that problem by flipping through the editorial pages of the best magazines of the 1880s and making a list of the leading illustrators, to whom he wrote asking that they accept commissions to do work for P & G advertisements. It was a long step forward for advertising art and a boon for illustrators, who were paid more for their work by P & G than they received from editors of magazines.

Each year Harley's advertising budget came as a shock to the older members of the firm. There was

no denying, however, that the money Harley spent on sales and advertising pulled in orders and swelled profits. Within a few busy years he had built a nationwide sales organization. Hundreds of buyers respected him as a salesman who knew his business and whose ideas were worth listening to. And as one of the first sales managers in America who thought in terms of the national market, he was a pioneer in the use of full-page advertising in national magazines. Through bold, creative selling and promotion he took an ordinary bar of soap and made it something rather special from Maine to California.

DON'T FORGET THE SMALL CUSTOMER

In the heyday of the steam locomotive, the words "steam engine" and "Samuel Vauclain" were practically synonymous.

Samuel Vauclain was a dynamo of a man who worked his way up from shop apprentice to general superintendent, president, and finally board chairman of the world-famous Baldwin Locomotive Works in Philadelphia. He was probably the greatest steam-locomotive builder in history, and he was a topnotch salesman, too.

In the highly competitive locomotive industry the major railroads—the Pennsylvania, the Southern Pacific, and a dozen or so others—were the blue-ribbon customers who handed out orders for ten to twenty million dollars' worth of engines at a single crack. Sam Vauclain got his share of those juicy orders, but he worked just as hard and enthusiastically to secure orders from the hundreds of smaller roads on this continent and in just about every country abroad. He was as proud and happy about an order from a sugar plantation in Cuba or Louisiana for a single locomotive as he was about a contract for one hundred and fifty steamers from the mighty Pennsylvania.

In his autobiography, written when he was seventy-three and still bristling with energy, Vauclain said, "I like to do business in large quantities, but I consider the loss of a small customer a calamity. Many small customers spell prosperity."

Sam Vauclain was salesman enough to overcome the sales resistance thrown up by the fiery James J. Hill and land a whopping order for Hill's Great

Northern. He was also salesman enough to hustle out of his Philadelphia office if he thought his presence would help Baldwin Locomotive get an order from a small narrow-gauge Colorado line or a logging outfit on the Pacific Coast. In other words, Sam Vauclain was too much a salesman and too wise a one ever to delude himself into thinking that any customer was too small to bother about.

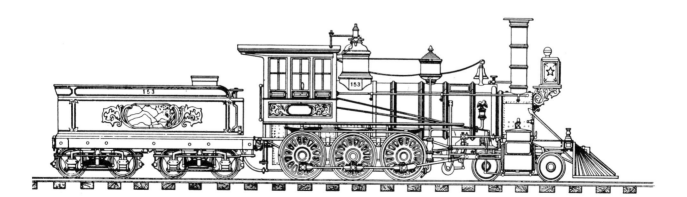

Many Ideas and Inventions

As we learned more about salesmanship and perfected our marketing system, ideas and inventions no longer remained buried away as laboratory curiosities.

THE MIDDLE YEARS of the last century ushered in what might be called the Golden Age of Invention in America. Ideas that men had been turning over in their minds for years became realities mainly because it was now possible for a new product to be of practical value to millions of people. Designs and working models were no longer laid aside by their creators and inventors as laboratory curiosities, for at last other men were beginning to understand the technique of marketing and the absolute need of selling a new product in the market place.

There is no valid reason why the typewriter, for example, should not have been in use at least a hundred years before the first Remington was sold in America. Men in England and France had worked out the practical theory of the typewriter and put together working models. These machines were not perfect, but had there been men with the imagination and perspicacity to devote their energies to selling the typewriter in Europe, improvements would have followed in short order. The first American typewriter was not perfect either. By today's standards it was, in fact, terrible, and there

Massive exhibits in Machinery Hall at the Centennial Exposition in 1876 symbolized America's growth as an industrial nation.

is no telling how many years might have passed before a really decent one would have been put together had not the typewriter fired the imagination of sales-minded men. They were intrigued by the potential market for such a machine. They were ready and more than willing to devote months and years of hard work to developing the market, and they goaded the inventor into improving his machine so that it would be more acceptable to millions of prospective buyers.

What is seldom recognized and rarely acknowledged is that public acceptance of all our great and near-great inventions was hastened, not by their inventors, but by salesmen and the merchandisers. By all means let us pay our respects to Benjamin Franklin for his dangerous lightning-rod experiment, but let us not forget to honor the legion of men who went from house to house and sold the rods that eventually sprouted from thousands of houses and barns. Who can say how long the typewriter or the sewing machine or Thomas Edison's electric light bulb would have remained unknown except to the readers of the venerable *Scientific American* had not men come along and taken on the job of selling these things?

Oddly enough, every great idea and invention that we now accept as essential to our welfare and creature comfort took a heap of selling. Human prejudice against new ideas has always been massive. Undoubtedly, thousands of wonderful dreams died along with the men who dreamed them simply because nothing was done to break down such resistance. The telephone, the automobile, the airplane, even the long-handled back-scratcher almost failed of acceptance because of public lethargy—and ridicule—before someone sold them as practical things to use and own. Nothing, not even the versatile vacuum cleaner, the passenger elevator, the lollypop, or life insurance, sold itself—or was easy to sell.

AN ANSWER TO A WOMAN'S PRAYER

The Singer sewing machine was the first household appliance to be sold successfully in America. The machine was, quite literally, the answer to the prayers of millions of women. As such it was a natural, and although Isaac M. Singer and his partner, Edward Clark, realized the size of the potential demand, they had no clear-cut idea of how to tap this market. There were no effective channels of distribution available to them in 1851, nor was there any system that they could imitate. They had to experiment and pioneer in creating nationwide sales of a consumer product.

The sewing machine was not a new idea. In 1790 Thomas Saint had been granted a patent in England which laid down certain of the fundamental and essential features of the sewing machine. Barthelmy Thimonnier, a Frenchman, actually made thirty machines for sewing army uniforms in 1830, and in 1846 Elias Howe, Jr., patented a sewing machine in America.

None of these early models had amounted to much. But Singer invented a radical improvement on the needle and shuttle Howe had used, and Clark got busy at selling. The two men formed a curious partnership. Singer was a hearty, robust

Working eleven days and as many nights, Isaac Singer perfected the sewing machine.

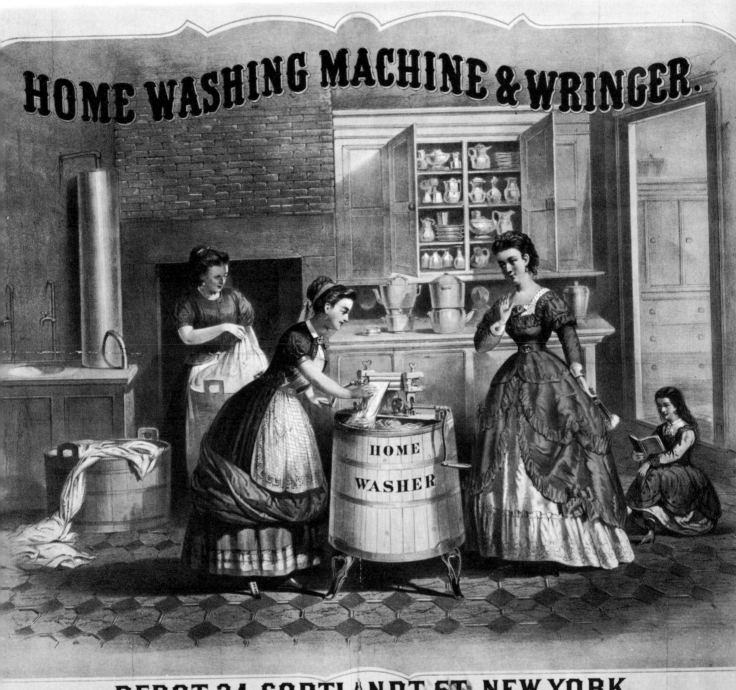

Woman's work was never done, but it was done more easily and quickly after inventors began tinkering with household appliances and salesmen went on the road to market them.

man thwarted in his ambition to be an actor and only moderately successful as an inventor. Clark was a quiet and methodical lawyer who, as it turned out after he took over the management of the Singer Company, had an unerring instinct for the principles of successful selling and merchandising.

Clark's first move in developing his sales organization from scratch was to establish branch sales offices (actually more like stores than offices) in such

Singer's New York salesroom. Agents with wives who could demonstrate the machines were paid six dollars a month extra.

principal cities as Boston, Philadelphia, Baltimore, and Chicago. He had opened fourteen such branches by 1856. Smaller cities and rural areas were covered by franchised agents. Clark was one of the few men of his time who insisted on thorough

186

training of branch-office personnel and franchised agents. Everyone connected with sales had to have an expert's knowledge of the construction and operation of the machine. They were expected to carry spare parts in stock, make repairs when necessary, and demonstrate the machine to prospective customers.

Clark was selling a fairly clumsy, rather formidable-looking machine in an age when, unlike today, most women looked askance at things mechanical. Thus the importance of Clark's insistence on demonstrations. A woman who might hesitate to work with a machine she did not understand—and a husband who balked at spending one hundred and twenty-five dollars—had little sales resistance left after she had watched a thorough demonstration of what the machine could do. In Singer branches women demonstrators (the prettier the better, to Clark's way of thinking) were employed.

Singer soon had competition, and plenty of it. When his sales boomed, many other manufacturers were lured into the business. The market was awash with sewing machines, but Clark far outdistanced his competitors in his carefully planned sales program. In 1856 he jolted the competition and delighted his customers by offering a fifty-dollar allowance for old machines turned in for new models— the first recorded instance of the now familiar trade-in allowance. Later the same year, Clark came out with a hire-purchase plan, an early form of installment buying in which a monthly rental fee of five dollars was applied against the purchase price of the machine.

These two marketing innovations pushed sales up 200 per cent within a year. Meanwhile, Isaac Singer, who was candid enough to admit that he did not care for the role of a businessman, built himself a baronial castle at Torquay, England, where he took up the life of a country squire. Edward Clark kept plugging away at sales and had the satisfaction of seeing a half-million machines sold annually before his death in 1882.

> "No longer is wrought the gusset and band
> With ceaseless stitch and wearied hand;
> For sewing is pleasure by magic art,
> Since curious machines well play their part."

Isaac M. Singer

The man who made it possible to change the skylines of the cities of the world got off to a slow and discouraging start. Elisha Graves Otis designed and built a freight hoist for use at the Yonkers Bedstead Manufacturing Company, where he was employed as a master mechanic. Actually, hoists were not new; men had been building them for several thousand years. But the hoist that Otis built had a unique feature. He had invented a safety device that would prevent the car from plummeting to the bottom of the shaft if the cable broke —a not infrequent occurrence.

Unaware of the enormous importance of his safety device, Otis was set to join the thousands of men headed for the gold fields in California. But before he took off to seek his fortune, fortune came to him in the form of an unsolicited order for the installation of two of his "safety hoisters" in New York City. Otis put off his trip, and in September 1853 opened a small shop and built the two hoists.

When no additional orders came along and the shop was as quiet as a churchyard, Otis must have

Elisha G. Otis

debated the wisdom of making a belated start for California. Instead of going west, however, he built another hoist, which he put on display at the World's Fair for the Exhibition of the Industry of All Nations, in the Crystal Palace, New York. With an eye toward publicity, Otis had himself hauled to the roof of the Palace in the hoist and then ordered the rope cut. The hoist, along with Otis, began to drop. The crowd gasped. Then the safety device stopped the hoist's sickening descent. This stunt vastly thrilled the spectators and earned Otis many columns of free publicity in the editorial pages of newspapers and magazines, but it sold less than three thousand dollars' worth of hoists.

Hindsight, the prerogative of all historians, tells us that Otis was trying to sell his elevators by the wrong methods. He was attempting to sell a product—or, more specifically, an improvement of an old product. It was not until he began selling an idea that he made any progress. Without a safe and reliable elevator the height of office buildings, department stores, and hotels was limited to five or six stories, which was about as high as anyone was willing to climb by stairs. The upper two floors were generally rented at heavy discounts or used for storage purposes. To building owners and to architects and builders Otis presented the idea of installing elevators so that the upper floors would become valuable and buildings could be built higher, perhaps as high as ten or twelve stories.

Hotel owners were the first to grasp the import of Otis' idea. They recognized that his new steam passenger elevator would make the upper floors "the most desirable in the house, whence the guest makes the transit in half a minute of repose and quiet, and, arriving there, enjoys a purity and coolness of atmosphere and an exemption from noise, dust and exhalations." Orders came from all the principal hotels in the country, including the famous old Congress Hotel at Saratoga Springs, where, it was said, "Van Derbilt and all the big guns of

This cut-away illustration shows a hotel lobby with the elevator mechanism in the basement which helped sell many elevators. The elevator, named the "Victorious," was made by Crane Brothers Manufacturing Company.

A demonstration by a lady "type-writer" never failed to perk up a prospect's interest.

New York pronounce it [the elevator] the best thing in the world."

Elisha Otis got the elevator industry off the ground by selling an idea. The safety device made the passenger elevator feasible, but the sale was clinched only when the buyer understood that an elevator would add to the value of his building.

THREE MEN AND THE TYPEWRITER

An invention that intrigued the best sales brains in the country when it made its debut was the type-writer.

The idea of a hand-operating writing machine had been rattling around in the minds of men ever since 1714, when Queen Anne granted a patent for such an invention to Henry Mills, but it was not until the 1870s, when Christopher L. Sholes, of Milwaukee, perfected his machine, that the type-writer attracted much attention. Unfortunately, most of this attention took the form of ridicule;

Sholes's machine was unkindly described as resembling a "large, complicated mousetrap." Ungainly though it was, Sholes's contraption was sufficiently impressive to interest Philo Remington of the Remington Arms Company, who was on the lookout for new products to manufacture. In September 1873 the Remington typewriter Number 1 was produced, a model described as follows: ". . . in size and appearance [it] somewhat resembles the family sewing machine. It is graceful and ornamental—a beautiful piece of furniture for office, study or parlor."

The public's sales resistance to the typewriter was monumental. For one thing, no one knew how to operate the machine, so typing a letter took longer than writing one by hand, thus clearly invalidating the inventor's claim that individuals and business houses would save valuable time by putting aside the pen for the keyboard. Secondly, the nation's business correspondence was then written by male

The first Remington typewriter. The foot pedal was used to return the carriage when the operator came to the end of a line.

191

REMINGTON TYPEWRITER.

1892 Model.

The history of the REMINGTON shows a steadily rising tide of popularity and success. It is absolutely unrivaled for all the essential qualities of a first-class writing machine.

1867. First invention of the Typewriter now known as the Remington Standard. A few machines were made by hand during this and the following years.

1873. The repeated experiments of the inventors having somewhat improved upon the first crude attempts, it was brought to the Remington factory at Ilion, N. Y.

1874. After more than a year of painstaking labor on the part of many able mechanical experts, the first Remington-made machines were put upon the market.

1880. Five years after, only one thousand machines had been sold. The public were slow to realize the value of the invention.

1882. The number had increased to twenty-three hundred machines.

1885. Five thousand machines were sold this year. It grew in popular favor. In

1890, Sales had risen to twenty thousand machines per annum.

1892. Finds our standing orders to our factory of one hundred machines per day inadequate to meet the rapidly increasing demand.

SEND FOR ILLUSTRATED CATALOGUE.

Wyckoff, Seamans & Benedict,

327 Broadway,

New=York.

William O. Wyckoff   Clarence W. Seamans   Henry H. Benedict

clerks possessed of a fierce pride in their penmanship and a jealous concern for their jobs. Their reaction to the advantages of the typewriter was a studied indifference.

Finally—and here was the greatest stumbling block—the typewriter sold for one hundred and twenty-five dollars at a time when many firms of considerable size paid not much more than that for a month's rent, and pens by the hundreds and ink by the barrel could be bought for a few dollars. Typewriter production in the Remington plant the first year was eight machines, one of which was purchased by Samuel L. Clemens, who pecked out on it his *Life on the Mississippi*, thus becoming the first author ever to submit a typewritten manuscript to his publisher.

It is no wonder, then, that typewriter sales were virtually nonexistent until three ambitious, self-confident men appeared on the scene and took a hand in developing them. These men were William O. Wyckoff, Clarence W. Seamans, and Henry H. Benedict. Together, in 1882, they formed the firm of Wyckoff, Seamans & Benedict, opened an office on lower Broadway in Manhattan and, with unbounded enthusiasm, set out to put a typewriter in every office in the city. They almost did, too.

Their technique was direct and effective and was built entirely upon the power of demonstration. Since the public had not taken to the typewriter, the three future kings of typewriter sales took the machine to the public—literally, and by hand. Day after day they lugged the heavy machines into offices and put on demonstrations, which, if not always convincing, never failed to arouse interest, for a young lady typist was taken along to show how dextrous one could become at the keyboard. When the demonstration ended, the machine was left on approval for a few days—with no down payment—so the employer and his curious staff could poke at the keys and examine the mechanism.

Typewriter sales got a boost when the firm of Dun, Barlow & Company, predecessor of Dun & Bradstreet, installed a battery of writing machines in its New York headquarters. For the pioneer typewriter salesmen this was a prestige account, and it is a sure bet that on all the calls they made subsequently the prospective purchaser was told that

The progress in improving the typewriter and in developing acceptance was summed up in this 1892 magazine advertisement. Wyckoff, Seamans & Benedict took great pride in the fact that the Prince of Wales and many members of royalty in Europe owned and used the typewriter.

193

this well-known firm was now typing its mercantile reports. A further order for forty machines for Dun, Barlow & Company's out-of-town offices was a real bonanza.

A few years later there was a flurry of typewriter-buying in the north woods. It seems that Sir Donald A. Smith, the managing director of the far-flung Hudson's Bay Company, sent a typewritten letter from London to the company's offices and outposts in North America. In no uncertain words Sir Donald let it be known that he was fed up trying to decipher the reports from the factors and commissioners at such places as Moose Jaw or Medicine Hat, no doubt written by candlelight with a goose quill held in fingers stiff with cold. Henceforth, ordered Sir Donald (whose own handwriting was nearly indecipherable), each post would equip itself with typewriters and no more handwritten reports would be sent to London.

ONE OF THE FIRST CANNED SALES TALKS

In 1884 a new owner took over control of an obscure little company located in Dayton, Ohio. The National Cash Register Company at the time employed thirteen people, produced four or five registers a week, and turned in an alarming deficit every year. The new owner was John H. Patterson, a wiry, energetic man of forty, who pioneered many of the fundamentals of good selling in use today.

Patterson had a compelling need to experiment with as many workable sales ideas as he could dream up. He had bought a company that made a product no one seemed to want. There were more reasons for not buying a cash register than Patterson could shake a stick at. The machine was an affront to thousands of clerks and cashiers in saloons, cafés, restaurants, and retail establishments where currency was handed over the counter in exchange for goods or services. With its bell that rang for all to hear when a key was pushed and a cash drawer that sprang open, the machine that recorded accurately and permanently the amount of a sale was regarded as a diabolical contraption designed to take from clerks their inalienable right to rob the cash drawer. Very probably these were honest people in most respects. Many of them simply did not consider it downright dishonest to purloin a few

dimes or nickels a day from the old cigar box or the drawer under the counter which served as the unguarded receptacle for cash received from customers. To a bartender's way of thinking, for example, a couple of nickels deftly slipped into his pocket was not much more than a few beers on the house.

Many a clerk who knew or as much as suspected that a man entering the establishment was a cash-register salesman did everything he could to keep him from seeing the boss. When a salesman asked if the proprietor was in, the invariable answer was no, or at least that he was too busy to see anyone that day. Sales material sent through the mail was intercepted and destroyed before the boss arrived in the morning. It was a game of mild deception, but it was one that both sides could play. National Cash Register salesmen learned to conceal their true identity from clerks. One man carried his sales material wrapped in a folded umbrella. Direct-mail selling and advertising literature was sent out in plain envelopes.

But getting past a clerk to the boss was only half the battle. It was no easy matter to convince a cynical owner of a saloon or a dry-goods establishment that the cash register would reduce the cost of petty larceny. The proprietors believed the sleight-of-hand artists would quickly hit on some ingenious method of outwitting the machine. Further, if there were three or four clerks working at different counters, it would be necessary to invest in as many cash registers at a considerable outlay of money. It was rather remarkable, then, that nearly twelve thousand registers were sold during the first three years after Patterson took over.

Of the thirty salesmen working for National Cash Register in 1887, Joseph H. Crane had the best record for overcoming the sales resistance and writing orders. Returning to Dayton from a field trip with a well-filled order book, Crane was asked by Patterson how he had sold as many machines as he had. Crane believed his success was due largely to a carefully prepared sales talk he had written. The sales talk, he explained, had come about in this manner: One day in Findlay, Ohio, three good prospects had visited the hotel room where Crane had installed a display of cash registers. Each of the prospects had shown a more than passing interest in the machines, but none of them had placed an order. At the end of the day Crane realized that something was wrong not with the registers or the market, but with him. He had muffed what should have been three good sales.

Crane told Patterson that he had thought back over his talk with the first prospect and analyzed it. As he reviewed the conversation, he realized he had neglected to mention several important points, any one of which might have clinched the sale. He made a note of these omissions. Then he reviewed what he had said to the other two prospects. Again, he realized, he had skipped over, or entirely omitted, salient sales points. He added these to his notes. From his analysis of what he had done wrong or inexpertly, Crane came to the conclusion that he was selling in a hit-or-miss fashion. So, in a hotel room in Findlay, one of the first "canned" sales presentations came into being. Crane wrote it, omitting nothing of importance. Furthermore, he memorized the presentation and never deviated from it when selling a prospect.

At the end of the explanation Patterson asked Crane to make his presentation on the spot. Patterson listened and realized it was good. It was so good, in fact, that Patterson had it printed in pamphlet form, with the title "The N.C.R. Primer" and the subtitle "How I Sell a Cash Register." The Pamphlet was circulated to all National salesmen and agents, who were told to learn the presentation word for word. So far as can be determined, National Cash Register was the first company to prepare for its salesmen such a set sales talk, covering, step by step, a presentation from the opening to the closing of a sale. This talk was just one of the developments in salesmanship which brought about public acceptance of an important new product.

The "first" cash register, showing only the mechanism and not the cash drawer. This appears in the improved model just installed in the grocery store, above.

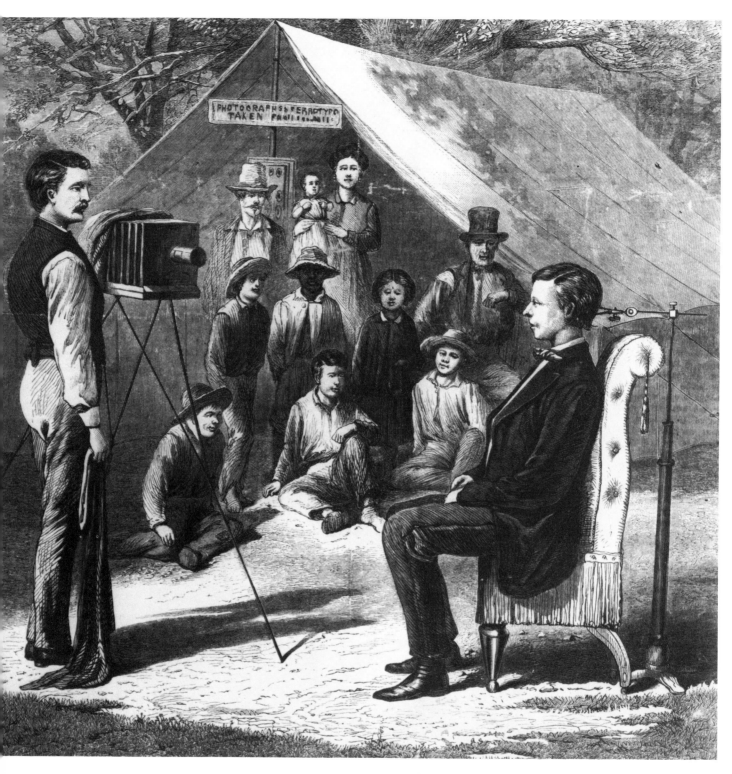

The thrill of a lifetime—posing for a portrait by an itinerant photographer. Before Eastman marketed his dry plates, photographers had to carry a darkroom along with them and develop their pictures on the spot.

"It would seem to me that you are in a fair way to fritter away your time in vague general efforts without getting down to specific business. . . . You and Jones were sent to New York to canvass the town, and you won't make much headway if one sits on his backside all day in the rooms. . . . What I want you to do is to make a list from day to day of the men you ought to see, and go see them. . . . You have been in New York a whole week and have reported no sales. Immediate results are what we are after, and I write plainly so that there may be no mistake as to our expectations. . . . Show this letter to Jones."

One might get the impression from this excerpt from a letter written in 1880 by George Eastman to two of his salesmen that he was a hard taskmaster who mercilessly rode herd on his men. Actually, he was not, but he did realize that the pioneer salesmen of dry plates and other photographic apparatus had to create a market from scratch, and he had a keen insight into these men's problems. His handwritten letters sent out from Rochester were models of specific advice, counsel, and guidance, combined with exhortation. In every letter he wrote to his men, Eastman got right to the point with candor and pungency: ". . . If you want to make an impression on the professional photographer, the best thing you can do is to select the most promising subject and go for him. If you can capture him on his own dunghill it will have more effect than anything else. . . . Make a thorough canvass and send to this office the name, address, and business of every man you visit. You have got the best field in the country and your efforts will be judged solely by the number of holders you sell. If you cannot sell the holders the company has no object to keeping you on the road."

A day later Eastman wrote to the same salesman: ". . . There is no lack of confidence, either in your ability or your energy, only I don't want them misdirected."

When George Eastman began making dry plates in 1880, his objective was to provide a more convenient photographic medium. The wet-plate system, with its cumbersome, fragile, and tempera-

George Eastman

197

Kodak salesman Frank Mosher leaving his hotel room to canvass the town for orders.

mental paraphernalia, annoyed him. Photography should be, he felt, not only easier but better. Up to the 1880s the inherent difficulties of wet-plate photography inhibited its popularity. Its practitioners were either professional portraitists or zealous, long-suffering amateurs who found joy in triumphing over the exacting and cranky medium.

Dry plates had been made in Europe. Eastman derived his formula from information published in the *British Journal of Photography*, making the changes his kitchen-brewed experimental emulsions indicated desirable. Once he had found a good, workable formula, his problem became how to produce many plates with uniform coating. He realized there existed a market for good dry plates. He could supply it, however, only if his plates were uniform. To achieve uniformity, he invented a coating machine (not unlike the time-honored wet roller used to "lick" stamps and envelope flaps) and patented it, first in England and then in the United States.

Once he had his uniform product, he was ready to sell, but there were few people to sell to. At that time there was only a handful of local dealers in photo supplies; stock houses in New York and a few other cities served both the professionals and the amateurs direct and by mail. Eastman and his salesmen had to make a market for his product.

One of Eastman's first objectives was to build a dealer organization, the bigger the better. "Work every town of any importance between Cleveland and Detroit," he instructed one salesman. "The small towns are not so thoroughly worked." In the matter of dealers, Eastman constantly reminded his men of the importance of good dealer relations. To a salesman in Chicago he wrote: "Orders are what we are after, but never do anything to get an order that will prejudice your customer when you see him again. Always remember that. I want to see you the most popular man in our line, and you can only accomplish that by carrying out this policy."

The policy of placing the interests of the customer and dealer first was further outlined in another of Eastman's letters: "The point that we endeavor to satisfy them on is that we are working for the interest of the photographer and also the interest of the dealer. We do not make any blow about taking care of our own rights. Neither the photographer nor the dealers care anything about this, whatsoever. . . . Under no circumstances can we work any sympathy for ourselves. The tocsins 'What have they done for the dealer?' and 'What have they done for the photographer?' are the ones that are going to carry us to victory."

Eastman did a great deal for both the photographer and the dealer. Between 1884 and 1886 he hired a number of demonstrators. These men were trained at the Eastman factory in Rochester and sent out to show customers and prospective customers how to use the company's products, how to get better results, and how to apply photography to new, specialized fields. They were instructed to call on architects, engineers, surgeons, museum directors, surveyors, and anyone else they could think of who could conceivably use a camera in his line of work. Eastman expected his salesmen to exercise ingenuity and imagination in seeking new uses for his products. He expected them also to sell with enthusiasm and pride in his products. When one salesman apparently disdained pushing enlargements as being mere peddling, Eastman came right back at him with a sharply worded letter: "Your favor of March 30 received. It refers to taking orders for enlargements and speaks of it as being a peddling business. The best salesman we have ever known would walk into a place of business, interest the proprietor in the goods that were desired to be sold, and present them in such a manner that he would be asked to ship goods. He did not hesitate to call himself a peddler. All our exertions are devoted to the business of selling goods at a profit. There is no object whatever in making them or advertising them or demonstrating them, unless it is to result in sale."

Persuading people to accept the telephone as a practical means of communication was a task vigorously executed by a man named Gardiner G. Hubbard, friend and father-in-law of Alexander Graham Bell. Of the many men who supported and encouraged Bell, probably Hubbard achieved the least fame, but he did the most to sell the idea of the invention to a skeptical public. He became a salesman

of the telephone in every sense of the word—talking to influential people everywhere, demonstrating the magic toy "at every opportunity." As historian Herbert N. Casson has said, "No possible listener was ever allowed to escape."

It was Hubbard who realized that the whole new idea of telephony had to be made familiar to the public mind; someone had to overcome the resistance that Casson has described in the following manner:

"The very idea of talking at a piece of sheet-iron was so new and extraordinary that the normal mind repulsed it. Alike to the laborer and the scientist, it was incomprehensible. It was too freakish, too bizarre, to be used outside of the laboratory and the museum. No one, literally, could understand how it worked, and the only man who offered a clear solution of the mystery was a Boston mechanic, who maintained that there was 'a hole through the middle of the wire.'

"People who talked for the first time into a telephone box had a sort of stage fright. They felt foolish. To do so seemed an absurd performance, especially when they had to shout at the top of their voices. Plainly whatever of convenience there might be in this new contrivance was far outweighed by the loss of personal dignity; and very few men had sufficient imagination to picture the telephone as a part of the machinery of their daily work."

So Gardiner Hubbard accelerated his promotion activities. He arranged a series of feats for Bell to perform, one of which was a "most severe test of the telephone": he had Bell and his friend Watson (of "Mr. Watson, come here. I want you" fame) borrow a telegraph line between Boston and the Cambridge Observatory, attach a telephone to each end, and conduct the first sustained telephone conversation. It lasted for more than three hours. The Boston *Globe Advertiser* published notes taken of the conversation on October 19, 1876, and the public's interest awakened.

Other demonstrations followed. Bell gave lec-

The sketch at the left was used to promote the telephone for social and business calls locally and out of town. The New York City Columbus Central Office served twenty-four hundred subscribers when the photograph below was taken in 1897.

tures "in the largest halls," and they became popular entertainment. Hubbard's activity was tireless, as was Bell's, and public incredulity began to fade. Then, one memorable day in May of 1877, the first money ever paid for a telephone was brought into Hubbard's office by a man named Emery, who leased two telephones for twenty dollars. The "toy" had been put across, at least to one man, by Hubbard. Now there remained the staggering problem of converting an entertaining gadget into profitable production and use.

Bell attracted the right men at the right time, it appeared. A young man named E. T. Holmes proposed that a few telephones be connected to the wires of his burglar-alarm business in Boston. Hubbard seized the opportunity. He lent Holmes a dozen telephones, and Holmes "was elated that I was to be the first one, and, on my own wires, to show off this wonderful new instrument to the public by connecting two or more parties together through a Central Office.

Soon afterward, relates Holmes, ". . . they sent me

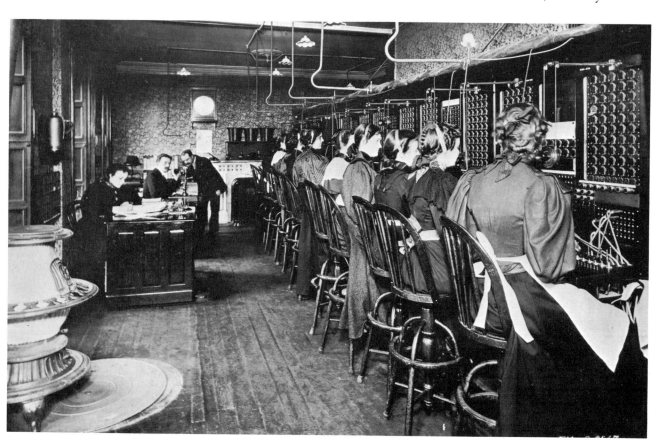

another telephone and after thinking where I would put it, decided to place it in the Revere Bank. After banking hours were over and nearly every one had left the bank, I took a man with me and we went over and connected it up. Our Burglar Alarm Department carried keys to all of the Banks. Until this time everyone had been greatly pleased to be selected as a telephone station, but the following morning a messenger from the Revere Bank brought word that the President would like to see me. I hastened down there expecting to receive the thanks of the President; instead, in a much injured tone, he said: 'Mr. Holmes, what is that play toy you have taken the liberty of putting up out there in my banking room?' 'That, Mr. Walley, is what they are going to call a telephone,' I said. 'What's a telephone?' he replied. 'Well, Mr. Walley, you can ring the bell in my office giving a certain signal, and throw a switch and you can say to my office that you would like to talk with them and you will immediately be able to converse with them.' Mr. Walley simply gave a grunt and quickly said: 'Mr. Holmes, you take that plaything out of my Bank and don't ever take such liberties again.' The *plaything* was quickly removed and the Revere Bank went on record as the FIRST TELEPHONE DISCONNECTION."

But other bankers and businessmen were quickly convinced of the soundness of the new means of communication, and in a short time an office was established in New York City as the center of Bell's activity. By August, 1877, there were 778 telephones in use. Hubbard decided that the time had come to organize the business, and Bell Telephone Association was formed, giving Bell, Hubbard, and Thomas Sanders (who had contributed more than a hundred thousand dollars to Bell through the early days of trial and error) each three-tenths interest in the patents and Watson one-tenth. These four men now had a monopoly of the telephone business, but no money with which to operate it. And to increase their worries, competition sprang up. But at least it seemed apparent from the competition that the telephone business had a future and, to Bell's surprise, it was his company that was besieged by applicants for telephone agencies despite the competitive efforts of the Western Union's American

Speaking-Telephone Company. Salesman Hubbard leased telephones at the rate of a thousand a month and knew that the time had come to find a man of good business ability to take over the management. He had sold the idea of the magic toy to the public; its future was now up to the management.

Theodore F. Vail, the new manager, successfully led the young company through its early days; telephones became normal and needed equipment for business people as well as a great convenience in social affairs. In September 1879 the Bell Telephone Company of New York received a polite but firm letter from James W. Boyle, a wholesale dealer in seafoods. Wrote Mr. Boyle: "We have just had the Bell telephone put in our office, and find it a great convenience, but we must say we would think still more of it if we could get communications early in the morning and late at night." A few weeks earlier, seventeen leading merchants and brokers on Fulton Street had drawn up a petition urging that the telephone exchange be opened for calls at five o'clock in the morning rather than eight o'clock. And, these petitioners added, it would be a help if the exchange remained open later than six o'clock in the evening.

By December 31, 1887, Boston, with the neighboring towns included as branch exchanges, had 5767 subscribers; Hartford, 1176; and New Haven, 1393. By March 29, 1881, the American Bell Telephone Company reported that there were in the United States only nine cities of more than ten thousand people and only one of more than fifteen thousand without a telephone exchange.

FOODTOWN, U.S.A.

In the early part of the nineteenth century, a cheap and abundant food supply and robust eating habits characterized the American way of life. True, there were times when belts had to be pulled tight, particularly in the ever growing cities. But when food was available, and this was most of the time, people ate—but not always the right kind of foods. Generally, they did not know or care much about a balanced diet, and they drank too much, taxing the inner mechanisms of their sturdy bodies. This situation was bound to change and change it did, gradually and with far-reaching marketing effects.

No place contributed more to the "eating revolu-

KIDNAPPED!

Find the Heartless Person.

Do you wake up in the night with a feeling of suffocation and dread?

Do you get dizzy and out of breath on exertion or feel faint when you rise suddenly from a sitting posture?

Does your heart flutter and palpitate at times?

You don't believe it's Coffee, but that is easy to prove.

Quit the Coffee 10 days.

That removes the cause—the poisonous drug, Caffeine.

Then use well-made Postum.

That supplies the food elements required by Nature to rebuild a broken down nervous system. The changed feeling settles all arguments.

These are incontrovertible facts.

Any physician can tell you this, but the best way to prove it is to quit Coffee and use well-made POSTUM for 10 days.

"There's a Reason" for

POSTUM

Postum Cereal Co., Ltd., Battle Creek, Mich., U. S. A.

Post's advertising copy of 1907 reflected his forthright convictions, combining commercialism with a health crusade.

tion" than Battle Creek, Michigan, often called "Foodtown." Here Charles Post, with one helper, Clark ("Shorty") Bristol, produced the first commercial batch of Postum Cereal, a coffee substitute, on January 1, 1895.

Postum Cereal was first put in paper bags and sold around Battle Creek from a handcart. But expan-

sion came quickly. In February 1895 Post went to Grand Rapids with a supply of Postum Cereal (later to be called simply Postum), a pot of cream, and an alcohol lamp to demonstrate his new product. Post boiled his substitute brew for the prescribed twenty minutes in the office of Willis H. Turner, the editor of the *Evening News*, remarking on the fragrance, potability, and caffein-free characteristics of his brain-child. He left with a credit of one thousand dollars for advertising. Then he went to see E. J. Herrick, a Grand Rapids grocery jobber. Herrick was discouraging, as Post liked to tell the yarn later, "showing some big bale-like packages called Caramel Coffee which he had bought a dozen or so eight years before."

"Nobody wants such a thing," Herrick said of Post's Postum. "There is absolutely no demand. Save your money, young man, have fun with it, or go into some business that there is some reason for. You simply cannot make anybody ask for an instead-of-coffee cereal drink."

But Post was insistent. He promised local advertising and consignment billing—no pay until the goods were sold. Thus a fundamental policy of the Postum Cereal Company was established, the guarantee of sale, which, of course, was also a guarantee of quality.

Post himself wrote all his advertisements at first, both for local and national publications. As an early and massive user of national advertising, Post put a "halo" around Postum, using a powerful brand of farmer English: "If coffee don't agree—use Postum." He gathered together the yeasty forces that had been working in Battle Creek for a generation—elements of religion, vegetarianism, Right Living, hydropathy, and Christian Science—and turned a health crusade into an attractive risk for a businessman. Within less than a decade the Postum plant became a spectacular city of wooden factory buildings painted white with green trim, recalling to thousands happy memories of their visit to the "White City" of the Columbian Exposition at Chicago in 1893.

It is a paradox of mass manufacturing that cash is always short in a strong growth period. Post had to struggle to get up the money to pay for his advertising. On one occasion he went to Chicago to ask a newspaper publisher for credit to advertise in his paper, on the basis that the sales of Postum were certain to liquidate the loan. The publisher at first declined but then reconsidered, and Post got a credit of ten thousand dollars, which was later increased to forty thousand.

The C. H. Fuller Company, an advertising agency

of Chicago, was also unable to resist Post's powers of persuasion and agreed to underwrite Postum advertising and place it in magazines and newspapers on a delayed-pay basis.

Postum developed a seasonal pattern of sales with the peak in the winter. Post needed another cereal product to sell in the summer. For several years, with the help of his daughter, he had prepared a granulated food for his own use and twice-baked it in the kitchen range. It was then put through a coffee grinder. These brown, hard-to-chew granules that resulted were christened "Grape Nuts"—Grape because the product contained maltose, which Post called grape sugar, and Nuts in honor of the nutty flavor of the new product.

Grape Nuts became a year-round seller, more than supplementing the seasonal sales of Postum. In addition, Post realized a substantial economy because the bran that was removed from the wheat in the manufacture of Grape Nuts was used to make Postum. The selling of Grape Nuts received a generous infusion of the Post advertising fervor. The new cereal food was advertised as an alternative to surgery for an inflamed appendix. It was recommended as a food for the brain and as a remedy for consumption, malaria, and loose teeth.

The health-food business has never faltered; we find a tremendous interest today in low-calorie foods, in vitamin-enriched breads and cereals, in polyunsaturated vegetable oils. America still eats well and robustly, but it also eats more intelligently, thanks in part to the pioneers of the "sensible" breakfast foods.

"COMMENCE FILLING UP THE FORMS"

The first faltering efforts to sell life insurance in America two centuries ago got almost nowhere for two good reasons. In the first place there was no accumulation of capital and very little cash income in this country at that time. As has been pointed out earlier, we were a nation of small farmers, tradesmen, and craftsmen, and a relatively large part of the

The Mutual Life Insurance Company of New York issued Policy Number 1 in 1843.

204

THE MUTUAL LIFE INSURANCE COMPANY OF NEW YORK.

This Policy of Insurance WITNESSETH,

ANNUAL PREMIUM.
$108 50/100

SUM INSURED.
$5000

That THE MUTUAL LIFE INSURANCE COMPANY OF NEW YORK, in consideration of the sum of *One hundred & eight* dollars, and *fifty* cents, to them in hand paid by *Sarah C. P. Ayres* and of the annual premium of *One hundred eight* dollars and *fifty* cents, to be paid on or before the *first* day of *February* in every year during the continuance of this Policy, Do Assure the Life of *Thomas N. Ayres* of the City of New York in the County of New York State of New York for the sole use of the said *Sarah C. P. Ayres* in the amount of *Five thousand* dollars, for the term *the whole Continuance thereof*

And the said Company do hereby Promise and Agree, to and with the said assured, her executors, administrators, and assigns, well and truly to pay, or cause to be paid, the said sum insured, to the said assured, her executors, administrators, or assigns, for her sole use, within sixty days after due notice, and proof of the death of the said *Thomas N. Ayres* And in case of the death of the said *Sarah C. P. Ayres* before the decease of the said *Thomas N. Ayres* the amount of the said insurance shall be payable after her death to her children, for their use, or to their guardian, if under age, within sixty days after due notice and proof of the death of the said *Thomas N. Ayres* as aforesaid.

Provided always, and it is hereby declared to be the true intent and meaning of this Policy, and the same is accepted by the assured upon those express conditions, that in case the said *Thomas N. Ayres*

shall die upon the seas, or shall, without the consent of this Company previously obtained, and endorsed upon this Policy, pass beyond the settled limits of the United States, (excepting into the settled limits of the British Provinces of the two Canadas, Nova-Scotia, or New-Brunswick,) or shall, without such previous consent thus endorsed, visit those parts of the United States, which lie south of the southern boundaries of the States of Virginia and Kentucky : or shall, without such previous consent thus endorsed, enter into any military or naval service whatsoever, (the militia not in actual service excepted ;) or in case he shall die by his own hand, in, or in consequence of a duel, or by the hands of justice, or in the known violation of any law of these States, or of the United States, or of the said Provinces; this Policy shall be void, null, and of no effect

And it is also Understood and Agreed, to be the true intent and meaning hereof, that if the declaration made by the said *Sarah C. P. Ayres* and bearing date the *twenty fifth* day of *January* 1843 and upon the faith of which this agreement is made, shall be found in any respect untrue, then, and in such case, this Policy shall be null and void : or in case the said *Sarah C. P. Ayres* shall not pay the said annual premiums on or before the several days herein before mentioned for the payment thereof, then and in every such case, the said Company shall not be liable to the payment of the sum insured, or any part thereof : and this Policy shall cease and determine.

And it is further agreed, that in every case where this Policy shall cease, or become or be null or void, all previous payments made thereon shall be forfeited to the said Company.

N. B. If Assigned, notice to be given the Company.

In Witness whereof, the said Mutual Life Insurance Company of New York, have, by their President and Secretary, signed and delivered this Contract. this *First* day of *February* one thousand eight hundred and forty *three*

Sam. Hannay Secretary.

M. Robinson President.

205

In one of the back rooms in the building at 44 Wall Street (left) Morris Robinson (above) and a staff of three assistants established the Mutual Life Insurance Company of New York, the first mutual life company in America.

population was on the move, exploring the opportunities offered in an enormous continent. In their own ways, and to the best of their abilities, men built estates for themselves. They cleared land for farms, opened stores, made things in their small shops, or went to sea. Their objective was not only to earn a living for themselves and their families, but to create going enterprises to leave as legacies. The idea of insuring one's life as a part of a legacy was new. Most men were unaware that this kind of financial protection for their families was possible.

Secondly, few men really understood how to sell so intangible a thing as life insurance. The rudiments of selling tangibles such as tinware or a plow were well known. Many a man could drive a hard bargain when swapping firewood for rum or trading salt fish for molasses or coffee. But the how of promoting and selling an *idea* was beyond their ken.

A start, of sorts, was made in 1759 when the Presbyterian Synods in New York and Philadelphia set up "A Corporation for the Relief of Poor Distressed Presbyterian Ministers and the Poor and Distressed Widows and Children of Presbyterian Ministers." This organization was distinguished not only for the remarkable length of its corporate name but also for being the first life-insurance underwriter in America. The idea was a noble one, but ministers eking out a living on an income of a few hundred dollars or so a year could hardly afford even the modest premiums charged by that worthy organization, and the number of policies written was insignificant. In 1794 the Insurance Company of North America was chartered in Philadelphia, the first commercial company in the United States to offer to write life-insurance policies. However, this company was interested primarily in fire and marine insurance, for which there was a ready market, and paid little attention to its life department, which

206

was discontinued after writing only six policies in five years.

The man who appears to have been the first agent for level-premium life insurance in America was Israel Whelen of Philadelphia, who, in 1807, was appointed agent for the Pelican Life Insurance Company of London, England. Nothing much is known about the volume of business he wrote. He must have made a few personal calls on prospective buyers, but for the most part his efforts were limited to low-key advertisements announcing that he offered life policies to anyone who applied. He gave up the agency after a few years.

What is notable about these pioneer insurance ventures is that no serious effort was made to *sell* life insurance. Admittedly, it was not easy to reach the market that existed except in the cities. But even there little was done to educate people to the value of life insurance. Except for Israel Whelen there were no sales agents. A few descriptive booklets were published, but copies were given only to people who requested them. Insurance was offered on a come-and-get-it basis, and the truth is that hardly anyone bestirred himself to go and get it. It is estimated that in 1800 there were fewer than one hundred life-policy holders in the whole country. The number increased hardly at all during the next thirty years.

The first man to come to grips with the lagging sales of life insurance and do something about them was William Bard, founder and first president of the New York Life Insurance and Trust Company. Since so few people were coming to the company for life insurance, Bard's idea was to further the availability of the insurance through the services of local agents. It was a good idea, and long overdue. Bard appointed physicians, lawyers, merchants, tradesmen, and other men of substance as agents. These novices to the field received booklets explaining the principles of life insurance, a batch of application forms, a small advertising allowance, and a cheery letter from Bard wishing them great success.

For their efforts Bard's agents were paid a 5 per cent commission, which hardly encouraged them to spend time selling insurance at the expense of their regular profession or business. Bard could not

have been surprised when one of them wrote: "Not having heard from me for so long a time you may think I have given up insurance entirely. The fact is that I have not sent but one policy this month as my business in the rag trade is so thriving that I have not had time to spare for you, but will hope for the best." Bard was hoping for the best, too. Selling by his agents was still on an if-you-want-it-come-and-get-it basis, but at least the agency system enabled a prospect to buy life insurance locally instead of applying to a distant home office.

Furthermore, these untrained and not very hard-working agents proved in a small measure that when a good idea is made known to even a few people, sales will go up. The number of policies written by New York Life increased so satisfactorily, all things considered, that other companies took notice and began setting up agency systems.

Another man recognized as a pioneer in marketing life insurance was Morris Robinson, the energetic founder of the Mutual Life Insurance Company of New York. Robinson was the first exponent of person-to-person selling. He exhorted his agents to solicit sales actively, and he set the pace for them by his own aggressive campaign of personal calls in New York. He wrote a large volume of business, as did those of his agents who followed his example.

Men in the industry were beginning to understand the importance of making many calls. That was progress. The country was making progress, too. There was more money in circulation than ever before. People who had roamed the country were settling down, and the public was becoming more conscious of the need for the financial protection and security offered by life insurance.

Thus, in somewhat more than eighty years, a tremendous potential market had been created for life insurance, and the industry had learned enough about selling to build up an agency sales organization that could tap that market. But there was still to come one important advance before the agency system could reach its maximum production. Men had to be trained to sell! An agent whose understanding of the fine points of life insurance was limited to what he had read in a booklet, and whose knowledge of the fine art of closing a sale was nil, was poorly equipped for his job. Not much could

The Metropolitan Life Insurance Company's Chicago staff of industrial-insurance agents posed for their picture in 1882. Superintendent S. Wyatt was one of the men brought over from England to organize district offices for Metropolitan.

humanly be expected of a man who, upon applying to a company for its agency, received the following written reply: "Herewith I send you such documents as are necessary to obtain Applications for Insurance, together with Pamphlets giving a sum-

208

mary of the subject. . . . I cannot by letter give you so good an exposition as you will acquire by reading the pamphlet."

This unhappy condition was not a result of home-office indifference to the trial and tribulations of inexperienced sales agents. Nor were the home offices callously pursuing a policy of turning loose a horde of solicitors unequipped to sell and let the devil take the hindmost while the company garnered such business as these men stumbled upon. Actually, the men in the home offices did not know much about selling life insurance either. They, too, were learning. One man who was learning, and making an honest effort to pass his knowledge along to his agents, was Guy R. Phelps, Secretary of the Connecticut Mutual. In 1848 Phelps included this worthy advice in a letter to a newly appointed agent: "In presenting the subject of Life Insurance . . . you will find, that however much convinced individuals may be, of the importance of being insured, they will be much inclined to postpone the subject to a more leisure time, and perhaps repeated interviews will be necessary to induce them to perfect their applications." Phelps had grasped a fundamental principal of successful selling. Some years later, a manual issued by the Metropolitan Life Insurance Company contained this advice to agents dealing with procrastinators: "Unless helped they will never cross the Rubicon. In such a case get out your forms of proposal, ask for pen and ink (or, better still, carry a portable inkstand with you) and commence filling up the forms."

Clearly what was needed in the industry was a group of highly trained salesmen who could go into the field and train other men to sell. It was time to build a force of general agents. The man who probably did the most to establish such a force was Henry Baldwin Hyde. In 1859, when he was twenty-five years old, Hyde organized the Equitable Life Assurance Society. Equitable began with a small amount of capital, a one-room office sparsely furnished with borrowed desks and chairs, and a thirty-foot sign across the front of a building on lower Broadway in New York. The first months, Hyde spent his mornings in the office at desk work, his afternoons and evenings out selling policies. He had unbounded energy and enthusiasm, two attri-

butes that were to earn him the accolade of "founder of aggressive marketing." Certainly, he was aggressive in his own person-to-person selling, and after he had got Equitable on its feet, he went out on the road and sold men on the idea of becoming agents for the company. Hyde had an extraordinary faculty for inspiring men with a passionate faith in the company and an enthusiasm for their job. He made selling "exciting and stimulating." But above everything else, Hyde recognized the need for adequate training. He realized, too, that he alone could not thoroughly train the hundreds of agents he was lining up to represent his company. For this work he employed traveling agents charged with the job of selecting and training new agents, who, in turn, would appoint subagents to work under their supervision. By thus building up his general agency system, Hyde was deploying trained forces for penetration of the life-insurance market in depth. Within a year after its founding Equitable had 229 agents, a highly creditable force for those days.

In insurance, as in every other industry, there existed a chronic shortage of qualified men to fill top positions in selling. Good men who had taken the time and made the effort to train themselves to become leaders of others were hard to find. This shortage was particularly accentuated in 1879 when the Metropolitan Life Insurance Company entered the field of industrial life insurance for wage-earners. The size of the market for small policies, with small weekly premium payments, staggered the imagination, as did the estimated manpower needed to sell industrial policies door-to-door in all our growing cities and then retrace the steps each week to collect the premiums. In those days workers were paid by cash on Saturday and had no checking accounts. The only way to collect a premium was to go to a policy-holder and get it in hard cash, preferably on Saturday afternoons and evenings, when chances were best that the policy-holder had not already spent his week's wages.

Metropolitan's president at that time was Joseph F. Knapp, who was determined that nothing would stop him from offering insurance protection to the masses, which, incidentally, included those people who needed it most. For some years Knapp had been following the activities of an English company, the Prudential of London, which wrote industrial insurance with considerable success. Knapp went to London to see how this kind of insurance was sold. While in England, he hit on an idea that partially solved his manpower problem. Not only would he import the British idea of industrial insurance; he would import men too. Soon afterward, he sent Brice Collard to England to engage men trained in industrial insurance sales. The first group, along with their families, arrived in America early in 1880. They were dispersed to key cities to hire and train local agents and establish district offices. Altogether five hundred and forty-four men with their families migrated from England to join the Metropolitan. Within three years the number of district offices had grown from three to fifty.

There were many pioneers in the development of marketing life insurance. The industry had more than its share of men with imagination, vigor, and abiding faith in themselves and their life work. And as in every other industry, insurance had its share of dullards and shirkers, too. This separation of the men from the boys, the sheep from the goats, is a continuing process. Success came no more easily to a life-insurance salesman a century ago than it does today. Failure was easily obtainable. The real test of the thousands of men who had brilliant careers in life-insurance sales was their determination to learn how to sell and their perseverance in applying what they had learned. An 1874 issue of the Equitable's agents' manual contained two items of advice as fundamental to success now as they were then: "When you work, don't suffer yourself to be drawn aside by anything from the idea of securing applications," and "Never have time on your hands unemployed during working hours."

The honeycomb of offices along lower Broadway was a rich territory for salesmen of life insurance, typewriters, and the telephone. The number of wires shown here near Maiden Lane in 1880 would indicate that the telephone salesmen had done their work well.

211

212

Through the Turn of the Century

This was a time of rapid transition for America. Momentous events and scientific developments affected the old methods of salesmanship.

AT NINE O'CLOCK on a Sunday night in January 1902, Paul Folwell, a jewelry salesman, left his home in West Philadelphia for a two weeks' trip through his territory in northeastern Pennsylvania. He walked to the corner, swung himself and his two heavy bags aboard a drafty streetcar, and rode for forty minutes to the Broad Street Station. At midnight he dropped his cigar butt in the cuspidor on the linoleum-floored smoking compartment of the sleeping car attached to the Buffalo Night Express and went to bed in Lower 8 to sleep his way through to Williamsport. Above his head a man snored in the upper berth; below him the steam pipes clanked and the wheels clacked over the switch points. It was all very familiar to Folwell, who spent about a hundred nights each year in a Pullman.

At six the following morning Folwell wriggled into his trousers with the acrobatic dexterity of a traveling man accustomed to dressing in a horizontal position, pulled on an undershirt, and made his way between the swaying curtains to the washroom at the end of the car, where he waited his turn at one of the washbowls. While waiting, he watched a man who traveled for a grocery wholesale house shave himself with a safety razor—made by a man in Boston named Gillette. To Folwell and the others,

Making up the berths.

busy with their morning ablutions, it was readily apparent that the safety razor greatly reduced the hazard of slitting one's throat when the car lurched.

At seven o'clock Folwell got off the train, walked to the Hotel Updegraff, registered, and had breakfast. It was only eight-fifteen when he said "Good morning" to the first merchant he called on that day. He made three more calls that morning, had a hearty lunch (fifty cents plus five cents tip), and at one o'clock took a trolley car for a call on a customer at the north end of town. He made two more calls in the afternoon, and left his last customer's place of business shortly after six o'clock.

The next day Folwell took the early morning local for a fifty-minute run to Sunbury, where he spent the day and made five calls. On succeeding days, by the use of local trains, interurban lines, and a pocketfull of well-thumbed timetables, Folwell got himself in and out of such places as Danville, Shamokin, Catawissa, Nanticoke, Tamaqua and a half-dozen other towns in the Pennsylvania anthracite region.

In each town the routine was the same. Calls were made on customers and prospects from as early as eight in the morning until closing time, which in some cases was as late as ten at night. Folwell was a conscientious salesman who did a thorough job of selling on every call he made. He suggested seasonal promotions to his customers and very often helped them prepare advertising copy. He advised them on reordering regular items and initiated orders for new lines his firm had added to its offerings. Many a Sunday afternoon was spent helping a merchant set up a new window display similar, perhaps, to an attractive display Folwell had seen in Reading or some other city. In short, he worked hard and knowledgeably at giving his customers service and advice in exchange for the business they placed with him. There was nothing flashy about his work. He did not, as some salesmen boasted, breeze into town and burn up the pea patch. But each year his volume was higher than the previous year and new customers were added to his list of regulars.

Friday night of the second week, Folwell took the sleeper for Philadelphia. He spent Saturday morning with the two partners of the firm he worked for. After lunch he repacked his sample bags, adding more sales literature and order books. He was home in West Philadelphia by three o'clock. That night Folwell and his wife had dinner at Kugler's excellent restaurant and took in the new show at Keith's

The morning ritual for a traveling man. By the 1890s there were six thousand Pullman sleeping cars in service.

Theatre. Sunday night, Folwell slept in Lower 12, Car 160, bound for Pittsburgh and a two weeks' trek through western Pennsylvania.

For Jerry Kent, who covered the Southwest for a Chicago hardware jobber, the routine was somewhat different from Folwell's. Instead of making many short trips, Kent took two long swings around his territory each year. Folwell's samples fitted easily into a single suitcase; Kent's samples filled two cumbersome trunks. The man who sells today from an attaché case will never know what a burden two trunks of samples were to Kent and the thousands of other men who traveled for jobbing and wholesale houses more than a half-century ago.

Upon arrival at Laredo, Texas, Kent hurried up the platform to the head-end baggage car and made certain that the trunks were taken off the train.

214

Paul Folwell made Reading (above) every six weeks. Jerry Kent, on his long swings through the Southwest, got into Topeka (below) twice a year. Both men rode trolleys and interurban cars to call on customers located outside the center of town or in nearby towns and villages.

The local stage line was often the best way to get from one small town to another in the Southwest.

He then arranged with one of the local livery wagons to bring the trunks around to the Hotel Hamilton, where Kent engaged two rooms, preferably on the second floor. Within an hour or so, two brawny porters had wrestled the trunks up the stairs (Otis had not yet sold the three-story Hamilton on installing an elevator) and deposited them in the room where Kent would display his wares. The trunks were packed with the same ingenuity that the old Yankee peddlers had displayed in stowing their trinkets. The entire room was soon filled with samples of a hundred or more hardware items plus dozens of catalogues and display signs. Several boxes of cigars were placed at strategic places amid the samples; less conspicuously displayed were a bottle of Kentucky bourbon and glasses. By early afternoon Kent was ready for business.

Some salesmen of the day, including Kent, wrote or telephoned ahead, advising customers of the dates they would be in town. These were the first people Kent called on after he had arranged his samples. An inexperienced salesman or one who was lazy might have used the telephone in the hotel lobby to announce his arrival and invite the merchant to come and look over his wares. Kent went out and personally invited merchants to visit his display. By so doing he had a chance to pre-sell the new lines he was carrying before his customers saw them. More important, he could take a quick look at the merchant's stock, making a note of the items in short supply and those of which there was considerable inventory.

There was more to Kent's job than walking the streets making calls and then selling the merchants who came to his display room. He had a delicate mission to perform for his firm's credit manager, who had become uneasy about the overdue accounts of a customer in Laredo. Also, Kent had heard, via the grapevine, that someone was planning to open a hardware store in a nearby town. It took four hours to find this man and get him over to the display room.

In almost every case a merchant brought his partner or one or two of his chief clerks along to Kent's room. This raised the problem of multiple selling. A clerk with a notion of impressing the boss could block a sale by expressing the opinion that a similar article could be bought cheaper elsewhere or, perhaps, by casually mentioning he had heard reports that the business outlook in general was pessimistic. Getting two or more men to agree on increasing their inventory or stocking a new item was a feat of persuasion and tact. Kent used both, with an occasional assist from the cigar box and the whisky bottle.

Kent wound up his business by noon of the fourth day in Laredo. Back into the trunks went the samples and down the stairs went the heavy load. Until train time Kent wrote reports to the home office and cleaned up his paper work. He saw his trunks safely loaded into the baggage car, then went aboard the train to enjoy one of the Missouri Pacific's six-course dollar dinners and to sleep through to his next stopping place.

Jerry Kent and Paul Folwell are fictional composites of the one hundred thousand or so traveling salesmen at the turn of the century. They worked hard and long under conditions that, by today's

216

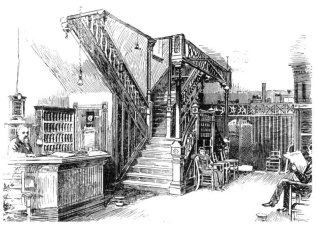

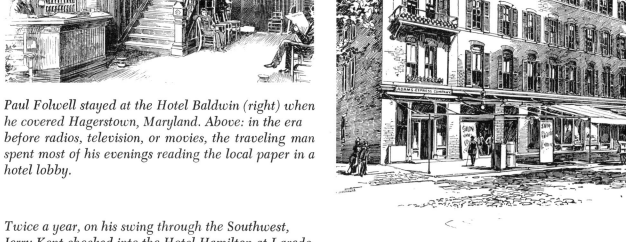

Paul Folwell stayed at the Hotel Baldwin (right) when he covered Hagerstown, Maryland. Above: in the era before radios, television, or movies, the traveling man spent most of his evenings reading the local paper in a hotel lobby.

Twice a year, on his swing through the Southwest, Jerry Kent checked into the Hotel Hamilton at Laredo, Texas, unpacked his sample trunks, and displayed his line of hardware items for inspection by the merchants who came to his room on the second floor.

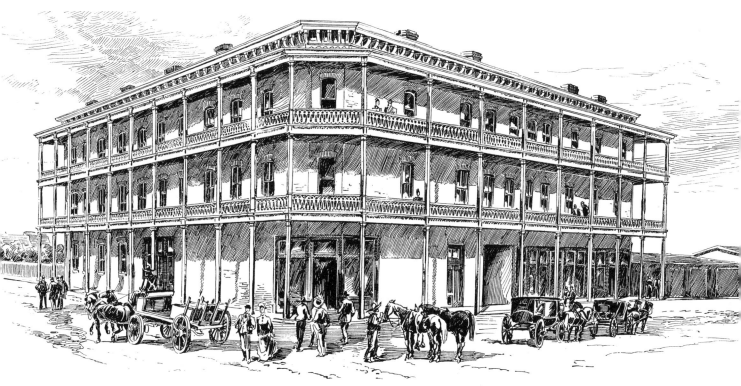

standards, would be considered intolerable. At night they were members of a fraternity of lonely men, swapping stories and experiences in drab hotel lobbies or, perhaps, playing penny ante in a sparsely furnished bedroom lighted by a naked bulb in the ceiling.

A HOLE IN THE GROUND

At about the time the Paul Folwells and Jerry Kents were traveling by train, shank's mare, trolley car, stagecoach, and buggy, two developments were taking place that would revolutionize selling in the twentieth century. These developments were destined to have irrevocably interlocked futures. The first concerned petroleum, which had virtually doomed the coal-oil industry in the early 1860s. The second was the emergence of the originally ludicrous horseless carriages into a respected means of locomotion.

On January 13, 1901, the front page of the New York *Times* was aglow with an account of the bridesmaids' dinner held prior to the biggest society wedding of the day. Miss Elsie French, of New York and Newport, had captured the heart of Alfred Gwynne Vanderbilt, who had just inherited some sixty million dollars, part of the original railroad fortune

amassed by his great-grandfather, Cornelius Vanderbilt. Tucked away at the bottom of that same front page, and hardly noticed by society-conscious readers, were a few paragraphs about an oil strike south of Beaumont, Texas. These same readers, sighing over the final details of the wedding a few days later, probably overlooked the paragraph on the same page telling that the crude-oil producers were rushing to sell their product to Standard Oil Company. Prices had dropped five cents a barrel. "No bomb," said the story, "has been thrown into the oil trade in late years that caused such wide consternation as the announcement of Col. J. M. Guffey's great strike in southeast Texas."

Big Hill, as the natives called it, was a circular mound, about a half-mile in diameter, rising no more than twelve feet above the surrounding swampy plain. The Neches River curled lazily nearby, emptying its waters and the barges that sailed it into the Gulf of Mexico a few miles farther south. There was not much to distinguish Big Hill from any other low mound anywhere except that near its crest the odor of sulfurous gas seeping from the soil was ever present. Venturesome schoolboys from Beaumont found rich satisfaction in lighting the gas and watching the earth burn.

On West Main, East Third, Elm, or Central Avenue, U.S.A., the salesmen and merchants were the market makers for American industry.

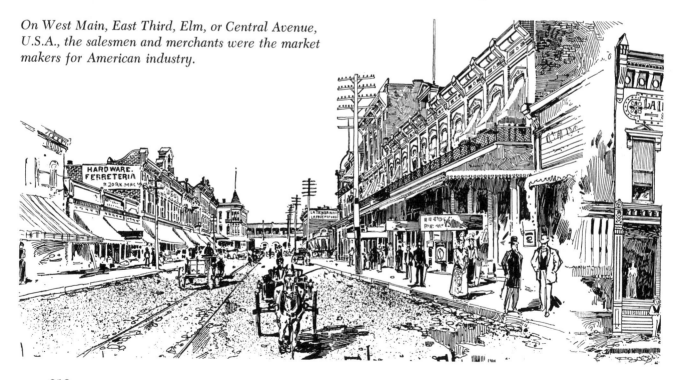

HONOR TO HIGGINS,
THE ORIGINAL OIL MAN OF BEAUMONT, TEXAS!

"Honor to Whom Honor is Due!"

PATTILLO HIGGINS was born in Beaumont, Texas, December 5th, 1863. He was educated there, and has resided in that city ever since.

Mr. Higgins located the Beaumont Oil Field in the year 1892, and contended that it was "worth millions of dollars."

PATTILLO HIGGINS.

RESOLUTION PASSED BY THE BEAUMONT OIL EXCHANGE AND BOARD OF TRADE:—

Be it Resolved, That in recognition of Pattillo Higgins' great service to his native city by locating the enormous wealth under its surface, the Beaumont Oil Exchange and Board of Trade do herewith unanimously elect Mr. Higgins an honorary member of this Institution. *Carried.*

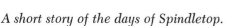

A short story of the days of Spindletop.

In the late 1880s Big Hill had attracted several people who suspected that where there was gas there was oil. Eventually, the first to try to release this treasure was Patillo Higgins, who dreamed of thousands of barrels of oil coming from the center of the mound. But after seven frustrating years he had exhausted his own financial resources and those of his backers. It remained for Captain Anthony F. Lucas to release the valuable contents from the unpretentious hill. Colonel Guffey achieved his moment of fame in finding the well, but it was Lucas who made the great strike.

Captain Lucas had graduated as an engineer from the Polytechnic Institute at Gratz, Austria, and had been commissioned in the Austrian navy. A job as an engineer in a salt mine in a Louisiana bayou led

Captain Lucas to perceive that oil, sulfur, salt, and mounds were somehow related. When he read an advertisement by Patillo Higgins, telling of a mound with gas and sulfur that Higgins believed would produce oil, Lucas immediately suspected the presence of a salt dome. Like Higgins, but for different reasons, Lucas began to believe in Big Hill. He took a lease on about six hundred acres of the hill, paying $11,050 and signing notes to pay $20,100 more. To Patillo Higgins went a 10 per cent interest in the Lucas lease.

On a hot July day in 1899 Lucas confidently started drilling with equipment he had brought from Louisiana. He expected to finish in a few weeks, but six months later he had managed to fight his way down through only 575 feet of the quicksands. Before he knew it, all his capital had been drained into that hole in the ground. Seeking addi-

Spindletop

tional financing, Lucas approached Standard Oil, whose production expert examined Big Hill and reported that Lucas was wasting his time and should go back to mining.

Luckily for the future of the oil industry, Lucas was a man of vision and determination. After many efforts he succeeded in obtaining financial backing from the Mellon family and prepared for another attack on Big Hill.

In the early part of January, 1901, when the drillers had lowered about seven hundred feet of pipe down the hole, the well suddenly began to spout mud. With no warning there was a deafening roar and the well erupted like a volcano—first mud, then gas, then oil and rocks shooting hundreds of feet into the air. America's first bona fide gusher had come in.

This gusher would be known as the Anthony F. Lucas gusher, and the whole oil field would be called Spindletop, a fabled name in Texas. Prior to Captain Lucas' strike, Gulf and Texaco had been minor factors in the oil business. Within a few years after Spindletop was tapped, they had become serious competitors of Standard in the oil business. For one thing, the Texas oil men developed a new demand, for their crudes were especially suitable for making the heavy fuel oil needed by locomotives and ships. In addition, the Texas producers were unencumbered with the burden of a heavy capital investment in the manufacture and sale of kerosene, as was Standard. Thus they were able to move quickly into the market with their light crudes when the growth of the automobile industry created an insatiable demand for gasoline.

BEFORE THE BIG STRIKES

In the early days, oil, like many other commodities, was peddled from door to door. Some was dispensed from tank wagons. But there were oil hucksters like Frederick Western, who for many years sold housewives gallon cans of kerosene from a mule-drawn wagon. Later he was transferred from wagon to tank truck and a new commercial route, but he always remembered the days with Stella and Annie, his beloved team of mules, as the happiest of his whole working life.

In those days Western's territory was the French Quarter of New Orleans. He had a different route for each day of the week, but he knew every customer by name, every courtyard by heart. In the morning he would set out, his wagon loaded with one-gallon cans of Standard Oil products and a handy supply of Perfection Oil Heaters. He would drive Stella and Annie slowly down the cobbled

Spindletop in 1929.

streets, his cry of "Oil! Oil!" breaking through the early morning quiet. Here and there a woman, clutching her coat against the chill, ran out of a doorway to exchange an empty kerosene can for a full one. In cold weather Western sold as many as six hundred gallons before the day was through.

At an impassable spot on one route, Western always left the mules with two elderly sisters who ran a grocery store and went off to deliver his cans of oil by wheelbarrow. It was a happy arrangement for the mules: the sisters and the children of the neighborhood vied with each other in stuffing them with bananas and lumps of sugar.

221

The Oil Man

While Frederick Western was pursuing a time-honored method of marketing, the industry for which he worked—the oil industry, with the Standard Oil Company its leader—was pioneering a new development in business in America. That development was bigness.

With the westward extension of the railroads and with industrialization and mechanization, consumer demand increased in the second half of the nineteenth century. People who had had little money now earned factory wages, which could be spent on things they no longer produced themselves. The volume of trade grew with this burgeoning purchasing power, and this, in turn, compelled businessmen to seek new ways of running their businesses with less risk and greater profit. One way, proved successful, was to buy out established companies with related operations, thereby reducing competition and increasing the opportunity for profit.

The oil industry was the first in which this new way of business reached a high development. Earlier, because of the possibility of high profits, many inexperienced men with little capital had been attracted to the oil fields. These marginal operators' efforts often resulted in bankruptcy, which worried the men of vision in the industry and prompted them to try various ways of strengthening themselves. The ultimate solution was the formation of combinations of several firms. Thus was formed the Standard Oil Company. Essentially, this formation meant reaching both backward and forward to obtain as large a measure of control of related operations as possible. Standard's organization provided a large volume of business and effective coordination of operations, from production of crude oil to the marketing of oil products. Efficient large-scale operations and strategic location of plants, combined with market and financial strength, enabled Standard to operate successfully in a highly dynamic sit-

"The Oil Man" was one of the many vendors painted by Calyo for The Street Cries of New York, a series immortalizing the once familiar peddler of goods who cried his wares as he strolled along the streets looking for customers.

uation. The pattern set by this giant was followed by the other successful oil companies and extended to virtually every other industry in the American economy.

The rise of big business has continued ever since without letup. With it have evolved changes in marketing which were developed and continue to be developed to suit special situations and to move the great mass of material and services created by American enterprise.

"FOR BUSINESS OR FOR PLEASURE"

The year 1904 was an eventful one on the national scene. This was the year Americans suddenly realized that the change of centuries was to mean more than just a change on a calendar. It was like awakening one spring morning to see the flowers and trees suddenly in bloom. There was prosperity everywhere. No longer were the luxuries of the telephone, the electric light, and plumbing to be exclusively for the very rich. Industries were learning the art of mass production with cheaper costs. Popular magazines, their circulations leaping, began advertising a bewildering abundance of improved necessities and fascinating new conveniences—at prices within the means of hundreds of thousands.

The year before, Orville and Wilbur Wright had made man's first powered flight. More and more people were becoming automobile conscious. There were at this time one hundred and seventy-eight automobile factories employing twelve thousand workers. Two pioneers drove a Franklin from San Francisco to New York in forty-three days. John Wanamaker's department stores in Philadelphia and New York sold automobiles—in addition to appropriate clothing to wear in them.

"Everyone can afford a Fordmobile," said Henry Ford. In June 1903, eleven years after making his first car, he had started again at forty with his third company, and by March 1904 he had sold six hundred and fifty-eight cars at seven hundred and fifty dollars apiece. The car was built "for business or for pleasure," his advertisement stated. "Built also for the good of your health—to carry you 'jarlessly' over any kind of half decent roads, to refresh your brain with luxury of much 'outdoor-

223

Born of the bicycle and buggy, the early automobiles were delightfully rakish, if somewhat unreliable. This 1902 Rambler quickly gave way to roomier covered vehicles which took the traveling salesman out of the steam cars and on to the road.

ness' and to fill your lungs with the 'tonic of tonics' —the right kind of atmosphere."

The lungs were perhaps more favored than the rest of the body, for in 1904 you could be carried "jarlessly" over only a few of the country's two million miles of roads. Ninety-seven per cent of the mileage was dirt, and "improved highways" were mainly gravel.

Although there was little doubt that all America would eventually be on wheels, few men anticipated how quickly the automobile, this child of the new century, would come of age. It would be another four years before Henry Ford would announce his Model T, the car by which many historians would date the birth of the automobile industry.

John D. Rockefeller and his Standard Oil associates, controllers of 77 per cent of the nation's oil business, were actually worrying about markets for their products in the midst of all this glorious change and prosperity. Before the automobile, gasoline had been discarded at refineries as a relatively useless product; production emphasis was on kerosene and other heavy products. Who could foresee that the spluttering little buggies that could drive up to fifty miles on a gallon of fuel would very soon number in the millions, creating a greater market for gasoline than all the lamps and stoves of America had ever created for kerosene, or that almost

The Model T Ford of 1908, the car that put America on wheels.

two million miles of dirt roads would be paved with products derived from oil to support the incessant travels of those buggies?

It did not take long, however, for salesmen to learn just how valuable the automobile was. In 1912 a New York City firm decided to buy an automobile for a salesman whose territory was New England and part of New York State. It seemed a gamble, but it worked out favorably. Not only were the salesman's expenses greatly reduced because of the time saved, but his orders increased 25 per cent and a number of new customers were secured. *Harper's Weekly* of March 2, 1912, had an explanation: "... The salesman in a trim, speedy little car produces an impression that the salesman on foot or in a horsedrawn buggy never could. The automobile shows, too, that the concern is enjoying prosperity. ... A new domain is forecast for the automobile, a field that is between that of the pleasure car and the motortruck. ... For city use an automobile with spacious storage space is revolutionizing the work of the salesman."

FROM TOY TO NECESSITY

Dedication to hard work and an unyielding persistence have always characterized the successful salesman in any U.S. industry. The importance of these qualities can clearly be seen in the history of the automobile, the product that was to become a major factor in changing the pattern of the American way of life. Once the automobile industry was on its way, those geniuses of American commerce,

225

the supersalesmen, began to emerge as leaders of that industry. The career of pioneer automobile salesman John North Willys is a fascinating case in point.

In 1900 Willys owned a sporting-goods store in Elmira, New York, which sold everything from fishing tackle to bicycles. That year he made a trip to Cleveland, where he saw his first automobile. It was a Winton, and Willys, just as most of America soon would, went automobile-crazy. He would probably have taken a Winton back to Elmira with him, but none was available at the moment.

When Willys returned home he discovered that a local doctor had just brought an automobile to town—a Pierce Motorette, manufactured in Buffalo and powered with a single-cylinder 2.75-horsepower motor. The Motorette had a light Stanhope body with bicycle wheels and a frame of bicycle tubing. This looked even better to Willys than the Winton,

John North Willys

and apprehensive lest someone beat him to it, he caught a train for Buffalo and went straight to George N. Pierce, manufacturer of the Pierce-Arrow bicycle. George Pierce was experimenting with automobiles but was not yet in production; the car he had sold the doctor in Elmira was the first and only one he had made. But the Willys gift of gab was not to be denied. He persuaded Pierce to sell him the next car he turned out and to assign him a Pierce-Arrow agency in Elmira. In 1901 Willys sold two cars; in 1902 he sold four. Irrevocably dedicated to automobile-selling by now, he went to Kenosha, Wisconsin, and obtained the agency for the Rambler car.

Willys, the little Motorette, and the Rambler went to town; in 1903 he sold twenty cars. Then, since in those days automobile factories had trouble turning out enough cars to go around to all their dealers, Willys took on another car, the Detroit, manufactured by the Detroit Auto Vehicle Company. But even with three suppliers Willys could not get enough cars, for by this time he had opened a sales agency in New York City.

By 1906 he had a stack of unfilled orders and knew he could sell any car that would run, so again he looked for another factory. He found it in Indianapolis, the Overland Automobile Company, an outgrowth of the Standard Wheel Company, which had been making automobiles since 1903. The company was just barely keeping its head above water, but there was nothing wrong with the Overland that a vigorous sales policy would not cure.

Willys, hungry for cars, contracted for the company's entire output of two models—a runabout and a touring car, designed to sell for six hundred and seven hundred dollars. The entire output of the company in 1907 was forty-seven cars. These, added to the Pierce-Arrows and Ramblers apportioned to him, netted Willys a healthy bank account and furthered his appetite for even more merchandise. He estimated that he could sell five hundred Overlands in 1908, and to help the firm increase its facilities he paid ten thousand dollars down against those five hundred cars.

But Willys had hardly returned home when word arrived that Overland was in financial trouble. Willys went back to Indianapolis to save the company, which owed its creditors eighty thousand dollars.

Probably Willys' greatest selling job came when he faced the Overland creditors, who looked grim and uncompromising when Willys went to work on them, promising he would have the company back on its feet if they would give him a chance. All they had to do was extend Overland more credit!

Willys must have been a man of great persuasion, for they bought his proposition. They not only gave him the additional credit he asked for but helped him establish credit elsewhere. After that he was made president, treasurer, sales manager, and pur-

This proud owner of an Overland, circa 1910, was undoubtedly admired as he drove about the country-side. His satisfaction, though he probably did not know it, derived in large measure from the enthusiasm of salesmen such as John Willys.

chasing agent of the rejuvenated Overland company. During 1908 he pushed four hundred and sixty-five cars through production. In 1909 the company built and sold more than four thousand cars, now called the Willys-Overland.

From then on it was easy. In 1910 annd 1911 those automobile firms that were doing well did very well, while those that were slipping found themselves headed toward disaster. More than twenty leading automobile manufacturers went bankrupt during that period. One of them was Pop-Toledo, with a big, well-equipped plant at Toledo, Ohio.

Willys bought the plant with all its machinery and material and moved his company to Toledo. In the next few years Willys-Overland absorbed a number of other firms. By 1915 Willys had made his company, with a production of 91,780 cars, the second largest automobile manufacturer in the world.

After the First World War, Americans in general developed a radically new point of view toward the automobile. No longer was the horseless carriage a luxury and mainly an instrument of recreation for the adventurous. It had become a year-round, day-and-night utility. In ten years the national registration of automobiles jumped from six million to twenty-three million.

Meanwhile, however, highway conditions throughout the country had improved little. But this was soon to be changed, and the country would be covered with a huge network of highways. Advertisers were already following the motorist, and billboards had become part of the American landscape.

The automobile was also precipitating an urban explosion throughout the country. Up to the turn of the century most American cities grew compactly outward from the business center. After that, suburban development cautiously followed the railroads and main turnpikes, but only to a limited distance. From 1920 onward, with increasing accel-eration, American cities burst their bounds and sprawled indiscriminately over the surrounding countryside.

The phenomenon of urban explosion, largely produced by the automobile, created a new type of "supercommunity." Every city in the United States had became, to some degree, the "center of a constellation of smaller centers." Traffic congestion in many cities became impossible. As early as 1920 traffic surveys conducted by the federal government indicated that most family shopping was accomplished within a radius of three miles of home.

In 1922 the National Department Stores made a novel departure from retailing tradition by erecting a branch establishment three miles out from the center of St. Louis, Missouri. Within the next twenty years this innovation was followed, at greatly extended distances, by many department stores of the larger American cities, by the principal mail-

The opportunity to advertise accelerated as rapidly as the production of cars, and those who had something to sell did not hesitate to take advantage of it.

The success of the early car salesmen led to more changes in selling. As the car became a necessity, the center of the city became more congested, and the retail merchants moved to the suburbs to be nearer their customers.

The rapid expansion of the automobile industry turned on the ability of the buyer to pay, and the solution was the installment plan, which eventually became a mainstay of the American economy.

order houses, and by leading operators of chain stores.

The mobility brought to America by the automobile strongly influenced the operations of Sears, Roebuck, for example. The status of the original Sears market, a rural one, was changing rapidly. No longer was the farmer isolated: he could go to town and shop there. The nation was becoming a homogeneous market. Sears, under the leadership of Brigadier-General Robert Wood, switched its emphasis from mail-order selling to retail stores equipped to serve both the motorized farmer and the city dweller.

Besides providing a bulwark of the economy during the boom of the 1920s and causing shifts in marketing patterns, the automobile was responsible for the growing use of installment credit. To find purchasers not only willing but also able to absorb the ever increasing output of the automobile factories would have been impossible had it not been for installment selling by dealers and installment buying by consumers.

Once established, the use of installment credit spread like wildfire. By 1950 dealers were called upon to find purchasers for about 6,700,000 cars and about twice as many used cars, to say nothing of 14,500,000 radios, 5,800,000 refrigerators, 4,300,000 washing machines, 3,500,000 vacuum cleaners, and many more millions of freezers, clothes driers, and other consumer goods.

The automobile industry, in fact, could not operate at its full capacity if it depended for its market on those who could actually afford to purchase cars and pay cash for them. Therefore it began inveigling Americans into leaning the present against the future. To develop a continuous mass market, it also persuaded them that prestige required their dissatisfaction with any model as soon as it had been superseded by a later one. The automobile industry had to sell both those who could not afford to buy and those who had bought but had not yet paid. Sell them it has.

230

The first salesman for King Gillette's new safety razor had no competition. Gillette's product was a brand new idea, but that did not make it any easier to sell. The salesman might have felt in his heart that every male in town would buy a safety razor, but the druggist he called on was not so sure. His customers already had razors and had acquired a dexterity at handling the long sharp blades without maiming themselves. What advantage was there to the safety razor that would prompt a man to spend five dollars for something he really did not need?

Gillette salesmen soon learned that there was nothing to be gained from long discussion of the merits of the different razors. Instead, they prevailed upon the druggist to step into the back room and try the safety razor. That usually did the trick. After shaving his own beard the druggist could speak with authority, as a man who used one himself, when a customer showed interest in the safety razor.

King C. Gillette, the inventor of the safety razor.

232

Selling Comes of Age

The years of World War I, the Roaring Twenties, and the Great Depression tested the mettle of the nation and the adaptability of the salesman.

IN MORE WAYS THAN ONE the sound of a gun fired on a hot day in June 1914, in far-off Sarajevo, marked the end of an era. This event indelibly affected the developments in marketing foreshadowed in the early years of the century.

Wars have a way of catching the world up with realities, be they physical or psychological. Wars are harshly urgent. Decisions must be made quickly; new methods and materials are utilized without long periods of testing. The very urgency of war brings about change, and after a war people do not go back to the way things were. They discard old ideas and methods, utilize the developments and advances brought into being by the exigencies of war, and go forward.

The period between World Wars I and II was one of dramatic change. Perhaps never in our history has the pendulum swung farther—from the lush, money-grows-on-trees period of the twenties to the bitter depths of the Depression in the thirties. Agonizing political changes, too, were a symbol of the period, as conservatism gave way to the New Deal, an ideological upheaval that has affected American ways even to the present day. In the selling profes-

Technological advances during and between the wars created more products to be sold.

sion profound changes kept pace with technology, the growth of the economy, the ever shrinking size of the world, and the developing patterns of urban living. The world—and salesmanship—were not to be the same again.

THE UNSEEN SALESMAN

It was Christmas Eve of 1906. Several vessels plying the Atlantic off the coast of the United States had been equipped with a newfangled apparatus called a wireless. On these vessels, in wireless rooms behind the bridge, operators wearing headsets were sitting at their instruments. Here and there on land, amateurs were tinkering with their homemade receivers, listening in, as usual, on any messages that might be traveling across space in the familiar dot-dash of Morse code.

Most of them, picking up the reiterated "CQCQ" that prefaced a message, eagerly awaited the buzzing of coded text. What followed this night could have afflicted one with a sense of hallucination. Faintly, through the earphones, there came the sound of a man's voice speaking. Presently, the music of a phonograph record followed. Then someone played a violin, and a voice was raised in song.

The wireless operators listening in on these ships at sea shouted for others to come and listen. Headsets were quickly passed from one person to another. The unnatural experience was not a hallucination after all. To the mystified listeners it took on the quality of a miracle, for nothing like it had ever been heard before. As far down the coast as Norfolk, Virginia, operators who heard that first radio broadcast began reporting its reception to the new wireless station at Brant Rock, eleven miles from Plymouth, Massachusetts.

In the lonely little Brant Rock station that Christ-

mas Eve, a few scientists, invited to attend the demonstration of wireless telephony, had joined the staff. Everyone had been eager and hopeful, but failure would have surprised none of them except the inventor himself, Professor Reginald Aubrey Fessenden.

So swift was the progress of science during the first half of the twentieth century that Americans reading about Fessenden's experiment almost sixty years later have difficulty understanding why it was invested with the quality of magic. Yet in 1906 wireless telegraphy, only a decade old, was the latest of marvels. Wireless telephony as a means of communication was held to be a dubious possibility.

The notion of sending music and song out into space hour after hour and day after day to entertain listeners had occurred to no one. It had not occurred even to Fessenden, who regarded his Christmas Eve demonstration partly as a scientific adventure and partly as a means of securing commercial publicity.

At about the time of Professor Fessenden's experiment, a fifteen-year-old named David Sarnoff was hired by the Marconi Wireless Telegraph Company of America as an office boy at a salary of $5.50 a week. He studied persistently to qualify himself for an operator's job, and in 1908 he was sent to the company's station in Nantucket.

As early as 1901 Marconi had established a sta-

Wireless telephony in its infancy. At left, the operator aboard a naval vessel places a call. At right is Reginald Fessenden, seated before his transmitting apparatus.

tion on the dunes of Cape Cod, near South Wellfleet. That station was blown down in the winter's blustery storms, but it was rebuilt. Then other stations were set up to the north, in Newfoundland, to attempt transmittal to the receiving station in Poldu, England. Those early years were full of trial and error, but faith in the certainty that messages could get through the air and that the venture would be a commercial success kept the trials alive. Marconi

was right. His efforts, bolstered by those of David Sarnoff, resulted in success.

By 1916 Sarnoff was assistant traffic manager of the Marconi Company. In that year he proposed the following innovation, which must have seemed fantastic at that time:

"I have in mind a plan of development which would make radio a household utility in the same sense as a piano or phonograph. The idea is to bring music into the house by wireless. . . . For example, a radio telephone transmitter, having a range of say twenty-five to fifty miles can be installed at a fixed point where instrumental or vocal music or both are produced. The receiver can be designed in the form

235

of a simple radio music box and arranged for several different wave lengths, which could be changeable with the throwing of a single switch or pressing of a single button."

Painstakingly, and in detail, the twenty-five-year-old visionary described his project and concluded:

"This proposition would be especially interesting to farmers and others living in outlying districts removed from cities. By the purchase of a 'radio music box' they could enjoy concerts, lectures, music, re-citals and so forth, which may be going on in the nearest city within their radius."

Sarnoff, in this memorandum, was the first to suggest a means of making wireless telephony a profitable service to the nation. This "proposition" was actually a major prophecy, and it added one vital new element—the "radio music box." Sarnoff understood, as no one else did at the time, that as long as listening was confined to individuals with headsets, the radio audience would be limited, and

David Sarnoff, wireless operator at Siasconset Wireless Station on Nantucket Island, Massachusetts, in 1908.

236

largely to adventuresome youthful fans. Not until listening could be made a group pastime would radio emerge from infancy. Only then could radio become a medium of mass communication, a social agency of incredible power, and a great independent industry.

It was not until 1920 that the first primitive radio station, with the call letters KDKA, was licensed by the Department of Commerce. The guiding spirit behind this was H. P. Davis, a vice-president of

David Sarnoff in 1912 at the Wanamaker Radio Station in New York City, still wearing the headset for individual listening which he believed could be replaced with a "music box" placed on a table, fitted with amplifying tubes and a loudspeaker, thus enabling a whole family to enjoy a broadcast program.

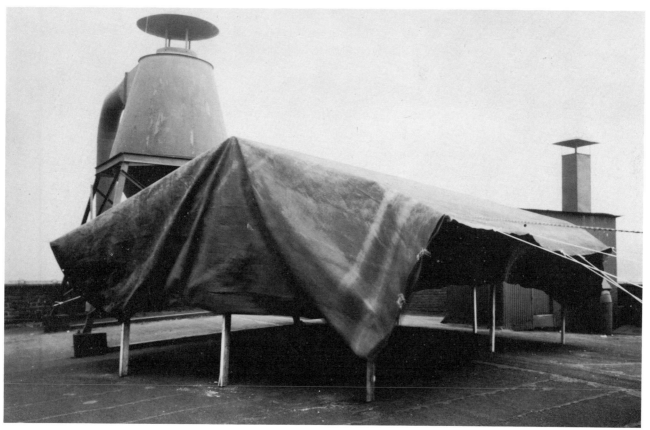

For the first six months of its existence, KDKA was a radio station without a studio. Most programs were originated either as phonograph records or from remote places. However, as the demand for live entertainment grew, this tent was pitched atop a roof at the Westinghouse East Pittsburgh Plant. The tent studio, until it blew down in the fall of 1921, served as an acoustical proving ground.

238

Studio broadcasting in the early thirties.

Westinghouse. Like Sarnoff four years earlier, Davis realized that radio could be a medium of instantaneous mass communication. Station broadcasting was inaugurated with the returns of the presidential election in which Senator Warren G. Harding and James M. Cox were the candidates.

Eighteen months after the first program from KDKA, two hundred and twenty stations were on the air in the United States and a new craze was

Frank E. Mullen, shown above left making an early KDKA broadcast, "The Farmers' Pioneer," was a young Sioux City, Iowa, farm editor when he was brought East in 1921. E. S. Bayard, Pennsylvania editor of the National Stockman and Farmer, *summoned him to take over the pioneering farm program.*

The returns of the Harding-Cox presidential election were broadcast by KDKA Radio on November 2, 1920. This, radio's most famous broadcast, marked the beginning of commercial radio broadcasting.

sweeping the country. "The rate of increase in the number of people who spend at least a part of their evening in listening in is almost incomprehensible," declared an editorial in the first issue of *Radio Broadcast*, in May 1922. "To those who have recently tried to purchase receiving equipment, some idea of this increase had undoubtedly occurred, as they stood perhaps in the fourth or fifth row at the radio center waiting their turn, only to be told when they finally reached the counter that they might place an order and it would be filled when possible. The movement is probably not even yet at its height. It is still growing in some kind of geometrical progression." Speculating about the future, *Radio Broadcast* surmised that "before the market for receiving apparatus becomes approximately saturated, there will be at least five million receiving sets in this country." And in the next issue the magazine's reporter on the Pacific coast described what

239

Listening in.

had happened there: "The average man on the street had never more than vaguely heard of radio until two months ago. . . . All of a sudden it hit us. The first most of us saw of it . . . was in first-page, first-column headlines from New York . . . proclaiming that the East had gone mad over radio. Within twelve hours, the interest swept the coast."

The injection of advertising into radio broadcasting took place in the summer of 1922. The first commercially sponsored radio program went on the air at five-fifteen on the afternoon of August 28 of that year. Probably no one connected with that broadcast realized it presaged a day when Americans, tuning in their radio sets, would find that every passing hour, as it struck, was the private property of a manufacturer of watches; that a half-hour program of music would be interrupted four times by eulogies of a brand of tobacco; or that the hucksters would be sovereign over the dimensions of time and space. Yet all these things were prefigured by the first commercial radio program, a ten-minute adver-

tising talk extolling Hawthorne Hall, a recently completed cooperative apartment house in Jackson Heights, across the East River from Manhattan Island.

By 1926 the era of network broadcasting had arrived; with the opening of this era, domination of the air waves by advertisers became inevitable. Broadcasters could now offer a larger audience than any other established medium of communication. There were already five million sets in use. Quite naturally, advertisers hurried to get on the air, gain good will through entertainment, and thereby increase their sales. They associated their trademarks as closely as possible with the names of popular performers, orchestras, newscasters, and commentators. Network broadcasting made radio the most powerful and pervasive of all advertising media.

Even though it might seem that broadcasting would have put the salesman out of business, it really only altered his function. Actually, broadcasting was a sales aid, performing a large part of the task of product identification. It created the desire for a product in advance of the salesman's pitch. And because of the enormous size of the audience it reached, it facilitated mass marketing. More salesmen were needed to open up the markets first tapped by radio. And a new kind of salesman was born, too—the announcer who delivered the radio commercials, a close relative of the old-time pitchman.

WHAT WILL THEY BUY?

While radio advertising was in its infancy, newspaper and magazine advertising continued to improve in sophistication and appeal. As an aid to salesmen it was excellent, but it could be made better still. From such scattered dissatisfaction "market studies" developed. It was Stanley Latshaw, advertising representative in Boston for the Curtis Publishing Company, who realized that neither space salesmen nor their customers knew much about markets, about the wants and habits of customers and dealers. Space salesmen talked about their publications, but they had no proof that advertising in a particular medium would help marketing a particular product. Latshaw realized that such information ought to be available to advertising salesmen and their customers. After selling the idea to Curtis, he hired Charles Coolidge Parlin, a schoolmaster from a small city in Wisconsin, and turned him loose with a roving commission to see what could be learned.

When in 1911 Parlin began to gather information useful to advertisers, the Bureau of the Census was collecting facts, but businessmen were unskilled in interpreting them. Parlin called his operation "commercial research." His first study was of the agricultural-implement industry. It was based on information taken from manufacturers' catalogues and from talks with manufacturers, wholesalers, and retailers. It resulted in a four-hundred-sixty page report—the first market-research study. Although questionnaire surveys had probably been used as early as 1824 by some newspapers, and in 1879 N. W. Ayres and Company had surveyed grain production by states for a client, Parlin's work was the first that developed into a continuing and organized research operation.

In 1912 Parlin visited all cities with a population over fifty thousand to document the volume of business done in department stores, wholesale dry-goods establishments, and principal merchant-tailoring

At this dinner to honor Parlin, he is seated between Stanley Latshaw and Dr. Joseph Willits of the University of Pennsylvania.

operations. The result, published that year, was a four-volume study, *Department Store Lines.*

The studies made by Parlin not only led to increased advertising in the *Saturday Evening Post,* but made commercial fact-finding a profession. Since Parlin's time, market research has become increasingly elaborate and the salesman depends more and more upon his company to furnish complete marketing information about its products. Motivational research, which investigates the "why" of a customer's decision to buy or not to buy, is an important outgrowth of market research.

ON THE EVE OF ANOTHER WAR

Although the Wright brothers had flown as early as 1903 which was the same year in which the Ford Motor Company got its start, the airplane took much longer than the automobile to get going. The U. S. Army became interested in the airplane around 1908, but neither the military strategist nor the tactician seemed to know what the plane might be used for in wartime. In 1917 automobile men, notably Howard Coffin of Hudson, John N. Willys, Henry Ford, and Henry Leland, made Liberty engines for aircraft, but American planes were not manufactured in time to affect the battle lines in France.

There were, however, exhilarating flying experiences in World War I, and young men came back from them unable to settle down to anything less exciting. In 1923, just a year after his belated graduation from Yale, Juan Terry Trippe quit his job as a bond salesman and with a friend, John Hambleton, bid a total of forty-five hundred dollars for nine Navy flying boats that were about to be junked. Trading off some of these planes for better models, Trippe and Hambleton tried running a plane taxi service around New York, only to find themselves going broke. In 1925, however, the Kelly Air Mail Act authorized the Post Office Department to sign contracts with private companies for carrying mail at rates running up to three dollars a pound, which made commercial flying a real possibility. Helped by Cornelius Vanderbilt Whitney and William H. Vanderbilt, Trippe and Hambleton scraped up enough cash to start Eastern Air Transport. This company joined forces with Colonial Airways to become Colonial Air Transport, which began to carry mail from New York to Boston. At about the same time Charles Lindbergh, then an Army reserve flyer, started to carry mail for the Robertson Aircraft Corporation on the St. Louis-to-Chicago run.

Between them, as it turned out, Trippe and Lindbergh did more than any two other individuals to set the United States on the road to developing air transport. In 1927 Trippe sewed up an exclusive landing permit from President Machado of Cuba which gave him control of the Caribbean region and so made Pan American Airways a possibility. And in that year Lindbergh made his historic flight across the Atlantic, sparking increased interest in the in-

Pan Am's first aircraft, a Fokker F-7, loading mailbags.

Juan Trippe with Mrs. Trippe (at right) ready for departure from San Juan to Paramaibo after a business visit with Postmaster del Valle. On this inaugural flight in September 1929 Colonel and Mrs. Charles Lindbergh (center) accompanied the Trippes.

243

On the sign in the image:

"GRAF ZEPPELIN"
RECEIVING DEP'T. FOR FREIGHT
HAMBURG·AMERICAN LINE
General Agents

This Record Air Shipment ——ded By

Domestic and Foreign
International Freight T—
VIA AIR, RAI—
Customs Bro—
JOHN H. F—
Phila—
New York
Pittsburgh

U.S.N.
2026

fant industry on Wall Street. There followed the formation of domestic carriers such as United Air Lines and Eastern (originally called Pitcairn after its founder). Meanwhile, Trans World Airlines developed as a midcontinent carrier, and Cyrus Rowlett ("C. R.") Smith began to build American Airlines into a transcontinental company. Other big domestic airlines came into being in the thirties, and scores of small lines were consolidated with them.

Trippe's Pan American Airways had air travel beyond the continental limits of the states much to itself at the start. Trippe was ever the salesman and practiced his art on the government, on shippers, on the general public, and on anyone else who needed to be shown that air travel was here to stay. Running his own private diplomatic service, Trippe negotiated flight-landing agreements with strategic countries on both the west and east coasts of South America. When mollifying arrangements were necessary, he did not flinch, but made the necessary

Air freight shipments, commonplace today, were a matter of wonder as recently as 1929, when the first aerially transported exhibition crossed the Atlantic on the Graf Zeppelin. The Philadelphia Business Progress Association assembled fifteen hundred pounds (the largest cargo ever carried by the airship) of Philadelphia-made goods, ranging from a lawnmower to pen points, bound for display in Berlin's largest retail store.

deals—with local airlines (often run by Germans) and with the Grace steamship interests, among others. But always he pushed the claims of Pan American Airways as a "chosen instrument," able to deliver services that lesser airlines could not guarantee. With a shrewd sense of public relations, he employed Lindbergh to pioneer some of his first Caribbean routes. Despite some stockholder reluctance, he pushed Pan American across the Pacific in the mid-thirties, establishing airports on lonely islands. They turned out to be of inestimable military value when war came in 1941.

244

THE SALESMAN'S LIFE BECOMES MORE COMPLEX

Salesmen traditionally received their compensation in terms of commissions—unless, of course, they owned their own businesses and thus earned the profits of their sales. Then gradually selling became less the realm of the entrepreneur and more another function of the corporation. This in turn seriously affected the salesmen. In many cases, compensation changed from commission to a salary plus incentive or bonus or commission. Sales training became an important factor, and many salesmen found themselves taking courses in salesmanship and reading literature on the psychology of selling. Many companies hired sales-training specialists or retained such outside counsel as the Psychological Corporation to train and guide their salesmen. The "born salesman" no longer existed; a man with an aptitude for selling was forced to become a "trained salesman" to enter the profession.

The growth of the technical industries, such as chemicals, brought about many changes for salesmen in the thirties. These industries required men who had degrees in the sciences, for manufacturing, research and development, and many administrative positions. Because of the technical nature of the products, salesmen, too, had to possess much more than a superficial knowledge. Consequently, there came about the rise of the "technical service representative," often a man with a degree in one of the scientific fields. These men actually sold, but they were equally concerned with helping customers to use products, with providing technical service and, often enough, with creating new products for them.

The distribution channels of domestic trade were influenced in the thirties by an enormous mass of regulatory legislation by federal, state, and municipal governments. Most of this was restrictive in character and tended to create a static condition. Indeed, this legislation promised to prolong the business life of a vast army of little storekeepers, whose annual sales volume was so small that it could not yield a living wage on the small margin of profit that was adequate for the large-scale retailers. The Census of Distribution of 1935 showed a total of 1,654,948 retail stores, of which 1,284,771 had an annual sales volume of less than twenty thousand dollars each; 686,347, or 41 per cent, had less than five thousand dollars each. Some states went so far as to pass laws deliberately aimed at taxing the chain stores out of existence, and thus, in effect, at subsidizing the local merchants, even if higher prices to consumers resulted.

Such federal legislation as the Robinson-Patman Act sought to promote fairer competition and, particularly, to abolish the unfair buying advantages that large-scale retailers might enjoy through preferential discounts, advertising allowances, and similar devices.

The use by large-scale retailers of well-known brands as "loss leaders" or "bargain-bait" was a competitive weapon that was most objectionable to small retailers and harmful to many manufacturers as well. Many states passed laws designed to curb the practice. Some of these laws prescribed minimum margins above cost for all sales, but such inelastic price fixing was not regarded with general favor. A more popular method, which by 1938 had been adopted by forty-three states, was by a fair-trade law, which made it legal for manufacturers and wholesalers to determine the minimum resale prices for their brands. A federal act made such contracts legal in interstate commerce.

Some legislative control of the market place was long overdue and certainly helped to stabilize the hit-or-miss methods of pricing which John Wanamaker had repudiated years before in his one-man effort at fair trade. Many others had followed his lead as a successful merchandiser, but it had been a matter of individual decision for far too long.

In spite of the Depression, however, the decade of the thirties was productive because of technology. Waterproof cellophane revolutionized packaging; Freon refrigerant, a chemical product, improved safe food-keeping; nylon, which became available just before World War II, unalterably affected the women's wear industry; plastics of all kinds were introduced by several manufacturers; agricultural chemicals stimulated increasingly abundant harvests; and many, many other products opened a whole new dazzling world. What an opportunity all these new goods offered to the salesman! However, the great war, soon to come, would remove that opportunity, at least temporarily.

245

America on the Move

With World War II technology moved into high gear. After the war a mobile, explosive population and widespread prosperity influenced the selling profession in countless ways.

NO EVENT OF OUR TIMES has influenced the buying habits of the American people with a magnitude equal to the effect of World War II. With the conversion of industry to the production of war goods Americans had to forego purchasing many consumer products. The automobile, that mainstay of our production-oriented economy for so long, was no longer traded in every year or two but remained with a family "for the duration," along with refrigerators, stoves, and other home appliances. At the same time, millions of American families found themselves suddenly prosperous. Unemployment had virtually disappeared with the war boom. Wages rose rapidly. Wives and other family members who in earlier years did not work were urged to do so to ease the manpower shortage. Overtime fattened millions of pay envelopes and savings accounts.

As a result, when the war ended, the appetite of Americans for goods of all sorts was nearly insatiable, their financial ability to buy practically limitless. Sellers found themselves in paradise. Almost

Today's account executive—or traveling salesman—arrives fresh for the day's work after a quick and easy flight from point to point. The strain now is seldom in traveling; it is in the number of people to see and how to handle situations on arrival.

anything sold. Waiting lists for new automobiles grew and grew. The public rushed to appliance stores, to war surplus outlets, and to the food stores, where, for the first time in years, their purchases were not limited by the number of red and blue stamps in their possession. Furniture, rugs, bric-a-brac, air and sea travel, garden tools, boats, clothing —there were buyers clamoring for them all. The same was true of industry. Steel, chlorine, caustic soda, building materials, plastics, wire, industrial fabrics, electronic supplies, machine tools—all were in too-short supply to fill the maws of industries suddenly reconverted to the production of peacetime consumer goods.

Hundreds of thousands of salesmen, many returning from the war, many having turned to other pursuits during the war years, took up the practice of their profession again—moving merchandise, ideas, and services through salesmanship. It was easy—too easy, in many cases. The challenge had been removed and the order-taker and the allotter were with us. Who does not recall stories of under-the-counter bonuses to assure delivery of a car, and the number of "extras" that had to be paid for when the vehicle finally arrived?

This prosperous situation was predicted by Paul Hoffman in the midst of the war years. His successful sales career for Studebaker automobiles began in Los Angeles at the age of twenty. Eighteen years later he was called to the home office in South Bend, Indiana, to take the vice-presidency and later the presidency of the firm. During World War II he asked a number of business leaders to join him in setting up a Committee for Economic Development to study the postwar needs of the country and the problem of rapidly converting production from armaments to civilian goods. Due to his energy and

persuasion, thousands of volunteers worked for C.E.D. on economic problems. They studied plant conversion, the growing backlog of civilian needs, and all other aspects of keeping the bottom from dropping out of our industrial economy.

Before the war ended, C.E.D. had prepared accurate forecasts of the millions of new automobiles, washing machines, refrigerators, houses, and hundreds of other items that would be wanted when peace came. Here was a pent-up demand for goods that astonished skeptics. It would take years, working at full capacity, to fill this need! Gradually, optimism began to replace pessimism. Industrialists began to plan for postwar peacetime production.

It is no exaggeration to say that Paul Hoffman, almost single-handedly, sold the nation a confidence and belief in its future. It was one of the greatest feats of salesmanship in our history. If Paul Hoffman had not acted when and as he did, the mental attitude could very easily have brought about a depression. As it was, Paul Hoffman and his C.E.D., working in hundreds of communities, changed this attitude to one of faith and hope. In short, he sold America a boom, instead of a bust.

WHY DO THEY BUY?

Along with the postwar seller's market came new problems. The average income of the American family had risen to such a point that there was now a great deal of so-called "discretionary income." Many Americans no longer had to spend the greatest portion of their annual wages on the necessities of life; food, housing, and clothing took up a smaller proportion of total income than ever before. The man in the street was in a position either to save his excess income or to spend it as he wished.

What did this mean for the marketers of the postwar period? Unless some way could be found to determine what people wanted, the marketers could eventually find themselves oversupplied with a mountain of unsalable goods. Discovering what people wanted—and why they bought—became urgent, particularly when the first postwar buying sprees were over and salesmen once more had to work to make a sale.

Motivational research—the name given to the technique of finding out why people buy—came into extensive use in the late 1940s. Essentially, it consists in delving into the psychology of people's purchasing patterns—the effects that color, packaging, smell, labeling, and a variety of other factors have on the consumer. Many merchandising firms learned that the findings of motivational research were informative and encouraging. A considerable number of consultants and consulting firms today devote much or all of their time to motivational research.

Why, for example, do people buy automobile insurance? The State Farm Mutual Automobile Insurance Company wanted to know this—as well as what qualities people look for in an insurance company. In large-scale consumer surveys and special "in depth" studies conducted by trained psychologists, the company learned some interesting things:

an insurance company may be resented unconsciously, yet at the same time be welcomed as a protector of individual welfare; even though people are generally happy not to have had an accident, they are inclined to resent having paid for a policy against which they have had no opportunity to collect; and policyholders are intensely interested in prompt, considerate service from a company agent after an accident.

Although the salesman is seldom involved directly in motivational research, he benefits from the results. If a product can be made completely acceptable to the consumer *before* it is offered for sale, the salesman's job obviously will be easier.

A study conducted for the Chicago *Tribune* on motives in automobile purchasing resulted in specific recommendations that changed automobile advertising. Found to be important were the purchaser's social situation and aspirations, and the specific "personality" attributes of an automobile which a purchaser can identify with himself.

A prune growers' association suffering a continuing decline in sales decided to find out what consumer's thought about prunes. In detailed interviews it was learned that they thought prunes dry, wrinkled, ugly, and of no particular food value except as a laxative. As a result of this survey, most prunes now are cooked and distributed in cans or jars labeled "prune plums." Resultant improved sales meant happier customers and a happier industry.

In his own way the salesman has always been

After the war thousands of families moved from the cities to rural areas, which were quickly transformed into thriving communities. The tranquil farmland at left quickly became Levittown, Long Island, right.

involved in motivational research. When the traveling peddler of yore arose at dawn and began brewing his coffee over an open fire, he must have thought about the people he was going to see that day. He could call upon previous experiences with the same people or with people in similar circumstances. He knew that showing his products in the proper sequence, interspersing luxuries with necessities, strongly influenced his sales success. And when, earlier in the year, back at his home base, he had selected his merchandise, he had done so on the basis of his "field" observations—which were not unlike modern "studies in depth." Actually, the good salesman of today must not only be able to use the findings of the professional researchers, but, like the peddler of long ago, he must have an inner feeling for people's desires and the know-how to stimulate them.

SUBURBIA AND THE SHOPPING CENTER

The population boom the United States experienced after World War II was almost literally an explosion. People had moved from the farms to the cities for many decades. Now, suddenly, there was no more room in the cities, and the move to the suburbs, which had begun around the turn of the century, was a force to be reckoned with.

The suburbanite male of the early 1900s was apt to be a member of the upper middle class who commuted to work in New York or Boston or Philadelphia every week day. Thanks to the development of the passenger car, the motor bus, and rapid transit systems, suburbia's population increased 60 per cent during the 1920s. The Depression years of the thirties somewhat slowed this movement, but after World War II millions of families that had been poor were now in the middle class. Transportation facilities were improving; urban housing and land supply were falling badly behind demand and the population was growing ever larger.

Thus a huge new boom in house-building began outside the city limits, where plenty of cheap land was available. Along with the thousands of new suburban homes came the need for more and better stores, more conveniently located than the downtown department store but offering equal-quality merchandise.

Actually, the idea of the shopping center is not new. Probably the first was the Roland Park Shop center established in 1907 in a Baltimore neighborhood about five miles north of the downtown area. Until 1923, however, there was no such thing as an integrated suburban shopping center. In that year

J. S. Nichols Company built Country Club Plaza on forty acres five miles south of Kansas City. It consisted initially of small, locally owned stores catering to automobile traffic and was located away from a mass-transportation terminal point.

Later came the move to the suburbs of downtown department stores, through branches such as Marshall Field's store in Lake Forest, Evanston, and Oak Park, Illinois, in the late twenties; Arnold Constable in New Rochelle, New York, in 1937; and Lord and Taylor in Manhasset, Long Island, in 1941. After the war the massive, integrated shopping centers we know today began to develop. In 1950 Allied Stores built a huge center in Northgate, Seattle, Washington.

One after another, shopping centers appeared in every section of the country. They became ever larger, from Shoppers' World near Boston in 1951 with 500,000 square feet of retailing space to gigantic enterprises such as the 1,480,000-square-foot development which includes the original Garden State Plaza in Paramus, New Jersey.

The nucleus of a shopping center is usually the supermarket.

Customers of the 1950s were attracted to the new Grand Unions, not only by their newness but also by the novel Food-O-Mat. This now familiar, gravity-fed dispensing unit was the invention of Grand Union's sixth president, Lansing P. Shields. It was designed to offer greater shopping convenience to customers and save floor space as the introduction of "convenience foods" increased overwhelmingly the number of items a food store was expected to handle.

The move to suburbia: where excess population flowed, the chain store followed (unless it had foresightedly bought a tract of land in a lonesome spot anticipating the onrush of housing developments after World War II). Grand Union, believing that the function of the supermarket is to provide the housewife with all the necessities for her table, her home, and her family, ventured further into the field of non-food merchandising than any of its competitors. Clothing, appliances, and goods of all sorts are available in many of the stores; all have the variety shown above.

One of the accepted axioms of selling is that when demand is created for a type of marketing institution, one will arise to satisfy that demand. The discount store was just such a response.

Fair-trade prices established by manufacturers during the 1930s to protect retailers against competition gradually became higher than economical shopping could bear. This, in turn, made it desirable for operators to open stores that would sell merchandise at prices well below established retail prices.

Even before World War II, discount houses existed in a few high-markup lines, such as jewelry and small appliances. Postwar discounting, though, has been vastly different—for several reasons. First, fair-trade prices have been widely publicized. Second, retail outlets such as department stores have ample stocks, making it possible for customers to inspect various makes of a particular product before going on to the discount house for the actual purchase. Third, the scarcity of merchandise in the early postwar years and the subsequent easy sell made many merchants apathetic about customers' needs. Finally, the customer gradually became better educated, more independent, and more determined to get his money's worth.

The first discount houses were much like the supermarkets of the early thirties. They operated in barnlike quarters on a low overhead and offered few services. The customer had to pay cash, but he reaped discounts of from 20 to 35 per cent of fair-trade or list prices.

At first the established department stores and other retailers contemptuously referred to the discounters as "parasites," "bootleg dealers," and "fly-by-nights." The demand for enforcement of the fair-trade laws and for laws to prohibit discount houses and discount operations was widespread.

Department stores and other established retailers then began to meet the discounters on their own pricing terms, in addition to offering services. And by this time the discounters were beginning to add services to meet the competition. By the middle of the 1950s it seemed that the discount store might only remain on the retail scene in large cities on a marginal operation with sales limited to the appliance business. However, it turned out differently.

A SUDDEN SURGE AHEAD

Dr. Malcolm McNair, for some time a distinguished educator in business administration and marketing at Harvard University, named his choice of the six greatest merchants in the United States history. They were F. W. Woolworth, J. C. Penny, John Wanamaker, Brigadier General Robert Wood of Sears, Roebuck, Michael Cullen, who opened the first food supermarket, and Eugene Ferkauf, the head of Korvette. The last of McNair's choices, Ferkauf, realized that the same bases of discount operations in selling appliances—low margin, minimum service, and high turnover—could be used to sell other kinds of merchandise. In 1954 Korvette opened its doors in the suburb of Westbury, Long Island. Since then, discount department stores have appeared in the suburbs of almost every large metropolitan area. Names range from Two Guys from Harrison to such substantial, old-line firms as F. W. Woolworth, Food Fair, Grand Union, and Allied Stores.

Eugene Ferkauf

The typical discount house today is still a large, barnlike, one-story building with plenty of parking space. Customers serve themselves, often loading goods into wire carts in an atmosphere much like that of a family fair and not much different from that of the general store of a century ago.

Ferkauf, a good salesman, discovered that discount stores appealed to suburbanites. Many suburban wives are busy with civic as well as family activities. Some hold full-time or part-time jobs. One of the greatest advantages of the discount store for these wives is that it offers the accessibility of the neighborhood store along with the range of merchandise available in a large shopping center, in which discount stores are usually located. In addition, many of these stores are open at night and frequently on Sunday as well.

The various discount stores came into being in a variety of ways. One factor they seem to have in common is that of being the brain child of a smart, aggressive salesman. An example is Ann and Hope, the first important soft-goods supermarket in New England, opened in 1954 almost by chance. Ann and Hope, in Lonsdale, Rhode Island (in the Providence metropolitan area), now does an annual business of over twelve million dollars in 120,000 square feet of selling space in an old mill building. Operating costs average less than 18 per cent, including pilferage losses. The retail margin runs from 20 to 23 per cent.

The founder, Martin Chase, had had some years of experience in the men's clothing business, including the operation of a small roadside "pipe-rack" clothing store. Later, he had operated a ribbon manufactory in an old mill in a comparatively isolated, hard-to-find area, just before he decided to liquidate and retire.

He opened a corner of the building for selling his left-over ribbon at low retail with no intention of undertaking an extended operation. However, the fantastically fast turnover that resulted induced him to stay in business. Other retailers, noticing the amazing customer traffic and sales volume, decided to get on the bandwagon with Chase. Those whose merchandise he accepted shared in his sales success.

Since Chase was a comparative novice in the de-

Connecticut's hat factories were once clustered around Danbury. Today the Factory Store sells everything from surplus hats to European imports.

partment-store business, many of his merchandising decisions were made by the salesmen of the manufacturers whose goods Chase accepted to sell in the old mill. Chase felt that the success of his store would be enhanced if competent people established similar businesses, helping to accustom the public to discount operations. Those experienced in conventional retail methods for low-priced soft goods were invited to investigate Chase's soft-goods merchandising venture and several of them later opened similar operations in other parts of New England.

253

What are the other retailers doing today to meet the threat of the discount houses? The variety chains have been hit harder by the discount store and by suburbanization than any other kind of retail outlet. To reverse the trend, a number of these chains have been trying to remake their "five and dimes" into junior department stores. J. J. Newberry recently opened a large store in Florida which carries a complete line of department-store merchandise. Other chains are opening their own discount houses.

Department stores are beginning to operate self-service and discount departments and high-fashion departments under the same roof. And supermarkets are moving into other enterprises besides the selling of food. Food Fair, for instance, is putting gas stations and auto-accessory stores in its shopping centers. Grand Union is opening huge discount stores containing a supermarket and a full-line general-merchandise operation under one roof.

Stores everywhere are getting larger, and the lines of demarcation between kinds of stores are becoming blurred. Supermarkets are handling general merchandise; mail-order firms are operating discount houses; and conventional department stores and apparel and variety chains are turning into junior and full-fledged department stores.

THE COIN-OPERATED ERA

Vending machines are not new. The first was invented about two thousand years ago in Alexandria by a Greek named Hero. A coin dropped into the machine tipped a balance bar, which opened a valve through which spouted holy water. The same principal is used today.

Hero's invention seems to have been essentially

Nathaniel Leverone, founder-chairman, and Patrick L. O'Malley, president, of Automatic Canteen Company of America, inspect the world's largest vending machine, the new "Dial-A-Sale" automatic vendor being manufactured in the company's plant in Frankfurt, West Germany. Purchases are delivered to a door by a unique "traveling compartment" elevator after the shopper has deposited the correct change and dialed a selection number. This particular model offers sixty-eight different selections from a stock of six hundred and forty-eight items.

forgotten until the late 1800s when a weighing machine was invented in Germany. Shortly after that, decorative vending machines sold colored balls of gum, supposedly health-giving charges of electricity, collar buttons, cigarettes, and cigar trimmers.

World War II brought to the vending-machine business its major impetus. Mobilization put many industries on a twenty-four-hour work schedule, creating a need for out-of-hours service. Machines dispensing cigarettes, candy bars, and soft drinks began appearing in factories throughout the land. Later, vending machines dispensed milk, fruit, books, ice cream, trip-insurance policies, hot sandwiches, women's hosiery, flowers, magazines, and hot coffee.

The story of one vending-machine company is intriguing. A friendly young man named Edward M. Sahagian is president of Consumers Automatic Vending, Inc., which operates about two thousand food-vending machines in South Carolina and in the New York area, where it furnishes over five thousand meals a day to employees in plants on Long Island. After being discharged from the Army Air Corps in 1946, Sahagian became a buyer for a British textile combine. He was sitting in his office one day when a life-insurance salesman named Philip Koff, whom Sahagian had turned down a week earlier, came back to try again. Koff was quite a salesman. He sold Sahagian a twenty-five-thousand-dollar twenty-year-payment policy. A few months later, Koff sold Sahagian on going into the vending-machine business.

They started by placing coffee-vending machines in subways, schools, and offices. The common arrangement was that they paid for the right to install the machine and took all the profits from it, if any. In their first six months they lost thirty thousand dollars.

Instead of folding up the operation, they decided to raise the stakes. Sahagian borrowed one hundred thousand dollars from his brother-in-law, and together with Koff incorporated as Coffee Vending Service, Inc. The corporation bought exclusive metropolitan New York rights to a machine that dispensed both hot coffee and cold drinks. Unfortunately, the machines were unreliable, and the partners had to re-engineer them one at a time as they

"The mechanical salesman" augments the personal service of the counter attendant at lunchtime. In-plant feeding is simpler and more efficient nowadays through the use of coin-ops. A dollar-bill changer, installed in many such places, makes a sale still easier.

The mechanics of an early coin-operated machine was illustrated in the Scientific American *magazine at the turn of the century.*

broke down. By the end of 1949 the corporation was in financial trouble.

Salvation came in the spring of 1950 when the company acquired the rights to another machine, which proved successful. In 1951 the partners added candy, cigarette-, and soda-dispensing machines. In 1955 they branched out, on a small scale, into a non-automatic in-plant feeding operation on a concession basis. In 1958 they added refrigerated equipment that automatically sold sandwiches, pastries, and desserts, and machines that sold hot platters.

Self-service—in discount stores, in supermarkets,

A future customer peers over the rim of the shopping cart set in the midst of a children's wonderland full of automatically dispensed delights.

and certainly at vending machines—which bypasses the salesman, who heretofore had had to persuade the customer to buy, has come to stay.

LOOK AT ME!

Attention to the appearance of a product and its container is as old as salesmanship. Early American peddlers learned that a colored flour sack or one bearing a design could effect a sale, as a simple country woman envisioned a new dress for daughter after the flour had been used. Many years ago the producers of Cream of Wheat initiated the packaging revolution when they used an illustrated box front for their cereal, an appealing innovation that brought greater sales. Today, the package has taken over many of the functions formerly performed by personal selling. As self-service and self-selection increased, the necessity for attracting the attention of the consumer demands that packaging and display use every trick of color and design. Motivation studies have shown that four out of ten purchases in supermarkets and three out of ten in drugstores are unplanned. In many cases it is an eye-catching pack-

age on display that creates a quick spark of desire resulting in a sale.

More and more efforts are being made to take the guesswork out of package design. A New York firm developed a small "black box" unit that is placed in supermarkets. Customers are asked to answer with a yes or no button such questions as "Which of the two packages on this shelf do you prefer?" Results are tabulated from several hundred locations and the producer can make a package-design decision on the basis of actual consumer preference. Another system compares the visual effect of a package in terms of retention of image and ability of the observer to remember what the copy said.

That stores handling prepackaged meats have a higher percentage of meat sales than stores that do not was discovered in a survey by DuPont. The consumer is attracted by the neatness and cleanliness of the package and by the transparent wrapping

257

Uneeda Biscuits were the first crackers to come out of the barrel and into boxes; Cream of Wheat the first package to draw customer attention with an illustrated box front. This ad ran in the old Literary Digest *in 1911.*

which protects the meat but permits the shopper to examine it unhurriedly.

Packaging is now accepted as a profession. The National Packaging Association is in its fifth decade of operation and has presented more than forty exhibitions of the packaging art at giant exposition halls. *Modern Packaging* magazine has been published for more than thirty years, and a considerable number of other publications have joined the field.

What of the salesman and the relatively new emphasis on packaging? Packaging has created new selling jobs. Someone has to sell design ideas, the effectiveness of packaging, the equipment used to make packages, the services of artists and design houses—even the devices used to measure the impact of packaging. None of the new approaches to selling has yet put the salesman out of business. The size and complexity of our present society have created more selling jobs than ever existed before.

THE IMPACT OF THE "IDIOT BOX"

What radio did to the practice of marketing in the 1920s, television far exceeded in the years immediately following World War II. Television com-

bines visual impressions with the spoken word. Prior to this phenomenon, these two conditions could be obtained only by using both radio and printed media. No other medium can present as much information about products as television, with its combination of sight, sound, and motion. And the message is delivered directly to the consumer in his home.

In the late 1940s small knots of people gathered in darkened living rooms across the nation, seated themselves on any available piece of furniture or on the floor, and intently watched a ten-inch square filled with flickering light. Few families had television sets in those days and there were not many programs worth watching, but Milton Berle had captured the fancy of almost everyone. There were a few sports programs—baseball and basketball, hockey, roller derbies, and the fights or wrestling nearly every night—sponsored primarily by cigarette, razor-blade, and beer advertisers. But Uncle Miltie was the first supersalesman of consumer products through the new medium of television.

The next decade brought a revolution in media

258

259

selection in the continuing battle to influence the consumer. In 1950 television accounted for only 6 per cent of the expenditure for national advertising; newspapers and magazines took in almost 60 per cent and radio approximately 20 per cent. A decade later, television accounted for 32 per cent of every dollar spent on national advertising. Magazines had slipped to second place with 22 per cent, and newspapers accounted for about the same amount. Radio had declined from 20 per cent in 1950 to only 7 per cent. That the one hundred top advertisers spent 51 per cent of their advertising dollars on television in 1960 points up the significance of this comparison.

Television greatly accelerated a most important marketing change. Today the manufacturer is the primary seller of his merchandise, reaching the consumer directly, a situation vastly different from that of the age when manufacturers relied on retailers to push their products just as consumers looked to the retailers for assurance of the value of a purchase.

In the modern marketplace the maker often sells the consumer before he enters a store. To a considerable extent the personal selling job has been taken away from the retailer, although he of course still exercises some influence—through control of shelf space and special promotions, for example. His primary function in many cases, however, is to stock and display merchandise that has been pre-sold to the customer. Constant consumer demand created by advertising has automatically become the great-

The soft sell on TV.

260

est pressure on a dealer to carry and display a particular product.

As with radio thirty-odd years ago, television has had a profound influence on the art of selling. It has created specialists in mass marketing, either through performances on television itself or in the marketing of television-advertised products to chain stores, discount houses, and individual outlets. It has in many cases changed the emphasis of retail selling from the taking of an aggressive initiative— necessary when the public knew few brand names —to tactfully guiding the consumer. Selling by television is salesmanship of a high order, and it has brought about the movement of more consumer goods than ever before in the nation's history.

MASS MARKETING AND THE COMPUTER

One of the most interesting developments in selling in the last decade has been the assistance that has come to the salesman from a complex and inanimate source—the man-made genius known as the computer, which seems to be almost a "controller" in our present way of life.

Today we are living in a "short order" economy, in which the problems of marketing are less and less those of production and more and more those of distribution. Since 1950, as the shortages of the immediate postwar period disappeared, getting and holding markets became more of a problem. With the buyer's market, the producer has to give delivery immediately, posing an additional challenge to industry. Thus has the computer come into its own, to help with the problem of keeping inventories as low as possible but consistent with "short order" delivery.

Actually, it seems that industry is facing an age-old sales problem which is merely more complex in our modern society. The old-time peddler, too, had to keep his inventory down to a minimum lest he burden either his back or that of his mule. And, too, he had to prejudge demand, for his service was that of providing delivery on the spot.

A pertinent example is the experience of General Foods, which, after World War II, was faced with such problems as giving the grocery trader faster, more reliable delivery and at lower cost. The company shipped most of its goods directly from its

The histrionics of the old-time traveling "medicine man" are matched by Milton Berle, here leading NBC's thirtieth anniversary program. Berle has pre-sold his television audience on scores of products since 1948, when he became the first major entertainer to head his own television show.

261

Revolutionizing today's record-keeping and making, the computer serves as a mechanical replacement for people. Above is the IBM 1404, designed to print either individual cards or continuous paper forms. Eight hundred one-line cards can be printed, two at a time, in one minute. One use: a salesman can pass by the machine in the morning, push a button, and pick up sufficient customer cards for a week's work, with all pertinent information at his fingertips.

plant to its customers—mainly supermarkets and chain stores—and frequently over long distances. The service was not very dependable.

To get physically closer to its customer, General Foods decided to build a network of central distribution centers to handle the company's products. These centers were to be so located that no customer would be farther away than three days' shipment by rail or overnight truck—a major undertaking because the company had many thousands of customers scattered all over the country. The best way of facilitating the function of these centers was to get customers on a regular, automated system of ordering so that there would be a steady flow of goods going to them. The plan has been a huge success. About half the goods shipped by General Foods today are ordered on such a routine basis that a salesman does not see the order for them until after the shipment has been made.

While overhauling its physical distribution, General Foods discovered that considerable changes had taken place in the salesman's job. These are not peculiar to General Foods or even to the food industry, but have been characteristic of every industry caught up in our "short order" economy.

The first change was a recognition on the part of General Foods that the end function of the manufacturer is not merely to place his products in his customer's warehouse. At General Foods the salesmen are customer-oriented. They must think about how best to push the product through to the hands of the ultimate consumer in the most efficient and most profitable manner.

Another major change is that automated ordering has freed the salesman from much of the drudgery and burden of making out orders and reports. Consequently, greater efficiency in the use of sales manpower has become possible.

262

One of the most gratifying developments of the postwar way of life is the revolution in bank salesmanship. The cool reserve of the bank teller of the mid-forties, the disdain with which an applicant for a loan was granted an interview—these are gone. Prosperity has brought about relaxed credit; more money in circulation has meant greatly increased banking activity. The consumer needs more banking services than ever before, more people to wait on

The friendly bank of today is a far cry from the forbidding fortress of years ago; bank officials make a real effort to sell their many services to new and old clients.

him and to advise him on his increasingly complex monetary situation. Suddenly after the war a small but hardy core of bank officials who had always believed that banking services were a commodity to be sold the same way as any other product found their counsel sought by their peers. A few banks led the way with advertising, public relations, sales-training, and branch-bank programs, and their almost instantaneous success in winning customer approval and new business made even the most dour old conservative take notice.

Today banks in the United States are courting the consumer as they never did before. No business has tried harder to revolutionize its public image. Once banks were aloof, forbidding, and austere; now they glow with warmth and friendliness as they try to sell the consumer a host of services. And a whole new corps of salesmen has been born. Bank officers have been given courses in salesmanship, shown how the services of the bank were not well known to customers, made aware that competition for deposits was fierce, and advised that they would benefit per-

sonally from increased business. In many cases they were told that they would be expected to make a specified number of sales calls each month and report on them. Some banks in suburban areas, where there is a constant influx of people, have worked out programs of personal calls on *all* newcomers.

The revolution in banking has worked wonders. Many of the men long involved in the business discovered they possessed real selling potential and responded to the new challenge not only with enthusiasm but with almost immediate results. Other bank men went on to become public-relations directors, sales-training supervisors, and new-business managers of their banks.

In the field of consumer credit, banks got off to a late start. The First National City Bank of New York was the first, in 1928, to make credit available to its depositors, and other banks rapidly followed.

The "Glass Bank" in New York is wide open and attractive, a visible symbol of the revolution that has occurred in banking.

Since the war, bank lending to consumers has more than quadrupled. Some banks now even have a charge-account plan by which, through the use of a bank credit card, a customer can charge a wide range of goods and services purchased at the various outlets that subscribe to the plan. One bank even sends out personal invitations at Christmastime to apply for a personal loan. And, of course, the competition for accounts has brought about the day when a new customer receives a premium when he opens an account.

WHAT OF THE SALESMAN TODAY?

We have reviewed some of the factors that so profoundly influenced our lives in the fifth and sixth decades of the twentieth century. By no means has this review been all-encompassing. There has been no other time in our country's relatively short history when the impetus of new developments has shattered old patterns so quickly or when the world of tomorrow has been so close to the world of today. It is a virtual impossibility to live today by patterns that sufficed for many decades. Business methods have changed so radically that it would be difficult —if not impossible—for a firm practicing methods even forty years old to survive. And as the times have changed, bringing with them changed business methods, so, too, have the salesmen's practices changed.

The influences on salesmanship have been manifold. The salesman of today has at his disposal communications methods not even dreamed of one hundred years ago. He is backed by advertising, sales-promotion and public-relations campaigns, and a veritable mass of other sales supports. He is trained to know his company's products, and those of the competitors in the industry he serves. He is taught the psychology and philosophy of sales. He attends conventions and other meetings where intensive courses in almost anything that bears on any phase of his business are open to him. His health is watched over by the company doctors, his outlook by the company psychiatrist, his security by a zealous personnel management that provides life and health insurance and a host of other benefits de-signed to relieve him of the stress and worries that have long beset mankind.

With all these modern accoutrements to the sales profession, what has happened to the sales drive that moved our pioneering ancestors? Has it been subdued by the regimentation and complexity of our way of life? Has the joy of selling, so much a driving force in our first salesman's outlook, been destroyed? Or is the spark still there, whether a man sells chemicals to soap companies, a line of canned goods to chain stores, or games and toys to variety stores?

Everything points to an affirmative answer to the last question. Just as the basic principles laid down in our Constitution have survived an almost unbelievable kaleidoscope of events, activities, and pressures, so the salesman retains characteristics that have always identified him.

Yet he has changed in many ways. The salesman today is no longer a "drummer" who merely pushes a product or lures into his employer's establishment a prospective customer visiting town. The new salesman is concerned with the whole distribution system, starting with determining his customer's needs and problems, helping with promotion and advertising, being "with it" right through to final delivery to the final consumer.

As technology advances and producers offer products that are increasingly complex, the salesman's sphere of activity grows. At General Electric, for instance, the salesman was once a specialist who sold only the line of a particular manufacturing department, even though the line went into a variety of markets. Now, instead of specializing in one product, the salesman is selling a whole group of products to a particular market, such as the air-conditioning industry.

Thus the man needed for this new kind of sales job has to be a generalist rather than a specialist. The technically trained salesman of a few years ago has been replaced by a man capable of absorbing stacks of information spewed out by the marketing department and applying it to his customers' problems. He sallies forth armed with a tremendous amount of data regarding his customers' needs, their products, their corporate organizations, and their supply and delivery schedules.

The new salesman has more executive ability

than his predecessor. A Boston sales manager describes the new salesman as a "businessman who travels."

The salesman of today has a tremendous advantage over his predecessors; he is armed with all sorts of technical and market-research assistance. A great many chores that used to take up his time —writing up orders and reports, checking the availability of goods and delivery schedules, for instance —have been largely eliminated for many salesmen.

An important factor in the development of the new salesman for industry is that he is likely to have fewer but larger customers than in the past. The industry salesman has become increasingly responsible for a larger portion of his customer's business. This creates the need for salesmen of sufficient stature to talk with the top management of his customer firms. It has also drawn top management of the seller more directly into the selling procedure. Personal selling is now company-wide, with contact with the customer taking place on many different levels.

When reading a book of this kind, which largely delves into the past, it is necessary to retain a sense of perspective. The strain, stress, and frustrating complexities of modern life encourage a tendency to look back on the past as the Good Old Days. A salesman today often cannot get through to a prospective buyer who is always "in conference" or is barricaded by a secretary instructed not to allow any salesmen into the Inner Sanctum. Understandably, he may envy the peddler of a century and a half ago who walked into a farm kitchen and interrupted nothing more important than the baking of an apple pie. So, too, may the salesman today, hounded as he is by an awareness that he has a dozen or more aggressive competitors, envy the man who sold the first work clothes or threshing machines or life-insurance policies. Those pioneers had the market to themselves, at least in theory. And the modern small merchant, bedeviled by the existence of chain stores, outlet stores, discount houses, direct-mail selling, minimum-wage laws, parking problems, and what not, undoubtedly sighs when he imagines how life must have been for the owner of a general store in a one-store village with no six-lane superhighway leading to a nearby shopping center. These are reflections induced partly by sentiment and nostalgia, partly by the harassments of the present age, partly by a psychological urge toward escape.

A popular misconception about the history of selling is that it records the deeds and successes only of great men—giants gifted with extraordinary talent and unduly rewarded by the gods of chance. Few, if any, of the men referred to in the preceding chapters of this book were endowed with genius or were lucky enough to stumble on a pot of gold with no effort on their part. They had brains, yes, and they used them. And they had talents, but these were mostly self-developed talents carved out of the knowledge acquired in the hard school of trial and error. Young Marshall Field had no evident talent for merchandising when he was apprenticed to a retail store in Pittsfield, Massachusetts. In fact, he had so little aptitude for merchandising that after he had worked in the store for a year, the owner recommended that Field consider taking up some other trade. R. H. Macy failed dismally several times before he got his company rolling in New York. Three out of the first five Woolworth stores folded in less than a year after opening. General Wood of Sears, Roebuck, referring to his company's entrance into the retail market, has said, "That first year, if there was any mistake we didn't make, I don't know what it was." John Deere was a simple blacksmith who got the idea for a better plow while working with an unsatisfactory old model.

Thousands of men whose names are lost in obscurity had dreams and ideas that never got anywhere because nothing was done about them. Thousands of people might have made decent work pants, but it was Jim Orr and Levi Strauss who were willing to go out and sell them. There was no great trick to selling advertising space in country newspapers or struggling magazines. In fact, hundreds of men did so. Those who stood head and shoulders above the others were men like Volney Palmer, F. W. Ayer, and Cyrus Curtis, who walked that extra weary mile, made that extra call, and thus were able to write the extra order that made the difference between notable success and mediocrity.

In both retailing and selling, very little was done prior to World War I to train personnel to be proficient. A young man who wanted to learn retailing

266

Future account executives listen carefully in their classes at Merrill Lynch, Pierce, Fenner & Smith, Inc. The eight-month training period is rugged and expensive, but worth it to the company in order to get the best salesmen possible. The men are carefully screened before the ten thousand dollar investment for each is made for training costs.

began by sweeping out the store, working in the stockroom, and running errands. When he was not busy at these chores, he might be permitted to wait on customers if there were more people in the store than the regular clerks could take care of. That is how J. C. Penney got his start.

Nor was the salesman of long ago who went on the road given much in the way of sales aids. Many a man made his first incursion into selling with nothing more than an outsized bag of samples, a pat on the back from the boss, and a few words of fatherly

advice about the evils of drink and high living—the latter somewhat superfluous in an era of small salaries and niggardly allowances for expenses.

The beginner often was assigned to a territory no one else wanted. It was usually long on real estate and scenery but short on prospective buyers for the salesman's wares. Such was the territory assigned to Harvey Firestone when he gave up a job as book-keeper in the office of a wholesale coal dealer for one as a traveling salesman for a small bottler of patent medicines, lotions, and flavoring extracts. Since he had no experience selling, twenty-year-old Firestone was given a route that included only small towns and villages in rural Ohio. He admitted that he was nervous when he climbed off the train at his first stop, the village of Applecreek. He was very much alone—and lonely—as he stood on the platform and looked the place over.

In Applecreek, Firestone found two fairly large

267

general stores. His good sense told him that he should call on them, but he lacked the confidence to tackle the big ones first. He decided to test his salesmanship on the owners of smaller shops—a move that got him nowhere. The small shops were not interested in his line; indeed, their owners would not even listen to Firestone's faltering sales talk. After several such fruitless calls, Firestone realized he would never earn his fifty-dollar-a-month salary plus expenses working like a peddler on the side streets, so he found the courage to call on one of the two larger merchants. To his surprise he came out of the store with an order.

Every salesman has to build his own self-confidence and test himself as Firestone did. What he learned in Applecreek when he called on the larger merchants was of value when he began to manufacture rubber tires and went after orders from the automobile manufacturers, including Henry Ford, who was well on his way to becoming the leader in the industry.

It is relevant to point out again that the untrained, inexperienced men who made good at selling or retailing were not exceptionally talented. And here, too, it should be noted that not every man who tried his hand at selling soared to success. Many failed; many more bogged down in the dreary rut of a barely eked-out existence. There were hundreds of reasons for failure and near-failure, and the most prevalent in selling, as in every other profession, was an unwillingness to work hard. Selling offered and still offers—opportunities and rewards, but the rewards have never been given on a silver platter.

W. H. Hoover once said that the biggest problem in selling vacuum cleaners was to find enough salesmen who really wanted to earn as much as thirty thousand dollars a year. Thomas L. Smith, when he was president of the Fleischman Yeast Company, put it another way when he remarked, "There is always plenty of opportunity for those who will take it, and more room at the top than can be filled with the present supply of ambitious men."

It would be presumptuous to predict what is ahead for the salesman. He will undoubtedly be influenced by further scientific approaches to the marketing of merchandise, services, and ideas. Perhaps he will be superseded by post-television types of communications. In other ways he will be made to adapt his ability to new outside influences. Chances are, however, that he will never be deterred from the pursuit of his profession and that he will remain the seller—a figure of historical importance in the growth of America.

BIBLIOGRAPHY

BOOKS:

ABBOTT, LAWRENCE F. *The Story of Nylic.* New York: New York Life Insurance Company, 1930.

ASHBROOK, WILLIAM S. *The Provident Life and Trust Company of Philadelphia, 1865–1915.* Philadelphia: Holmes Press, 1915.

ASHER, LOUIS E., AND EDITH HEAL. *Send No Money.* Chicago: Argus Books, 1942.

ATHERTON, LEWIS E. *The Southern Country Store, 1800–1860.* Baton Rouge: Louisiana State University Press, 1949.

BARRETT, WALTER. *The Old Merchants of New York City.* New York: Carleton Press, 1862.

BARTELS, ROBERT. *The Development of Marketing Thought.* Homewood, Ill.: Richard D. Irwin, Inc., 1952.

BOYNTON, HENRY WALLCOTT. *Annals of American Bookselling, 1638–1850.* New York: John Wiley and Sons, Inc., 1932.

BRANCH, E. DOUGLAS. *Westward.* New York: Appleton-Century-Crofts, 1930.

BRIGHAM, CLARENCE S. *Journals and Journeymen.* Philadelphia: University of Pennsylvania Press, 1950.

BRUCHEY, STUART WEEMS. *Robert Oliver, Merchant of Baltimore, 1783–1819.* Baltimore: The Johns Hopkins Press, 1956.

BUCK, SOLON J. AND ELIZABETH. *The Planting of Civilization in Western Pennsylvania.* Pittsburgh: University of Pittsburgh Press, 1939.

BULEY, R. CARLYLE. *The Old Northwest.* 2 vols. Bloomington: Indiana University Press, 1951.

CROW, CARL. *The Great American Customer.* New York: Harper and Row, Publishers, 1943.

CURRENT, RICHARD N. *The Typewriter and the Men Who Made It.* Urbana: University of Illinois Press, 1954.

DEPEW, CHAUNCEY M. (ed.). *One Hundred Years of American Commerce.* New York: D. O. Haynes and Company, 1895.

CASSON, HERBERT N. *The History of the Telephone.* Chicago: A. C. McClurg-Ribel Company, 1913.

DOW, GEORGE FRANCIS. *Everyday Life in the Massachusetts Bay Colony.* Boston: The Society for the Preservation of New England Antiquities, 1935.

DUBLIN, LOUIS I. *A Family of Thirty Million.* New York: The Metropolitan Life Insurance Company, 1943.

DULLES, FOSTER RHEA. *The Old China Trade.* Boston: Houghton Mifflin Company, 1930.

FAIRBURN, WILLIAM ARMSTRONG. *Merchant Sail.* Center Lovell, Me.: Fairburn Marine Educational Foundation [1956].

GARDINER, DOROTHY. *West of the River.* New York: Thomas Y. Crowell Company, 1941.

GREGG, JOSIAH. *Commerce of the Prairies.* Cleveland: Arthur R. Clark Company, 1905.

HARRINGTON, VIRGINIA D. *The New York Merchant on the Eve of the Revolution.* ("Studies in History, Economics and Public Law, ed. by the Faculty of Political Science of Columbia University," No. 404.) New York: Columbia University Press, 1935.

HATCH, ALDEN. *Remington Arms.* New York: Holt, Rinehart and Winston, Inc., 1956.

HOLBROOK, STEWART H. *Machines of Plenty.* New York: The Macmillan Company, 1955.

———. *The Story of American Railroads.* New York: Crown Publishers, Inc., 1947.

HOLMES, EDWIN T. *A Wonderful Fifty Years.* New York: Privately published, 1907.

HOWER, RALPH M. *The History of an Advertising Agency; N. W. Ayer and Son at Work.* Cambridge: Harvard University Press, 1939.

JAMES, MARQUIS. *Metropolitan Life.* New York: The Viking Press, 1947.

JONES, JOHN BEAUCHAMP. *The Western Merchant.* Philadelphia: Grigg, Elliott and Company, 1849.

JORDAN, PHILIP D. *The National Road.* Indianapolis: The Bobbs-Merrill Company, Inc., 1948.

KELEHER, WILLIAM A. *The Fabulous Frontier.* Santa Fe: The Rydal Press, 1945.

KELLY, P. C., AND N. A. BRISCO. *Retailing.* Englewood Cliffs, N.J.: Prentice-Hall, Inc.

KILGOUR, RAYMOND L. *Messrs. Robert Bros., Publishers.* Ann Arbor: The University of Michigan Press, 1952.

KNOWLES, RUTH. *The Greatest Gamblers: The Epic of Oil Exploration.* New York: McGraw-Hill Book Company, 1959.

LANIER, HENRY W. *A Century of Banking in New York, 1822–1922.*

LEHMANN-HAUPT, HULLMUT. *The Book in America.* New York: R. R. Bowker Company, 1951.

LEWIS, OSCAR. *Sea Routes to the Gold Fields.* New York: Alfred A. Knopf, Inc., 1949.

LIEF, ALFRED. *It Floats; The Story of Procter and Gamble.* New York: Holt, Rinehart and Winston, Inc., 1958.

McCAFFERTY, E. D. *Henry J. Heinz, A Biography.* Pittsburgh: Henry J. Heinz Company, 1923.

McCORMICK, CYRUS. *The Century of the Reaper.* Boston: Houghton Mifflin Company, 1931.

McNAIR, M. P., AND OTHERS. *Cases in Retail Management.* New York: McGraw-Hill Book Company, 1957.

MARCOSSON, ISAAC F. *Wherever Men Trade.* New York: Dodd, Mead and Company, 1948.

MAY, EARL CHAPIN. *A Century of Silver, 1847–1947.* New York: Robert M. McBride and Company, [1947].

MORISON, SAMUEL ELIOT. *Maritime History of Massachusetts, 1783–1860.* Boston: Houghton Mifflin Company, 1921.

ROWE, WILLIAM H. *The Maritime History of Maine.* New York: W. W. Norton and Company, Inc., 1948.

SCHUYLER, PHILIP N. (ed.). *The Hundred Year Book.* New York: A. S. Barnes and Company, Inc., 1942.

STALSON, J. OWEN. *Marketing Life Insurance.* Cambridge: Harvard University Press, 1942.

STERRY, I. H., AND WILLIAM H. GARRIGUS. *They Found a Way.* Brattleboro, Vt.: Stephen Daye Press, 1938.

VESTAL, STANLEY. *The Missouri.* New York: Farrar, Strauss and Company, Inc., 1945.

WILSON, LYNN W. *History of Fairfield County, Connecticut, 1639–1928.* Chicago: S. J. Clarke Publishing Company, 1029.

WRIGHT, R. L. *Hawkers and Walkers in Early America.* Philadelphia: J. B. Lippincott Company, 1927.

YORKE, DANA. *Men and Times of Pepperell.* Boston: Pepperell Manufacturing Company, 1945.

ZIMMERMAN, M. M. *The Supermarket, a Revolution in Distribution.* New York: McGraw-Hill Book Company, 1955.

PERIODICALS:

Bulletin of the Business Historical Society. Cambridge: The Graduate School of Business Administration, Harvard University.

The Business History Review. Cambridge: The Graduate School of Business Administration, Harvard University, 1926–.

The Connecticut Magazine (also known as *The Connecticut Quarterly*). Hartford, Conn.: The Connecticut Quarterly Company, 1895–1908.

The Deseret News. Salt Lake City, Utah.

Des Moines Register. Des Moines, Iowa.

Historical publications of the Tercentenary Commission of the State of Connecticut. New Haven: Yale University Press.

Johns Hopkins University Studies in Historical and Political Science. Baltimore: The Johns Hopkins Press, 1883–.

Journal of Political Economy. Chicago: University of Chicago Press, 1893–.

Mississippi Valley Historical Association Proceedings. Cedar Rapids, Iowa, 1907–1924.

Mississippi Valley Historical Review. Bloomington, Ind., 1914–.

Missouri Historical Review. Columbia, Mo., 1906–.

New England Magazine (continued as *American Monthly Magazine*). Boston, 1831–1835.

The Quarterly Journal. Albany: New York State Historical Association, 1919–.

The Saturday Evening Post. Philadelphia, Curtis Publishing Company, 1821–present.

UNPUBLISHED MATERIAL:

BAILEY, ROBERT. Letter Book. Philadelphia, Historical Society of Pennsylvania.

DOUGLAS, WILLIAM. Account Book, 1766–1774. New Haven, New Haven Historical Society.

HILL, SAMUEL. Journal and Log of Two Voyages, 1815–1822. New York: Manuscripts Division, New York Public Library.

KIRK, JOHN. Letter Books. Chicago, Chicago Historical Society.

Log of Betsy. Mystic, Marine Historical Association of Connecticut.

OGDEN, LEWIS. Letter Book, 1787–1798. New York: Manuscripts Division, New York Public Library.

PAYTON. Letter. Watertown, Mass., William Underwood and Company.

THOMPSON, GLENN EDWARD. "The Acquisition, Dispersal, and Influences of the James Watson Fortune, 1783–1839." Unpublished Ph.D. dissertation, University of Pennsylvania, 1958.

INDEX

PICTURE CREDITS (by pages)